DATE DUE

DEC - 1 1994	
JAN 2 8 1995	
MAR 0 3 1995	
OCT 2 0 1995	
APR 0 3 1999	
AUG 0 5 1999	
MAY 2 7 2000	
GAYLORD	PRINTED IN U.S.A.

Architecture of Skidmore, Owings & Merrill, 1963-1973

Introduction by Arthur Drexler · Commentaries by Axel Menges

Architectural Book Publishing Co., New York

725
APC

Collaboration on commentaries: Oswald W. Grube and Nora Krehl-von Mühlendahl
Translation of introduction into German: Brigitte Weitbrecht in collaboration with Axel Menges
Translation of commentaries into English: E. Rockwell

104073

Published 1974 by Architectural Book Publishing Co., Inc.
All rights reserved
including the right of reproduction in whole or in part in any form
Published simultaneously in Canada
by Saunders of Toronto, Ltd., Don Mills, Ontario
© Copyright 1974 by Verlag Gerd Hatje, Stuttgart
ISBN 8038-0014-2
Printed in Germany

Contents / Inhalt

Introduction

What is called modern architecture has now survived more social upheavals, transformed more of the built environment, and established hegemony over more disparate cultures than any architectural manifestation of the Western world since the Roman Empire. Roman in its claim to universality, the international style, like science, is practiced and understood everywhere. Merely to be Chinese or Russian or African is no excuse for mismanaging its techniques and configurations. There is no other way to build.

A style that began under the aegis of utilitarianism, invoking economy of means along with a taste for "simplicity", now embraces extravagance as well as poverty. The rich, like the poor, cannot escape modernism; even wealth must pretend to prudent "solutions" to "problems". The movement abounds in masterpieces, but these are seldom considered to be the product of private inspiration, essentially incommunicable. At all levels of accomplishment excellence is understood to be the result of right practice, which can be taught; those who have learned it can work together and we may expect continuous improvement. Experience confirms the theory – or at least does not disprove it. Why then has modern architecture lost so much of its original coherence? Why has the certainty that once struck with the force of revelation turned first to uneasy icnoclasm and, lately, to a nervous ecumenism? More awkward still: how is it possible for an international movement of such magnitude to have reached its present age without serious philosophical probing of its fundamental assumptions?

Any answer must begin with the fact of success: modernism prevails, and must now take responsibility for the ills its exponents claimed it could overcome. These ills were not diagnosed as afflictions of the aesthetic sense, except as poor vision might be considered a side effect of cancer. They were held to be the result of society's unwillingness, or inability, to fairly distribute and intelligently use the wealth made possible by industrialization. Therefore every solution to an architectural problem was expected to serve as a prototype, a model for the eventual reconstruction of the village, the city, the world. But the notion that architecture is a suitable instrument for effecting social reform is as foolish now as it has always been. Architects are servants, not masters, and like all good servants they can persuade their masters to modify bad habits whenever it makes no serious difference. Unlike other servants, however, they will be blamed for their masters' failings.

For those who await the revolution from moment to moment, what provokes unease is not the succesls of individual architectural achievements but rather their appropriation by the very peop e whose lives such good works were supposed to transform. The oppressors continue to oppress, only now they do so from headquarters whose good design was meant to be morally redeeming. To this indignity we may add the disgrace of a social apparatus incapable of coping, at least in the United States, with the most urgent and obvious problems – housing, for example, and transportation.

Despite the servitude of architects, economic and social factors are not the sole determinants of built urban form; the will of the architect and the dogma of modern architecture have played their part. Bromidic as the Marxist complaint about formalism may be, it does take account of a phenomenon which, at the same time, it fails to explain: the architect's will to make form can and does impose itself on society, sometimes with disastrous effect, sometimes with saving grace. Our judgements of quality, inseparable from our notions of what is desirable, continue to be predicated on ideas about architecture, technology, economics and social well-being that have their origin in circumstances we no longer find humanly acceptable. Yet with or without a re-examination of theories and assumptions, the formal possibilities of the new architecture continue to unfold. Not every interesting possibility has been tried; the store of useful ideas is by no means exhausted, and already much that was rejected, or undervalued, at the beginning of the movement is being re-integrated in a more generous perspective. (The process starts with neglected Italian work of the 'thirties and will no doubt soon reach its counterparts in Austria, Czechoslovakia, and Hungary.)

There is another body of neglected work, even harder to see whole. It constitutes current normative practice and seldom engages in the polemics that are thought to make up architectural history. Perhaps that alone is sufficient reason to examine the work of the most able practitioners, as distinguished from the few initiating geniuses. Several candidates are eligible for such consideration; none more so than Skidmore, Owings and Merrill. For more than 35 years in the United States, and since World War II in other countries as well, the firm has tested the viability of most assumptions of the modern movement.

Einleitung

Die sogenannte moderne Architektur hat bis heute mehr gesellschaftliche Umwälzungen überlebt, einen größeren Teil der gebauten Umwelt verändert und eine beständigere Herrschaft über verschiedenartige Kulturen aufgerichtet als jeder andere Baustil der westlichen Welt seit dem römischen Kaiserreich. Der Internationale Stil ist römisch in seinem Anspruch auf Universalität und wird wie die Naturwissenschaft überall verwirklicht und verstanden. Chinese oder Russe oder Afrikaner zu sein, ist noch lange keine Entschuldigung dafür, mit seinen Techniken und Gestaltungsmöglichkeiten unsachgemäß umzugehen. Es gibt heute keine andere Möglichkeit, sich baulich zu artikulieren.

Dieser Stil, der unter der Ägide des Utilitarismus geboren wurde, auf Sparsamkeit der Mittel zielt und der »Einfachheit« huldigt, umfaßt heute den Luxus wie die Bedürftigkeit. Die Reichen können sich dem Modernismus ebensowenig entziehen wie die Armen; auch der Wohlstand muß abgewogene »Lösungen« für »Probleme« vortäuschen. Die Bewegung brachte eine Fülle von Meisterwerken hervor, die jedoch selten als Produkt der wesensgemäß nicht mitteilbaren Inspiration eines Einzelnen gelten. Auf allen Leistungsebenen hält man das Hervorragende für das Ergebnis des richtigen Verfahrens, das gelehrt werden kann; die es erlernt haben, können zusammenarbeiten, so daß stetige Verbesserungen zu erwarten sind. Die Erfahrung bestätigt diese Theorie oder widerlegt sie wenigstens nicht. Warum hat aber dann die moderne Architektur so viel von ihrer ursprünglichen Einheitlichkeit verloren? Warum ist die Sicherheit, die einst mit der Kraft einer Offenbarung wirkte, zuerst in eine krampfhafte Bilderstürmerei und jüngst in einen reizbaren Ökumenismus umgeschlagen? Noch seltsamer: Wie ist es möglich, daß eine internationale Bewegung dieser Größenordnung ohne ernst zu nehmende philosophische Untersuchung ihrer Grundvoraussetzungen ihr jetziges Alter erreichen konnte?

Jede Antwort auf diese Fragen muß von dem Faktum Erfolg ausgehen: Der Modernismus herrscht und muß jetzt die Verantwortung für die Mißstände tragen, die er nach Aussage seiner Repräsentanten überwinden sollte. Diese Mißstände wurden nicht als Beleidigung des Schönheitssinnes diagnostiziert – höchstens so, wie man die Abnahme des Sehvermögens als Nebenwirkung von Krebs betrachten könnte. Sie galten vielmehr als Folge der mangelnden Bereitschaft oder der Unfähigkeit der Gesellschaft, den durch die Industrialisierung erschlossenen Reichtum gerecht zu verteilen und verständig zu nutzen. Man erwartete daher von jeder Lösung eines architektonischen Problems, daß sie als Prototyp, als Modell für die künftige Neugestaltung des Dorfes, der Stadt, der Welt zu dienen vermöge. Die Auffassung jedoch, daß die Architektur ein geeignetes Instrument zur Verwirklichung sozialer Reformen sei, ist heute so töricht wie je. Architekten sind Diener, nicht Herren. Wie alle guten Diener können sie ihre Herren dazu veranlassen, schlechte Gewohnheiten abzulegen, wenn keine schwerwiegenden Folgen daraus entstehen. Im Gegensatz zu anderen Dienern werden sie aber für die Fehler ihrer Herren gescholten.

Das Unbehagen derer, die die Revolution von einem Augenblick zum andern erwarten, entzündet sich daran, daß die gute Architektur jenen, deren Leben sie gerade verändern sollte, durch Vereinnahmung anheimfällt. Die Unterdrücker unterdrücken weiterhin, nur eben jetzt von Hauptquartieren aus, deren gekonnter Entwurf eigentlich zur moralischen Wiedergutmachung bestimmt war. Zu diesem Fehlschlag kommt die Schande eines Sozialapparates, der – wenigstens in den Vereinigten Staaten von Amerika – unfähig ist, mit den vordringlichsten Problemen, zum Beispiel dem Wohnwesen und dem Verkehr, fertig zu werden.

Obgleich die Architekten als Diener fungieren, bestimmen wirtschaftliche und gesellschaftliche Faktoren nicht allein die Baugestalt – der Wille des Architekten und das Dogma der modernen Architektur spielen ebenfalls eine Rolle. So abgedroschen die marxistische Klage über den Formalismus auch sein mag – sie berücksichtigt doch ein Phänomen, das sie allerdings nicht zu erläutern vermag: Der Formgestaltungswille des Architekten kann sich der Gesellschaft auferlegen und tut es auch, manchmal mit verheerender Wirkung, dann wieder mit befreiender Kraft. Unsere Qualitätsurteile, die untrennbar mit unseren Auffassungen vom Wünschenswerten verbunden sind, beruhen nach wie vor auf Vorstellungen von Architektur, Technologie, Wirtschaft und sozialem Wohl, deren Ursprünge in Verhältnissen liegen, die wir heute nicht mehr menschenwürdig finden. Doch mit und ohne neuerliche Überprüfung von Theorien und Voraussetzungen entfalten sich weiterhin die formalen Möglichkeiten der modernen Architektur. Nicht jeder interessante Weg wurde beschritten; der Vorrat an erfolgversprechenden Ideen ist keineswegs erschöpft, und heute wird schon vieles, was am Anfang der Bewegung abgelehnt oder unterbewertet wurde, in einer groß-

SOM comprises approximately 1,000 architects, engineers and technicians. From within the firm they are able to provide complete services in planning, designing, engineering and construction supervision. Seven principal offices – New York, Chicago, San Francisco, Portland, Oreg., Washington, D.C., Paris, and Los Angeles – are directed by twenty-five general partners. Working arrangements on a given project, headed by a partner in charge of design, vary from the close association of colleagues to the execution of design decisions made by one man. The firm's commissions range from the exotic – a Presidential library, for example – to such more or less routine matters as industrial or transportation facilities; whether they are conspicuous or recessive all of these buildings receive an attention to detail vital to the philosophy and ethics of modern architecture. In this connection Bruce Graham of the Chicago office relates a significant story. Faced with having to design a hospital, he remarked to Mies van der Rohe that it presented endless technical problems and little opportunity for the pleasures of architecture. To this, according to Graham, Mies responded: "*I* do not have to design such buildings, but *you* must." It is indeed the compulsion to solve the least rewarding problems, as well as the most interesting, that has given SOM its enviable reputation.

Once praised for the consistent quality and character of its work, then sometimes criticized for being too consistent, SOM's recent practice often draws simultaneous praise and blame – to the same building – for the consistent quality of its innovations. The present variety may be a product of those accidents of temperament and personal inclination which so often determine the character of large enterprises. Certainly some of it reflects, if it is not actually caused by, a more willing acceptance of the fact that responsibility for buildings ultimately rests on individuals. Each of them has a name, and where twenty years ago the firm was reluctant to identify individual members, it does so now as a matter of course.

SOM no longer has a single house style – it never really did – but it does have distinct regional habits. The difference between the Chicago and the New York office is conspicuous; both offices differ even more from the San Francisco approach, and within each of these three main divisions there are individual variations. The most important of these is undoubtedly the direction taken by Walter Netsch in Chicago, setting aside the organization of buildings according to their structural systems in favor of complex plan geometries. Netsch's preoccupation with geometry also has roots in Chicago through Frank Lloyd Wright, yet in the present American architectural scene one might have expected this idea to have been pursued on the West Coast; certainly the San Francisco office is more relaxed about the management of structure.

The Chicago office has distinguished itself by developing several structural systems more efficient for highrise towers. Some of these continue in the direction inaugurated – or at least clarified – by Mies van der Rohe, and insofar as there may be a center of gravity, a continuity that by now takes on the character of tradition, it is the relatively constant Chicago preoccupation with buildings that are structurally "tough". To the extent that they have themselves done more to enlarge the scope of this tradition than any other architects in the United States, SOM's Chicago office may be said to stand at the center of American practice. Yet it is in New York that some of these ideas have been given interpretations no less forceful, and certainly more surprising, than in Chicago. The notion of minimal form as skin rather than bones, for example, reaches its apogee in New York with Gordon Bunshaft's Marine Midland Building at 140 Broadway. The expressive power of massive steel framing is carried to what might seem to be its logical conclusion not in Bruce Graham's John Hancock Center in Chicago, but in Roy Allen's U.S. Steel building in New York. And although its point of departure is structural efficiency, Bruce Graham's Sears Tower in Chicago is of still greater interest for solving a visual rather than a structural problem: its massing as a set of towers of uneven height reduces apparent bulk and restores a more varied skyline – the kind of problem that might have been expected to attract the attention of architects in New York. And again, it is not Walter Netsch's penchant for the more emotionally subtle response, or Bruce Graham's and Fazlur Khan's for the technically sophisticated, that has yielded SOM's few exercises in architecture as part of an organic "ecological" whole, but rather Edward Bassett's Weyerhaeuser building near Tacoma and Gordon Bunshaft's office complex for the American Can Company near New York, both on suburban meadowland and both concerned with enhancing their sites.

In some way that probably cannot be demonstrated, SOM's work is a dialogue between its regional offices. Regional distinctions alone, however, provide no adequate framework for evaluation. It would seem more logical to consider SOM's work according to building types, as in fact they have been grouped in this book. Useful enough for purposes of comparison,

zügigeren Perspektive miteinbezogen. (Dieser Vorgang beginnt mit übersehenen italienischen Bauten der dreißiger Jahre und wird zweifellos bald auf Österreich, die Tschechoslowakei und Ungarn übergreifen.)

Ein weiterer Bereich unterbewerteter Tätigkeit läßt sich noch schwerer in seiner Gesamtheit erfassen, nämlich die alltägliche Baupraxis, die selten in die Polemiken eingeht, aus denen angeblich die Geschichte der Architektur besteht. Vielleicht genügt dies schon als Grund für eine Betrachtung der Arbeit der fähigsten Praktiker im Unterschied zu den wenigen genialen, epochemachenden Geistern. Mehrere Kandidaten kommen für eine solche Betrachtung in Frage, allen voran die seit über 35 Jahren in den USA und seit dem Zweiten Weltkrieg auch in anderen Ländern praktizierende Firma Skidmore, Owings & Merrill.

Die Firma beschäftigt heute ungefähr 1000 Architekten, Ingenieure und Techniker. Sie bietet aus einer Hand umfassende Dienste in Planung, Entwurf, Konstruktion und Bauüberwachung. Sieben Hauptbüros – New York, Chicago, San Francisco, Portland, Oreg., Washington, D.C., Paris und Los Angeles – werden von 25 Hauptpartnern geführt. Die Arbeitsarrangements für ein Projekt reichen von engen Zusammenschlüssen mehrerer Personen zu einer Arbeitsgruppe bis zu Einmannunternehmungen und die Aufträge von so exotischen Dingen wie einer Präsidentenbibliothek bis zu mehr oder weniger alltäglichen wie Industrie- und Verkehrsanlagen. Bruce Graham vom Chicagoer Büro hält eine für diesen Zusammenhang bezeichnende Anekdote bereit. Sich der Aufgabe gegenübersehend, ein Krankenhaus zu planen, bemerkte er gegenüber Mies van der Rohe, daß damit endlose technische Probleme verbunden seien, jedoch kaum architektonische Freuden. Gemäß Graham antwortete Mies hierauf: »*Ich* brauche solche Gebäude nicht zu entwerfen, aber *Sie* müssen es.« In der Tat verdankt die Firma ihr beneidenswertes Ansehen dem Zwang, sowohl die undankbarsten als auch die interessantesten Probleme lösen zu müssen.

Einst wurde sie für die Konsequenz und den Eigencharakter ihrer Arbeit gerühmt, dann wurde sie gelegentlich wegen zu großer Konsequenz kritisiert, und ihre jüngsten Errungenschaften ziehen wegen der Konsequenz ihrer Neuerungen häufig bei ein und demselben Gebäude Lob und Tadel zugleich auf sich. Der heutige Abwechslungsreichtum ist vielleicht eine Folge jener Zufälle von Temperament und persönlicher Neigung, die so oft das Wesen großer Unternehmen bestimmen. Zweifellos spiegelt sich in ihm auch eine größere Bereitwilligkeit, anzuerkennen, daß die Verantwortung für Gebäude letzten Endes auf Individuen ruht – wenn nicht diese Bereitwilligkeit den heutigen Abwechslungsreichtum gar erst ermöglicht hat. Während die Firma noch vor 20 Jahren ungern die jeweiligen Mitarbeiter nannte, ist dies heute eine Selbstverständlichkeit.

Der Unterschied zwischen dem Büro in Chicago und dem in New York ist auffallend; beide Büros heben sich noch stärker vom Ansatz in San Francisco ab, und innerhalb jeder dieser drei Hauptabteilungen treten wiederum individuelle Richtungen auf. Die wichtigste davon ist zweifellos die, die Walter Netsch in Chicago eingeschlagen hat. Die Organisation von Gebäuden beruht bei ihm nicht mehr auf strukturellen Systemen, sondern auf komplexen Grundrißgeometrien. Netschs Geometrie-Besessenheit läßt sich zwar mit Frank Lloyd Wright in Chicago historisch beheimaten; trotzdem hätte die derzeitige amerikanische Architekturszene erwarten lassen, daß diese Idee zuerst in San Francisco verfolgt worden wäre, denn unstreitig ist man dort hinsichtlich der Behandlung der Struktur freizügiger als anderswo.

Das Büro in Chicago zeichnete sich bisher besonders dadurch aus, daß man sich hier um möglichst effiziente Struktursysteme für Hochhaustürme bemühte. Mit einigen werden die Wege verfolgt, die Mies van der Rohe einst eröffnet oder wenigstens gebahnt hatte. Soweit man von einem Schwerpunkt, einer Kontinuität, die jetzt schon Traditionscharakter trägt, sprechen kann, ist damit die fast ständige Beschäftigung des SOM-Büros in Chicago mit strukturell »harten« Gebäuden gemeint. In dem Maß, wie es mehr als jedes andere Büro in den Vereinigten Staaten dazu beigetragen hat, den Rahmen dieser Tradition zu erweitern, kann man vom SOM-Büro in Chicago behaupten, es stehe im Mittelpunkt der amerikanischen Praxis. In New York jedoch wurden einige dieser Ideen nicht weniger überzeugend und zweifellos überraschender als in Chicago verwirklicht. So gelangt die Auffassung von der Fassade als Haut, nicht als Skelett, mit Gordon Bunshafts Marine Midland Building (140 Broadway) in New York zu voller Ausprägung. Die Ausdruckskraft eines massigen Stahlskeletts erreicht ihren logischen Höhepunkt nicht mit Bruce Grahams John Hancock Center in Chicago, sondern mit Roy Allens Hochhaus der U.S. Steel (One Liberty Plaza) in New York. Und obgleich sein Ausgangspunkt die Tragfähigkeit ist, also ein strukturelles Problem, ist Bruce Grahams Sears Tower in Chicago von noch größerem Interesse für die Lösung eines optischen Problems: Durch die Bündelung einer Reihe von Türmen ungleicher Höhe verschwindet der Eindruck der Unförmigkeit und entsteht ein abwechslungsreicherer

analysis by building type merely reveals that there are four or five ways to generate variations on the same type; the subdivisions are so numerous as to render analysis by function as misleading as analysis by structure. What seems inescapable is analysis according to intent. That this may require mind reading, as well as a certain skepticism toward what is avowed, should not obscure the fact that intent is often enough self-evident – more often, indeed, than structural systems or building programs.

Structure and materials at one level, detail and integrating composition at another, are the means with which intent is signified.

Even though it has been largely rejected during the last decade, the idea that architecture can be produced with structure alone has had an authority that is still all-pervading. The structural motif continues to signify the attitude of responsibility, like a business suit or a briefcase or whatever other accoutrement may be selected to indicate a fixed position near the top of a hierarchy. The structural systems that constitute accepted form language for this emotional message have of course been established by Ludwig Mies van der Rohe. To Mies structure meant one material: steel. His concern was to develop an absolute structure whose logical validity would transcend any particular condition of site or program. He defined the ideal building as a one-story pavilion with a flat, clear-span roof, coffered because the equal distribution of stresses justifies the equal distribution of perimeter columns on identical elevations. But the intent is not structural clarity for its own sake. It is rather to respond to the contingent world with a sobriety that can withstand or evade the unexpected. There is no inherent reason why structure in steel, or any other material, must be deployed to signify sobriety, and although the mood, the material and the forms have together dominated consciousness for so long that they now seem inseparable, and are characteristic of much of SOM's work as of everyone else's, there are obvious alternatives. Structure can be used to signify frivolity, if that is the opposite of sobriety, and all shades of deportment in between.

Removed from sobriety but not yet frivolous is the one-story office and printing plant designed for the newspaper "The Republic" in Columbus, Indiana, by Myron Goldsmith. A long, rectangular block, with columns evenly spaced on all sides, it signifies its mood by the thinness of its structural members: here we do what we have to, neither apologizing nor explaining. Thus the square bays are not expressed on the perimeter, where closely spaced columns each carry slim I beams to the larger central spans. Box-like lighting fixtures under a ribbed ceiling complete the range of structural detail, so that the assemblage of component parts tends to look manufactured rather than built. Two relatively subjective design decisions are allowed: first, glazing is divided into two lights of identical height, the upper section treated as an opaque plane concealing the column structure on the end elevations. Second: the steel is painted white, a color Mies reserved for the relaxations of the countryside. The effect is calm, insistent but not compulsive, and with a vague affinity for the thin-walled boxes of Japanese architecture in its abrupt change from solid to void at the corners. What is less relaxing is that only by keeping his eyes on the ground can the visitor hope to find his way to the entrance; the elevations offer no clue, and the plan provides no more than an orderly containment of necessary spaces.

Nothing in this building's program requires that a visit to it should constitute a momentous event in someone's life. Architecture like this – and it is Architecture, not building – rejects more opportunities to amuse than it accepts. That is not the case as one moves toward the other end of the emotional scale for which structure is the significant form.

Two examples that bring home the point are the central engineering building for Armstrong Cork, by Roy Allen, and the office building for the Boots Company by Bruce Graham. Both buildings emphasize the roof plate as a massive horizontal plane, justified at Armstrong by using it to accommodate mechanical equipment; both set glass walls behind their perimeter columns; and both accommodate a lower floor as a subordinate element, almost concealed for Boots (where it is expressed as a base or pedestal related to the ground plane rather than the columns) and articulated at Armstrong where the top floor reads as a *piano nobile.*

The Boots building makes use of square bays in a classic 3 to 5 ratio, its evenly stressed elevations concealing the fact that the main internal feature of the building is a sunk garden to which both floors open. The rectangular structural bays of the Armstrong building, in a ratio of 4 to 16, provide a more insistent rhythm in the long elevations, but on the narrow ends the perimeter columns are eliminated for the upper floor, so that the roof plate appears to be a clear span. On neither building is structure modified for any purpose; only the approach road, for example, can find the door, which is otherwise unaccented, yet the cage-like character of the structure is contradicted by its tactical impenetrability.

Publishing house and printing plant of the newspaper "The Republic"/Verlags- und Druckereigebäude der Zeitung »The Republic«, Columbus, Indiana.

Central engineering building of the Armstrong Cork Company / Technisches Zentrum der Armstrong Cork Company, Lancaster, Pennsylvania.

Headquarters of the Boots Pure Drug Company / Hauptverwaltung der Boots Pure Drug Company, Nottingham, England.

Umriß. Von einem solchen Problem hätte man annehmen können, es ziehe die Aufmerksamkeit der Architekten in New York auf sich. Und wiederum sind es weder Walter Netsch mit seiner Neigung zur subtilen Anpassung noch Bruce Graham und Fazlur Khan mit ihrem Bemühen um eine zu sich selbst gekommene Technik, die bei SOM zu einer Architektur gelangten, welche Teil eines organischen »ökologischen« Ganzen ist, sondern vielmehr Edward Bassett mit seinem Weyerhaeuser-Gebäude bei Tacoma und Gordon Bunshaft mit seinem Komplex für die American Can Company bei New York, die beide auf freiem vorstädtischen Grund errichtet wurden und im Dienst einer ästhetischen Überhöhung ihres Standortes stehen.

Auf eine Weise, die wahrscheinlich nicht demonstriert werden kann, ist die Arbeit von SOM ein Dialog zwischen den Regionalbüros. Regionale Unterschiede allein ergeben jedoch noch keine geeigneten Anhaltspunkte für eine Wertung. Logischer ist es dann schon, die Arbeit von SOM in Kategorien von Bautypen zu beschreiben, wie es im vorliegenden Buch geschieht. Doch die Analyse nach Bautypen, so nützlich sie für Vergleichszwecke sein mag, offenbart lediglich, daß es vier oder fünf grundlegende Varianten für einen und denselben Typ gibt; die Spielarten innerhalb der einzelnen Varianten sind dermaßen zahlreich, daß die Analyse nach der Funktion so irreführend wird wie die Analyse nach der Struktur. Unabdingbar erscheint deshalb die Analyse nach der Intention. Daß dies Gedankenlesen sowie eine gewisse Skepsis gegenüber dem Eingestandenen erfordert, sollte nicht darüber hinwegtäuschen, daß die Intention oft genug klar zutage liegt – häufiger sogar als Struktursysteme oder Bauprogramme.

Struktur und Materialien auf der einen, Detail und Komposition auf einer anderen Ebene, dies sind die Medien, in denen sich die Intention kundtut.

Obgleich die Ansicht, Architektur könne allein mit der Struktur geschaffen werden, seit einigen Jahren weithin verworfen wird, ist ihre Autorität keineswegs schon gebrochen. Auch weiterhin signalisiert das strukturelle Motiv Verantwortlichkeit (wie ein dunkler Anzug und ein Köfferchen, mit denen man sich herausputzt, um eine feste Position in den Spitzenbereichen einer Hierarchie zu demonstrieren). Die Struktursysteme, die eine allgemein anerkannte Formsprache für diese emotionale Botschaft darstellen, wurden bekanntlich von Ludwig Mies van der Rohe entwickelt. Für Mies war Struktur gleichbedeutend mit Stahl, und er trachtete danach, damit einen absoluten, über alle Sonderverhältnisse des Terrains oder des Programms hinaus gültigen Bautyp zu entwickeln. Das ideale Gebäude definierte er als eingeschossigen Pavillon mit identischen Seiten und kassettiertem Flachdach, getragen von gleichmäßig verteilten Außenstützen. Die Intention war jedoch nicht strukturelle Klarheit um ihrer selbst willen, sondern Reaktion auf die zufallsbedingte Welt mit einer Nüchternheit, die das Unerwartete ertragen oder vermeiden kann. Es gibt keinen zwingenden Grund dafür, mit einer Konstruktion aus Stahl (oder irgendeinem anderen Material) Nüchternheit zu assoziieren, und obschon die Vorstellung des Zusammenhangs von Atmosphäre, Material und Form das Bewußtsein schon so lange beherrscht, daß die drei heute untrennbar zu sein scheinen, und obschon dieser Gedanke einen großen Teil der Arbeit von SOM wie auch aller anderen Architekten prägt, gibt es offenkundige Alternativen. Mit Struktur kann man auch Leichtfertigkeit – wenn dies das Gegenteil von Nüchternheit ist – und alle dazwischenliegenden Werte zum Ausdruck bringen.

Abseits der Nüchternheit, aber auch der Leichtfertigkeit steht das einstöckige Büro- und Druckereigebäude, das Myron Goldsmith für die Zeitung »The Republic« entwarf. Es ist ein langgestreckter, rechteckiger Block mit auf allen Seiten gleichmäßig gereihten Stützen. Seine Atmosphäre wird bestimmt durch die Schmalheit seiner strukturellen Glieder, die zu sagen scheinen: Hier sind wir und leisten, was wir leisten müssen, ohne Entschuldigungen oder Erklärungen abzugeben. Zwei verhältnismäßig subjektive Entscheidungen schlugen sich im Entwurf nieder: Zum einen ist die Verglasung in zwei Felder gleicher Höhe unterteilt, wobei das obere Feld an den Schmalseiten undurchsichtig ausgebildet ist, um die Trägerkonstruktion zu verbergen. Zum anderen erhielt der Stahl einen weißen Anstrich – den Mies für Erholungsbauten in ländlicher Gegend vorbehalten hatte. Der Eindruck ist der von Ruhe, von ungezwungener Eindringlichkeit; im abrupten Übergang vom Offenen zum Geschlossenen an den Ecken zeigt sich dazu eine gewisse Ähnlichkeit mit den dünnwandigen Gehäusen japanischer Architektur. Weniger erholsam ist, daß der Besucher den Blick auf den Boden richten muß, wenn er den Weg zum Eingang finden will, denn die Fassaden geben kaum Aufschluß. Auch im Grundriß zeigt sich nichts als eine geordnete Folge der notwendigen Räume.

Im Programm dieses Gebäudes ist nichts enthalten, das eine Besichtigung zu einem unvergeßlichen Erlebnis machen würde. Eine solche Architektur – und es ist Architektur,

Both of these buildings are pavilion types widely used by SOM for a variety of purposes. The type derives from Mies' School of Architecture and Design at Illinois Institute of Technology, with its thin roof plate suspended from enormous trusses to provide uninterrupted loft space for a *piano nobile*, and a basement floor whose actual means of support is in no way visible from the elevations but is in fact a normal distribution of interior columns (as is the case with the Boots building). The ambiguities inherent in this parti have been variously resolved by minimizing the difference in structural treatment or by implying that the lower floor is in some way a separate structure related to the ground plane. However it is treated, the main force of the design depends on the visual plausibility of the structure as column-and-roof. Suppression or emphasis of detail becomes particularly important. Thus, stiffening flanges on both Boots and Armstrong help to place the buildings in the realm of engineering; the rigorous expression of a module in all interior fittings sustains the aura of inevitability, the choice of exterior color – dark – sustains the mood of earnest endeavor. And although the programs for such buildings seldom demand the articulation of some particular feature, neither do they demand equalization within a single rectangular container. The real advantage is that extended, regular elevations suggest that there is no rational alternative, and offer a structural system in such abundance that, if there were less of it, its muscularity might seem somewhat exaggerated. Yet in both buildings the Miesian objective of craft and purity is achieved in fact as well as in fancy. From mechanical equipment to furniture, interior fittings are pleasingly if relentlessly integrated. At all scales the precision of detail is beautiful. Yet the result is curiously frustrating, perhaps because the energy, persistence and intelligence brought to bear on structural detail cannot be related to any purpose other than their own. The dilemma is fundamental to "rational" architecture.

The expressive range indicated for these three structures by no means indicates the gamut; it does suggest the plausible limits for low, moderately large structures of essentially utilitarian character. A change in scale from low horizontal building to vertical slab or tower obviously increases the opportunities for structural invention, and it may be useful to consider first what may be the SOM skyscraper equivalent to Myron Goldsmith's "The Republic" building. In the context of the work included in this book, that equivalent is the 19-story Business Men's Assurance Co. office building in Kansas City. It is quite simply an unadorned structural cage, a rectangle in plan of three to five bays, all square, standing on a low paved platform. A slight, almost imperceptible increase in height differentiates the ground floor arcade from the rest of the structure; columns and beams are of the same dimension and the glass wall is set well back so that the cage stands free and clear. In a sense this is the archetypal skeleton structure, abstracted of all superfluous detail and apparently capable of receiving whatever one chooses to put inside it, given the limits of the 36' bays. Since it stands alone in a park, and since its frame is clad with white marble whose slight grain is invisible at a distance, it seems like an abstract architectural model that happens to have been built full scale. Considering that the formal idea has precedent in Giuseppe Terragni's Casa del Fascio, built at Como in 1932, and was subsequently elaborated by Terragni and others in the years just prior to World War II, it is surprising that it had to wait until the mid-60's before anyone actually built it in the United States. Terragni's Casa del Fascio explored the ambiguities that result from articulating a rectangular column and beam structure and, in the same wall plane, leaving it undifferentiated from a solid infill. The contradiction between structure and non-structure was reinforced by a uniform veneer of white stucco; the white marble cladding used in the Business Men's Assurance building serves the same purpose of abstracting the form so that it ceases to look "built" (although joints and marble veining are a minor distraction). But between the Italian manipulation of column and wall, and the Business Men's Assurance building stands Mies van der Rohe. What we have now is a structure purified by suppressing the wall and abstracting the structure itself. Beyond that, design decisions consist essentially in the elimination of detail, or at least in making detail unobtrusive, and the building carries no particular emotional tone. On the other hand, although it is not exactly lighthearted, it can only make its point by avoiding the portentous accents of engineering. Indeed, it comes amazingly close to being just what it looks like: a rudimentary skeleton structure.

What happens when the same theme does take on structural detail can be seen in the Tenneco building. Though substantially larger – 33 stories, seven bays to each side with interior columns replaced by central utility cores – Tenneco is nevertheless the same structural cage with recessed glass walls. Here, however, the cage is articulated. Columns are pulled slightly forward to stress the vertical line; the street level arcade is three stories high; the columns receive an extra "buttress" up to the middle of the first fascia; and a

Headquarters of the Business Men's Assurance Co. of America / Hauptverwaltung der Business Men's Assurance Co. of America, Kansas City, Missouri.

Tenneco Building, Houston, Texas.

nicht einfach Bauen – verzichtet auf mehr Möglichkeiten des Gefallens, als sie ausschöpft. Dies trifft um so weniger zu, je mehr man sich dem anderen Ende der emotionalen Skala, wo die Struktur zur Hauptdeterminanten der Baugestalt erhoben ist, nähert.

Zwei Bauten ragen hier besonders hervor: das technische Zentrum der Armstrong Cork Company von Roy Allen und das Verwaltungsgebäude der Boots Pure Drug Company von Bruce Graham. Bei beiden Gebäuden tritt das Dach als wuchtige horizontale Platte hervor, was bei dem Armstrong-Gebäude dadurch gerechtfertigt ist, daß darin technische Einrichtungen untergebracht sind; bei beiden sind die Glaswände hinter die Außenstützen gesetzt; bei beiden ist das Erdgeschoß ein untergeordnetes Element. Beim Boots-Gebäude ist es fast unsichtbar, als Basis oder Sockel auf das Erdniveau und nicht auf die Stützen bezogen, während es beim Armstrong-Gebäude, dessen Obergeschoß sich als piano nobile darstellt, stärker in Erscheinung tritt.

Beim Boots-Gebäude wurde mit quadratischen Stützenfeldern im klassischen Verhältnis von 3:5 gearbeitet. Die regelmäßigen Seiten verbergen das wichtigste innere Element, einen vertieften Innenhof, auf den sich beide Geschosse öffnen. Beim Armstrong-Gebäude verleihen rechteckige Stützenfelder, angeordnet im Verhältnis 4:16, den Längsseiten einen eindringlicheren Rhythmus als den Schmalseiten, an denen sich zudem im Obergeschoß keine Außenstützen befinden, da die Dachplatte frei über die gesamte Gebäudebreite spannt. Bei keinem der beiden Gebäude wurde die Struktur für irgendwelche Zwecke modifiziert; so kann nur die Zufahrt den im übrigen unbetonten Eingang finden. Der taktischen Uneinnehmbarkeit widerspricht allerdings der käfigähnliche Charakter der Struktur.

Beide Gebäude sind Flachbauten, wie sie von SOM für die verschiedensten Zwecke verwendet werden, und haben als Vorläufer Mies van der Rohes School of Architecture and Design am Illinois Institute of Technology. Deren Merkmale sind ein piano nobile, das von einer an riesigen Überzügen hängenden, nach unten völlig glatten, dünnen Platte überdacht wird, und ein Basisgeschoß, dessen Tragwerk von außen nicht sichtbar ist, in Wirklichkeit aber (wie beim Boots-Gebäude) aus ganz normal angeordneten Innenstützen besteht. Die hierin liegenden Mehrdeutigkeiten wurden auf verschiedene Weise überwunden: durch möglichst geringe Unterschiede in der strukturellen Behandlung oder durch eine Anordnung, die erkennen läßt, daß das Erdgeschoß in gewisser Hinsicht ein gesonderter, auf das Erdniveau bezogener Bauteil ist. Wie dem auch sei – die entwurfliche Überzeugungskraft beruht auf der visuellen Glaubwürdigkeit der Struktur als Dach-Stützen-Konstruktion. Das Weglassen oder Betonen von Einzelheiten wird hier besonders bedeutsam. So tragen Versteifungsflansche an beiden Gebäuden dazu bei, sie ins Reich der Bautechnik zu versetzen; die strenge Einhaltung eines Moduls bei der gesamten Innenausstattung schafft eine Aura der Zwangsläufigkeit; die dunkle Außenfarbe unterstreicht die Atmosphäre ernsthaften Bemühens. Obgleich die Programme für solche Gebäude selten verlangen, daß ein Merkmal besonders hervorgehoben wird, erfordern sie eigentlich keine Gleichmacherei innerhalb eines einzigen, rechteckigen Behälters. Dessen Vorteil besteht jedoch darin, daß seine großen, regelmäßigen Außenseiten den Eindruck erwecken, es gebe keine vernünftige Alternative. Bei beiden Gebäuden wurde im Entwurf wie in der Ausführung Mies van der Rohes Leitbild – technische Perfektion und Reinheit – verwirklicht. Von den technischen Anlagen bis hin zum Mobiliar ist die Inneneinrichtung gefällig, wenn auch unerbittlich integriert. Überall ist die Präzision des Details schön. Trotzdem wirkt das Ergebnis seltsam frustrierend, vielleicht weil die auf das strukturelle Detail verwandte Energie, Beharrlichkeit und Intelligenz offensichtlich nichts als Selbstzweck ist. Dies ist ein fundamentales Dilemma der »rationalen« Architektur.

Die für diese drei Gebäude genannten Ausdrucksmöglichkeiten umfassen keineswegs die ganze Skala; sie deuten lediglich die begreiflichen Grenzen für niedrige Bauwerke mittlerer Größe und vorwiegend zweckgebundenen Charakters an. Ein Wechsel von flacher, horizontaler Bauweise zum vertikalen Turm- und Scheibenbau eröffnet zweifellos weitere konstruktive Möglichkeiten, und es ist vielleicht angebracht, zuerst zu fragen, welches Hochhaus von SOM wohl dem Gebäude der Zeitung »The Republic« von Myron Goldsmith entspricht. Es ist der 19geschossige Turm der Business Men's Assurance Co. of America in Kansas City. Der Bau ist ganz einfach ein schmuckloser struktureller Käfig auf einer niedrigen, gepflasterten Plattform, im Grundriß ein Rechteck aus quadratischen Stützenfeldern, angeordnet im Verhältnis von 3:5. Das Erdgeschoß ist durch eine leichte, fast unmerkliche Überhöhung von den übrigen Geschossen abgesetzt; Stützen und Träger haben die gleichen Maße, und die gläserne Außenwand ist so stark zurückgesetzt, daß der Käfig frei und deutlich dasteht. In gewisser Beziehung haben wir hier den Archetyp der Skelettstruktur vor uns, bar aller überflüssigen Details und offenbar aufnahmefähig für alles, was man

horizontal sun shade hangs from each floor like an upside down parapet. Dark metal cladding helps to suggest that these details are derived from structural considerations. The result is without the abstract, nearly scaleless quality of the Business Men's Assurance building, nor is it yet so engineered as to seem like more effort than the problem requires.

The Tenneco building takes form derived from "minimum" structure to something just short of the mid-point of its expressive possibilities; beyond this the form derives either from improved structural efficiency or from some other quality implicit in the building as a whole. Lightness and grace, or horizontal stacks of floors, or verticality, for example, are all available for expressive elaboration, but what tends to be selected for emphasis is the idea of massive power, strength, and weight, characteristics which are not necessarily in the spirit of a developing technology of light, efficient, high-rise construction. An example is the United States Steel building in New York at 1 Liberty Plaza, which in fact does achieve a remarkable economy of materials despite its massive appearance, but before considering its formal implications it may be more useful to review the SOM structural innovations that seem to indicate the future of skyscraper design.

It is not necessary to recapitulate in detail the variations, which begin with the introduction of larger spans and evolve in relation to the demand for greater height at a reasonable cost. The main line of development has, of course, been concerned with the problem of stabilizing structure, and has focused attention on the contradiction between an expressed orthogonal frame and the lateral bracing normally concealed within core walls. Precedent for expressing the diagonal has been variously cited as going back to the Eames House of 1949, the Crystal Palace of 1851, or the buttressing of gothic cathedrals. It would be conceded that the truss walls of Mies' Convention Hall project of 1953 revealed some of the design possibilities of expressed lateral framing, although it is sometimes forgotten that Mies first explored the idea in 1934, with a project for a glasswalled house cantilevered from a hillside. In skyscraper design, however, Mies continued to reject expressed lateral framing. Like Japanese architects of the classical period, he apparently regarded such framing as something to be concealed at all costs. Psychologically the attitude is akin to that of the Greeks in the Hellenistic period; they understood quite well the principle of the arch but preferred to reserve such excessively dynamic construction for sewers. As the distinction between the art of architecture and the science of engineering has blurred, that attitude is no longer psychologically persuasive. But the first experiments with this technique are cast in the language of engineering, not "art" – the distinction is still operative. One result is that the idea seems at first sight grotesquely in excess of what is required, despite its demonstrable economic advantages. Thus SOM's San Francisco office rejected a 1957 study for a building with expressed lateral framing because it was only 17 stories high, and not until the 27-story Alcoa building of 1967 was there a suitable occasion to try it out. Interesting as the Alcoa building may be, it too seems not quite big enough to justify its structure and the attendant, albeit minor, inconveniences to the building's occupants, whose views out are interrupted by unintelligible fragments flying across the windows.

The first suitable opportunity occurred with the 100-story John Hancock Center of 1970. This combines accommodations in one massive, tapered, rectangular tower for department stores on the ground, third and fourth floors; parking from the sixth to the twelfth floors; offices from the thirteenth to the forty-first floors; apartments from the forty-sixth to the ninety-second floors; and restaurant-observation level, TV studio and mechanical space above. These are incorporated in a structure and a height module that in no way differentiates their diverse functions. In the apartments the sloping perimeter walls and massive beams and columns, including the slanting ones, produce an effect not unlike that of a renovated garret in Berlin or Paris, although the distractions of obtrusive structure are compensated by spectacular views, if not by garret rents.

Seen from the other side of Chicago the tapered profile of the Hancock building is an extraordinarily compelling urban image. As one approaches the building, catching glimpses of it in the kaleidoscope of urban forms, and as its detail becomes visible, its mesmerizing effect increases. Approaching it at ground level, close up, introduces a rude shock: this gigantic construction stands on a one-story travertine pedestal, as if it were a paperweight. All striving to express the dynamics of a maximally efficient structure ends abruptly some twelve feet above ground level. The solidity implied by a stone base is disrupted by shop windows and minimal entrances, compounding the confusion. The contrast between a very low entrance and a massive superstructure may of course be used to advantage, and is not problematic in itself. But mediating between the scale of the street and the scale of the building is certainly one of the functions of an entrance; it is a function that architects

Alcoa Building, San Francisco, California.

innerhalb des Stützenrasters von etwa 11×11 m unterbringen möchte. Der Turm steht für sich in einem Park, sein Skelett ist mit weißem Marmor verkleidet, dessen leichte Körnung aus einem gewissen Abstand nicht mehr wahrgenommen wird, und er gleicht einem abstrakten Baumodell, das zufällig in voller Größe gebaut wurde. Wenn man bedenkt, daß sich diese Konzeption bereits in Giuseppe Terragnis 1932 erbauter Casa del Fascio in Como findet und danach von Terragni und anderen in den Jahren unmittelbar vor dem Zweiten Weltkrieg weiterverfolgt wurde, ist es erstaunlich, daß sie in den Vereinigten Staaten erst um die Mitte der sechziger Jahre verwirklicht wurde. Terragnis Casa del Fascio war ein Experiment mit der Mehrdeutigkeit, die dadurch entsteht, daß eine streng orthogonale Stützen- und Trägerstruktur von festen Ausfachungen gänzlich undifferenziert bleibt. Der Widerspruch zwischen Struktur und Nicht-Struktur wurde noch durch eine einheitliche Ummantelung aus weißem Stuck verstärkt. Die weiße Marmorverkleidung an der Hauptverwaltung der Business Men's Assurance Co. dient ebenfalls dem Zweck, die Gestalt zu abstrahieren, so daß sie nicht mehr »gebaut« aussieht (wenngleich die Fugen und die Äderungen des Marmors etwas ablenken). Aber zwischen dem italienischen Umgang mit Stütze und Wand und dem Gebäude der Business Men's Assurance Co. steht Mies van der Rohe. Was wir heute vor Augen haben, ist ein Bau von großer Reinheit, die darauf beruht, daß die Wand in den Hintergrund tritt, die Struktur selbst auf das Äußerste abstrahiert ist und das Detail ausgeschieden oder wenigstens unauffällig ausgebildet wurde. Tatsächlich ist der Bau erstaunlich nahe daran, das zu sein, was sein Aussehen verspricht: eine rudimentäre Skelettstruktur.

Was geschieht, wenn bei gleicher Konzeption mit strukturellen Details gearbeitet wird, sieht man beim Tenneco Building. Obwohl es erheblich größer ist – 33 Geschosse und sieben Stützenfelder pro Seite, wobei der zentral angeordnete Erschließungskern die inneren Stützen ersetzt –, ist es doch der gleiche strukturelle Käfig mit zurückgesetzten Glaswänden. Der Käfig ist jedoch gegliedert: Die Stützen springen etwas vor, so daß die Vertikale betont wird; die Arkade auf Straßenniveau ist drei Geschosse hoch; die Stützen sind bis zur Mitte des ersten Randbalkens mit noch weiter vorgezogenen »Diensten« versehen; von jedem Stockwerk ragt ein waagrechter Sonnenbrecher wie eine umgestürzte Brüstung vor. Die dunkle Metallverkleidung verstärkt den Eindruck struktureller Vielfalt. Das Gebäude ist weit von der Abstraktheit und nahezu vollständigen Maßstabslosigkeit der Hauptverwaltung der Business Men's Assurance Co. entfernt; es ist aber auch nicht so technisiert, daß der Beschauer das Gefühl hätte, man habe mehr Mühe darauf verwendet, als das Problem überhaupt erforderte.

Das Tenneco Building läßt sich als eine »Minimal«-Struktur, der durch strukturelle Details ein expressiver Charakter verliehen wurde, beschreiben. Bei den übrigen Hochhäusern leitet sich die Gestalt entweder von einer statisch effizienteren Tragwerksform oder von einer anderen dem Gebäude als Ganzem zugeordneten Determinanten her. Leichtigkeit und Anmut, horizontale Differenzierung oder Vertikalität sind die naheliegendsten Ausdrucksmittel der zweiten Kategorie; man neigt allerdings heute vielfach dazu, wuchtige Kraft, Stärke und Schwere zu betonen, also Merkmale, die nicht unbedingt dem Geist einer aufstrebenden Technologie des leichten und stabilen Hochhauses entsprechen. Ein Beispiel dafür ist das Hochhaus der U.S. Steel (One Liberty Plaza) in New York, bei dem jedoch trotz des massiven Aussehens eine bemerkenswerte Materialökonomie erreicht wurde.

Es ist hier nicht notwendig, die neuere Entwicklung des Hochhausbaus, die mit größeren Spannweiten begann und mit der Erfüllung der Forderung nach größerer Höhe zu erschwinglichem Preis fortschritt, im einzelnen zu rekapitulieren. Das Hauptinteresse galt selbstverständlich dem Problem der Skelettversteifung und konzentrierte sich auf den Widerspruch zwischen einem sichtbaren orthogonalen Skelett und der normalerweise in den Kernwänden verborgenen Versteifung gegen Horizontalkräfte. Verschiedentlich wurde die Ansicht vertreten, die Vorläufer der sichtbaren Diagonalen gingen auf das Eames House von 1949, den Kristallpalast von 1851 oder die Strebepfeiler gotischer Dome zurück. Man räumt ein, daß die Fachwerkwände in Mies van der Rohes Convention-Hall-Projekt aus dem Jahr 1953 etwas von den formalen Möglichkeiten sichtbar gelassener Versteifungselemente offenbarten, vergißt dabei aber gelegentlich, daß Mies diesem Gedanken schon 1934 nachging, und zwar mit der Skizze eines frei über einem Hang schwebenden Glashauses. Beim Entwurf von Wolkenkratzern lehnte Mies jedoch beharrlich sichtbare Diagonalen ab. Wie die japanischen Architekten der klassischen Epoche hielt er offenbar eine solche Versteifung für etwas, das um jeden Preis versteckt werden muß. Psychologisch ähnelt diese Ansicht der Einstellung der Griechen während der hellenistischen Periode; sie hatten das Prinzip des Bogens sehr wohl erfaßt, verwendeten aber eine derart dynamische

John Hancock Center, Chicago, Illinois.

around the world have grappled with but have rarely solved with complete success in the urban high-rise context. SOM's intelligence has not yet been applied to the problem with anything like the energy concentrated on solving structural problems. In the John Hancock Center, where engineering ends it is improvisation, not architecture, that takes over.

Another Chicago structural exercise seems to hold more intrinsic architectural significance: the 109-story Sears Tower. The theme is essentially a building made up of buildings: nine towers packed in a square rise to different heights. Each tower is 75 feet square and each is a structural tube whose clear spans are framed by perimeter columns spaced six to a side, including the shared corner columns which are of larger dimension. During construction an extraordinary and beautiful space sequence is revealed in looking from one tower into the others; on completion, of course, office partitions will obliterate this internal clarity. But the unquestioned structural efficiency and economy of the Sears Tower, while it may be the only justification necessary to its brilliant engineer, is not itself the most interesting aspect. The form is doubly persuasive precisely because it can be built with other structural systems. The clear articulation of component towers equal in all dimensions except their height provides what now seems an obvious solution to several problems at once. It suggests possible ways of differentiating functions for buildings intended to accommodate so-called "24 hour" programs, such as the John Hancock. It suggests ways in which the composition of a tower can be made more responsive to its immediate environment, since its component parts can be oriented to advance or recede in relation to what goes on around them. And finally it suggests that height expressed through dominantly vertical detail might perhaps take second place to height expressed through massing itself – the building affords pure vertical ascent for each of its parts with the advantages of set-backs in its totality. What is left to refine is the articulation of the skin, and most particularly the treatment of the column where one tower stops and the adjacent tower continues upward. Perhaps because the formal idea came first, and a suitable structure was applied to it, the Sears Tower can be experienced as technique in the service of form rather than the other way around. It is difficult to think of another skyscraper put up in the United States during the last 15 years that opens up as many possibilities of form and structure alike.

If the Hancock building casts architecture in the idiom of civil engineering, and if the Sears building rationalizes towers of varying heights by a suitable structural technique, the 54-story tower for U.S. Steel, at 1 Liberty Plaza in New York, occupies a more ambiguous territory. Here the intent is to use steel as visibly and assertively as possible: it is what the client sells. Initial studies were directed toward the use of plate steel to make a bearing wall, but the time required for research and legal clearances ruled it out in favor of what is essentially a conventional skeleton frame with a stabilizing core. The significant innovation is that greater stress loads are carried on the perimeter, through spandrel girders whose great depth allows reduction of the web to a thickness of 1/4": Besides reducing the role of a stabilizing core, there is an additional economy in taking care of one half of the skin with the steel structure itself.

The U.S. Steel tower is a rectangle with a bay ratio of three to five. These bays are 50 feet on the long elevations, with the dimension increased almost imperceptibly on the narrow ends (where the central bay is wider still). The 6'3" height of the spandrel girders equals the height of the windows, and is enough to absorb the suspended ceiling as well as the parapet and heating element on the floor above. Because the webs of each of the spandrel girders are not fireproofed on the outside, their flanges have been extended (over a core of sprayed-on fireproofing material) to act as a flame shield. With the addition of these shields the total set back for the glass is more than two feet, so that the bottom flange acts as a sunshade.

Columns, however, are conventionally fireproofed and steel-clad. With the flange of each column articulated as an element slightly more than one foot wide, the actual column face is made to read as an unusually wide reveal. Spandrels and columns are thus part of the same grammar of steel girder construction, brought up to a scale normally associated with elevated highways or railroad crossings and contradicted by every building in the vicinity. The immediate visual impression is that if the U.S. Steel building is structurally sound, then everything around it must be unsafe; if the others are safe, then the U.S. Steel building must be something of an exaggeration. The sheer quantity of metal displayed to the eye is perhaps no more than would be consumed by dividing the structural bays with closely spaced vertical mullions, or using some other cladding system; it is, of course, the reversal of proportions between solid and void that makes the difference. This is not a glass building with a skeleton frame; it is a steel wall with glazed slots, hypnotically compelling, especially as

Sears Tower, Chicago, Illinois.

U.S. Steel Building, New York, New York.

Konstruktion lieber für Abwasserkanäle. Da sich die Unterschiede zwischen der Kunst der Architektur und der Wissenschaft der Bautechnik verwischt haben, ist diese Haltung psychologisch nicht mehr überzeugend. Die ersten Experimente wurden jedoch in der Sprache der Technik und nicht der »Kunst« verwirklicht – der Unterschied ist immer noch lebendig. Eine Folge davon ist, daß für uns das Prinzip auf den ersten Blick in grotesker Weise das Erforderliche zu übersteigen scheint – obwohl wir uns der wirtschaftlichen Vorteile durchaus bewußt sind. Das SOM-Büro in San Francisco verwarf noch 1957 eine Studie zu einem Gebäude mit sichtbarer Diagonalversteifung, das allerdings auch nur 17 Geschosse hoch war; erst mit dem 27geschossigen Alcoa Building von 1967 wurde ein Anfang in dieser Richtung gemacht. So interessant das Alcoa Building auch sein mag, es wirkt doch ebenfalls nicht groß genug, um seine Struktur und die damit verbundenen, wenn auch geringfügigen Beeinträchtigungen für die Benutzer – deren Sicht nach draußen durch ärgerliche, quer über die Fenster verlaufende Bauelemente behindert wird – zu rechtfertigen.

Die erste dem Prinzip angemessene Gelegenheit ergab sich mit dem 100geschossigen John Hancock Center von 1970. Der massive, rechteckige, sich verjüngende Turm bietet Platz für Lobbies, Geschäfte usw. vom Souterrain bis zum 5. Geschoß, für Garagen vom 6. bis 12. Geschoß, für Büros vom 13. bis 41. Geschoß, für Apartments und Wohnungen vom 46. bis 92. Geschoß sowie für Restaurants, Aussichtsräume, ein Fernsehstudio und technische Anlagen in den letzten acht Geschossen. Struktur und Höhenmodul sind in keiner Weise entsprechend den verschiedenen Funktionen differenziert. In den Apartments rufen die schrägen Außenwände und die massiven Träger, Stützen und diagonalen Versteifungsglieder eine Wirkung hervor, die der eines ausgebauten Dachstocks in Berlin oder Paris nicht unähnlich ist. Die Nachteile der sichtbaren Struktur werden zwar durch fabelhafte Ausblicke, leider aber nicht durch Dachstockmieten ausgeglichen.

Aus der Ferne gesehen ist der sich verjüngende Turm ein höchst eindrucksvolles städtisches Wahrzeichen. Wenn man sich dem Gebäude nähert, im Kaleidoskop des Stadtbildes immer wieder einen Blick darauf erhascht und allmählich Einzelheiten wahrnimmt, steigt die von ihm ausstrahlende Faszination noch an. Steht man dann ganz dicht davor, so erlebt man eine böse Überraschung: Das riesige Bauwerk steht auf einem eingeschossigen Travertinsockel, als sei es ein Leichtgewicht. Das Bemühen um die architektonische Bewältigung einer höchstleistungsfähigen Struktur endet abrupt 3,60 m über dem Boden. Die von einer Steinbasis ausgehende Wirkung der Solidität wird von Schaufenstern und von winzigen Eingängen gebrochen, so daß die Verwirrung vollständig ist. Zweifellos ist die Vermittlung zwischen dem Maßstab der Straße und dem Maßstab des Gebäudes eine wichtige Funktion des Eingangs. Mit dieser Funktion haben sich Architekten auf der ganzen Welt beschäftigt, doch selten haben sie bislang im Hochhausbau eine zufriedenstellende Lösung gefunden. Auch die Firma SOM hat ihre Intelligenz auf diese Frage noch nicht mit gleicher Energie wie auf die Lösung anderer Probleme gerichtet.

Einer anderen Chicagoer Strukturübung, dem 109geschossigen Sears Tower, scheint eine größere architektonische Signifikanz zu eignen. Ein Gebäude aus Gebäuden, dies ist das Grundthema. Neun in ein Quadrat gepackte Türme erheben sich zu verschiedenen Höhen. Jeder Turm ist im Grundriß ein stützenfreies Quadrat mit einer Seitenlänge von etwa 22,80 m. Der Durchblick durch die noch offenen Türme zeigt eine außergewöhnlich schöne Raumfolge; nach Fertigstellung werden natürlich die Trennwände die innere Klarheit verbergen. Unbestrittene strukturelle Leistungsfähigkeit und Wirtschaftlichkeit mögen dem glänzenden Ingenieur zur Rechtfertigung genügen, stellen jedoch nicht den interessantesten Aspekt des Gebäudes dar. Seine Gestalt ist doppelt überzeugend, weil sie auch mit anderen strukturellen Systemen zu realisieren ist. Die deutliche Aufgliederung des Baukörpers in einzelne Türme, die in allen Abmessungen außer der Höhe gleich sind, stellt für mehrere Probleme zugleich eine zwingend erscheinende Lösung bereit. Sie weist Wege zur Differenzierung von Funktionen bei Gebäuden, die wie das John Hancock Center sogenannte 24-Stunden-Programme aufnehmen sollen. Sie erschließt darüber hinaus Möglichkeiten zur besseren Anpassung eines Turmhauses an seine unmittelbare Umgebung, da die Bestandteile je nach dem, was um sie herum vorhanden ist, vor- oder zurückspringen können. Und schließlich zeigt sie, daß Höhe nicht nur durch vorherrschend vertikale Details, sondern auch durch Massengruppierung ihren architektonischen Ausdruck finden kann. Verbesserungsbedürftig ist noch die Gliederung der Außenhaut und insbesondere die Behandlung der Stützen an der Stelle, an der ein Turm endet und der Nachbarturm weiter aufsteigt. Weil die formale Idee zuerst da war und eine geeignete Struktur für sie gefunden wurde, kann der Sears Tower wohl als technisches Experiment im Dienst der Gestalt gelten und nicht umgekehrt. Man kann sich kaum einen anderen Wolkenkratzer der

the eye climbs the rungs of the facade and the glass disappears altogether. Inevitably the black paint makes the effect still more sinister, and the fortress quality is emphasized by the one-story height of the ground floor surmounted by a double height floor accommodating a bank. The only such change in vertical rhythm, this mezzanine level appears to be the true entrance, but, alas, it is no part of the public thoroughfare.

Because the site slopes down to the west, the building sits on a kind of podium of giant steps whose soft, rolled edges make them impossible to use (steel bollards and chains prevent the foolhardy from trying), and real steps are cut into them. The height of the U.S. Steel building was the result of a trade-off with the city, whereby an adjacent narrow block was acquired by the company and turned into a "plaza". The same ground treatment is used here, with the addition of trees regularly distributed. Chiefly because of the hostile steps, the result is a singularly grudging public accommodation all the more remarkable in view of the opportunity that was missed. The desire to repel, even when prompted by the client, would perhaps be more intelligible if there really were some reason why the public should be discouraged from using the plaza or entering the building: here we may again note the phenomenon and delay for a moment a guess as to what it means.

The U.S. Steel building displays the rhetorical possibilities inherent in the design of structure. A quite different statement, but no less rhetorical, is found in Gordon Bunshaft's Marine Midland building nearby at 140 Broadway. Here the architectural statement is not about the nature of structure but of office space. The "function" of the building is recognized as analogous to that of a package; what is offered is a commodity: portions of space. Marine Midland is thus a commodity in a glass and metal wrapping so flat that it appears to have been printed rather than built. If the BMA tower looks like an architectural model, the skin of Marine Midland relates it to recent painting, perhaps the work of Ad Reinhardt, as well as to graphic design in its contrasts of shiny bronze-tinted glass and matte-black metal, seemingly silk-screened over a high-gloss paper. At the same time, its perfect surfaces are contradicted by its actual shape. Marine Midland follows precisely the limits of its site – a block that narrows from east to west, so that the building is a trapezoid four bays wide on the east, three on the west, and seven bays long, the dimensional discrepancy being absorbed in the central core spaces. The reduction of width on the west elevation, although probably unnoticed by thousands of people passing every day, is nevertheless conspicuous when the building is seen from an opposite corner. There is no particular reason why a skyscraper should not follow the contour of an irregular site; what is unnerving here is the distortion of perspective, experienced simultaneously with a prismatically pure, flat mass whose every detail suggests a rigorous formal logic, utterly independent of anything as contingent as a defect in New York's street grid.

Detail is essential to this building, but with one exception it may be said to consist in its own absence: no element on the facade protrudes more than half an inch. The detail that asserts itself as such is a mullion recessed in the center of each column, making the flat surface on either side read as part of the single element incorporating the windows, and yet the extreme delicacy of the mullion (3″ wide) as well as of the glazing bars and the cladding joints, reasserts an underlying affinity with *baukunst*.

The building is surrounded by a field of travertine paving and this, together with a bright red metal cube designed by Isamu Noguchi, completes a tripartite composition. The metal cube, itself out of square and alarmingly balanced on one point, complements the building's distorted perspective. Together the three elements – building, paving, cube – are somehow more than they seem to be, as if the composition had been created by a sculptor of the minimal school intent on transposing the empiricism of architecture into the metaphysics of abstract form. (Are they perfect forms deteriorating toward earthly imperfection, or imperfect forms aspiring to the Platonic Idea?)

That the building follows a now familiar pattern of double height mezzanine with a single height floor at street level, and that its entrances are not generous, seems in this case beside the point. Delicacy of detail tends to overcome an implied indifference to the immediate environment. Marine Midland achieves substantial economies through the design of its flat skin; the formal qualities that derive from this are made explicit through the use of the site. What happens when the flat, two-tone dark skin is applied by the acre to bulk buildings without other distinction is a less happy story. Marine Midland's ubiquitous progeny have not yet matched its distinction, and have introduced a new note to the keyboard of perfunctory solutions to real estate problems; on the other hand they are no more tedious en-masse than the army of vertically pin-striped buildings launched by Mies. In some respects they are more straightforward in recognizing the limits of their own possibilities.

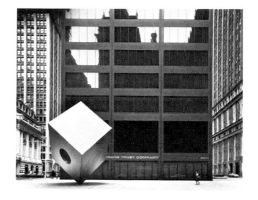

Marine Midland Building, New York, New York.

letzten 15 Jahre in den Vereinigten Staaten denken, der so viele Möglichkeiten sowohl der Gestalt als auch der Struktur eröffnet.

Während man beim John Hancock Center die Architektur der Sprache des Ingenieurbaus unterwirft und beim Sears Tower durch ein geeignetes strukturelles Verfahren die Rechtfertigung für Türme verschiedener Höhe findet, gehört der 54geschossige Turm der U.S. Steel (One Liberty Plaza) in New York einem mehrdeutigeren Bereich an. Hier war beabsichtigt, Stahl so sichtbar und auffällig wie möglich zu verwenden, denn Stahl ist das Verkaufsobjekt des Bauherrn. Im Gespräch war anfangs vor allem eine tragende »Rohr«-Haut aus Stahlplatten, die aber angesichts des hohen Zeitaufwandes für die Bewältigung der mit dieser Konstruktion verbundenen technischen und gesetzlichen Probleme zugunsten eines im Grunde konventionellen Skeletts mit Aussteifungskern verworfen wurde. Dessen besonderes Merkmal liegt darin, daß ein überdurchschnittlich hoher Lastanteil auf die Gebäudeaußenseiten entfällt; wegen ihrer großen Höhe konnten die Randträger trotzdem sehr schlank dimensioniert werden – so beträgt die Dicke der Stege nur etwa 6,5 mm. Das Hochhaus ist im Grundriß ein Rechteck mit einem Stützenfeldverhältnis von 3:5. Die Spannweite beträgt in Gebäudelängsrichtung ungefähr 15 m, in Gebäudequerrichtung etwas mehr (wobei die Mittelfelder nochmals weiter sind). Die Randträger sind mit einer Höhe von rund 1,90 m ungefähr so hoch wie die Fenster; sie verbergen zum einen die abgehängte Decke und bilden zum anderen auch die Brüstung des darüberliegenden Geschosses, wodurch gegenüber einer üblichen Vorhangfassade etwa 50% an Hautfläche eingespart wurden.

Die Stege der Randträger sind außen nicht feuergeschützt; dafür sind die Verkleidungen der Flansche so weit vorgezogen (über einem Mantel aus aufgesprühtem Feuerschutzmaterial), daß sie als Hitzeschild wirken. Unter Berücksichtigung dieser Schilde ist die Glaswand um mehr als 60 cm zurückgesetzt, so daß der untere Flansch zugleich als Sonnenbrecher dient.

Die Stützen dagegen sind konventionell feuergeschützt und stahlverkleidet. Da der Flansch jeder Stütze als ein etwas über 30 cm breites Element ausgebildet ist, wirkt der noch sichtbare Stützensteg wie eine außergewöhnlich breite Fuge. Randträger und Stützen sind somit Teil einer einheitlichen Stahlprofilkonstruktion in einem Maßstab, den man normalerweise mit Hochstraßen oder Eisenbahnbrücken verbindet und der sämtlichen benachbarten Gebäuden widerspricht. Folgender optischer Eindruck drängt sich unmittelbar auf: Wenn das Hochhaus der U.S. Steel strukturell stabil ist, müssen alle Bauwerke der Umgebung gefährdet sein; wenn jedoch die anderen Bauten stabil sind, muß man beim Hochhaus der U.S. Steel stark übertrieben haben. Die Stahlmenge, die sich dem Blick des Beschauers darbietet, ist vielleicht nicht größer als bei einem üblichen Hochhaus mit enggestellten vertikalen Sprossen; die Umkehrung der Proportionen zwischen dem optisch Offenen und Geschlossenen ist es, die den Unterschied ausmacht. Dies ist kein Glasbau mit Stahlskelett, sondern eine Stahlwand mit verglasten Schlitzen, die eine hypnotisch zwingende Wirkung ausübt, besonders wenn der Blick an den Profilen der Fassade emporklettert und das Glas nicht mehr erfaßt. Zwangsläufig verstärkt der schwarze Anstrich die düstere Wirkung, und das festungsartige Aussehen wird dadurch betont, daß über dem ein Stockwerk hohen Erdgeschoß ein Stockwerk von doppelter Geschoßhöhe folgt, das eine Bank beherbergt. Dieses Zwischengeschoß, das die einzige Abwechslung im vertikalen Rhythmus bringt, scheint das eigentliche Eingangsgeschoß zu sein, ist aber leider für Passanten nicht erreichbar.

Weil das Gelände nach Westen abfällt, steht das Gebäude auf einer Art Podium, dessen riesige, mit abgerundeten Kanten versehene Stufen jedoch nicht begehbar sind (stählerne Poller und Ketten sollen Vorwitzige daran hindern, es trotzdem zu versuchen); nur an einigen Stellen sind echte Treppen in diese Stufen eingeschnitten. Die Turmhöhe ergab sich aus einem Handel mit der Stadt, bei dem die Gesellschaft einen benachbarten schmalen Block erwarb und in eine »Plaza« umwandelte. Die Gebäudebehandlung ist hier dieselbe wie beim Hauptblock; hinzu kommt eine Bepflanzung aus gleichmäßig gesetzten Bäumen. Vor allem wegen der fußgängerfeindlichen Stufen ist dieser öffentliche Platz seltsam trübsinnig, was angesichts der vorhandenen, jedoch nicht genutzten Möglichkeiten bedauerlich ist. Der Wunsch nach Unzugänglichkeit wäre, selbst wenn er vom Bauherrn geäußert worden wäre, vielleicht verständlicher, wenn wirklich ein Grund dafür vorläge, das Publikum an der Benutzung der Plaza oder am Betreten des Gebäudes zu hindern. Auch hier wieder können wir nur das Phänomen festhalten.

Das Hochhaus der U.S. Steel stellt die im Tragwerk beschlossenen rhetorischen Möglichkeiten zur Schau. Eine ganz andere, aber nicht minder rhetorische Sprache spricht Gordon

Hancock, U.S. Steel, and Marine Midland have been observed to lack satisfactory relations with the street. In startling contrast is a building that solves this problem, and yet has been criticized because the total form for which its entrance is a necessary solution is unsympathetic to adjacent buildings. The 50-story office tower at 9 West 57th Street in New York City is inserted on an east-west block, where buildings of such height have previously been avoided. Unlike most crosstown streets in Manhattan, 57th is an unusually wide avenue that can absorb 50-story buildings. Since the city exists to make and manage money, it is fatuous to pretend that higher considerations, such as civility, comfort or common sense, can halt the intrusion of these profitable giants; only money can stop what it starts. 9 West 57th Street is controversial, as they say in the newspapers, not because it is tall but because it does not rise straight up from the street (as architects have taught everyone to expect). Ostensibly the result of interpreting the zoning envelope to avoid setbacks, without trading off too much ground area for a "plaza", the building pitches back in a sweeping curve for the first nineteen floors and then rises vertically. This disrupts the continuity of the street and leaves the sides of adjacent buildings exposed; their intersection with the curved glass plane is politely described as unfortunate. However, the bottom of the glass wall is terminated by an enormous trough extending across the full width of the building, carrying off rain water and at the same time providing a generous and explicit entrance canopy. 9 West 57th Street is one of the few skyscrapers recently constructed in New York City of which it can be said that the entrance is neither an inconvenient interruption the architect would rather have avoided, nor an extraneous addition imposed on something else, but is an indispensable part of a unified configuration. Perhaps it is just this contrast, between the agreeable scale at street level and the glass ski-jump looming overhead, that disturbs critics more than the conjunction with buildings on either side. And though critics may agree that it demands a block to itself (imagine it, for example, as a replacement for the UN secretariat) the layman's response is disarmingly contrary to learned opinion. Indeed this building quite literally stops people in the street; the immense curved glass wall is an exhilarating spectacle, not as architecture but as urban theater, as fascinating as a fountain.

The discrepancy between architecture in the service of technique, and architecture in the service of a content for which technique is only the means to an end, generates today's significant arguments about the future of the art. Most of the SOM buildings conceived as expressive form are solutions to non-commercial problems: they are either museums or libraries or schools. Such buildings come into existence because they celebrate something pleasant that has resulted from the accumulation of money, rather than the process by which the money is made. Client and public usually agree that such occasions justify architecture formed, or at least conditioned, by a diet more nourishing than utility. But conventional criticism still finds it necessary to eschew expression (which implies a content to be expressed). If there is such a thing as aristocratic taste (however reluctant it may be to assert itself as such) its distinguishing characteristic in our own time has been its fatigued disavowal of any content other than form itself: there is no message because there is nothing worth saying. Thus "advanced" music denies the emotionally energized expansion and contraction of time, preferring instead the duration of silences between sounds; painting may be nothing more than the sensation of color; architecture only "skin and bones". Arrived finally at its popular level of misunderstanding, the reductionist view achieves ultimate vulgarity in Marshall McLuhan's "the medium is the message": pseudo-technical justification for the vacuous. For Zen priests and Christian mystics perhaps: emptiness and silence are authenticated by the religious disavowal of the self in an indifferent universe, so that emptiness and silence may be filled by ineffable understanding. For us the disavowal of meaning leads more naturally to the empty head.

How difficult it is, then, to understand buildings that assert a content other than that attributable to their own substance. If the content is intelligible because society has already agreed upon it, the architect may have an easier time. Churches, for example, we do generally agree should look, feel, and be, different from supermarkets, if one feels that churches should exist at all. But monuments? Should they exist? And if so, who is worthy of commemoration? Is a good building honoring an unworthy man all the more reprehensible for accepting the notion of architectural grandeur as psychologically therapeutic and, perhaps, redeeming? The questions are painfully real, despite the infrequent opportunities given to architects to answer them, and criticism seldom rises to the occasion. Thus it is predictable that a monument to an American President, regarded by his enemies as well as his friends as larger than life, should produce critical attacks on the idea of monumentality, rather than on the man himself. The Lyndon Baines Johnson Library in Austin, Texas, matches the idea to the

9 West 57th Street, New York, New York.

Bunshafts Marine Midland Building (140 Broadway). Hier bestimmt nicht die Struktur, sondern der Büroraum die architektonische Aussage. Die »Funktion« des Gebäudes wird darin gesehen, Verpackung zu sein; es wird eine Handelsware in einer flachen Glas- und Metallumhüllung angeboten. Während der Turm der Business Men's Assurance Co. einem architektonischen Modell gleicht, steht das Marine Midland Building in Beziehung zur modernen Malerei, etwa zum Werk von Ad Reinhardt, ebenso zur Graphik, scheint doch seine Haut mit ihren Kontrasten zwischen glänzendem, bronzefarben getöntem Glas und mattschwarzem Metall im Siebdruckverfahren auf Hochglanzpapier hergestellt zu sein. Zugleich widerspricht aber der Grundriß dieser Vollkommenheit der Oberfläche. Das Marine Midland Building folgt genau den Grenzen des Baugeländes; es ist ein Block, der von Osten nach Westen schmaler wird. Das trapezförmige Gebäude ist an der Ostseite vier Felder und an der Westseite drei Felder breit; die Längsseiten sind in sieben Felder unterteilt. Die unterschiedlichen Dimensionen werden vom zentral angeordneten Kern aufgefangen. Die geringere Breite auf der Westseite fällt wahrscheinlich den meisten Passanten kaum auf, ist jedoch unübersehbar, wenn man das Gebäude von gegenüber betrachtet. Es gibt keinen besonderen Grund dafür, daß ein Wolkenkratzer dem Umriß eines unregelmäßigen Geländes nicht folgen sollte; aufregend ist an diesem Gebäude, daß die scheinbare perspektivische Verzerrung mit einer prismatisch reinen, flachen Baumasse einhergeht, die in all ihren Einzelheiten auf eine strenge, von etwas so Zufälligem wie einer Unregelmäßigkeit im New Yorker Straßennetz unabhängige formale Logik schließen läßt.

Das Detail ist für dieses Gebäude wesentlich, doch mit einer Ausnahme scheint es darin zu bestehen, nicht vorhanden zu sein: Kein Fassadenelement springt um mehr als 1,5 cm vor. Die Einzelheit, die als solche ins Auge fällt, ist ein vertieft in der Mitte jeder Stütze liegendes Profil. Es bewirkt, daß man die Flächen zu beiden Seiten als Teil eines einheitlichen, die Fenster umschließenden Elements auffaßt.

Um das Gebäude zieht sich ein mit Travertinplatten belegter Platz, auf dem eine von Isamu Noguchi entworfene leuchtend rote Metallskulptur steht. Der Rhomboeder, der gefährlich auf einer Ecke balanciert, ist wie das Gebäude nicht rechtwinklig. Zusammen sind die drei Elemente Gebäude, Platz und Skulptur irgendwie mehr, als sie zu sein scheinen; es ist, als sei die Komposition von einem Bildhauer aus der Schule der minimal art mit der Absicht, den Empirismus der Architektur in die Metaphysik der abstrakten Form zu übertragen, geschaffen worden. (Handelt es sich um vollkommene Formen, die zu irdischer Unvollkommenheit entartet sind, oder um unvollkommene Formen, die nach der platonischen Idee streben?)

Was herauskommt, wenn massige Gebäude in großen Mengen und ohne Unterschied mit einer flachen, in zwei dunklen Tönen gehaltenen Haut überzogen werden, ist weniger rühmlich. Die überall anzutreffenden Abkömmlinge des Marine Midland Building erreichen dessen Rang nicht. Sie bilden lediglich ein neues Glied in der langen Kette unbefriedigender Versuche, schwierige Grundstücksprobleme zu lösen. Freilich sind sie in der Masse auch nicht langweiliger als das Heer der von Mies ausgegangenen senkrecht profilierten Gebäude.

Am John Hancock Center, am Gebäude der U.S. Steel und am Marine Midland Building wurde bemängelt, sie hätten keine zufriedenstellende Beziehung zur Straße. In krassem Gegensatz dazu steht ein Gebäude, das dieses Problem löst und doch kritisiert wurde, weil seine Gesamtgestalt, die von seinem Eingang nicht zu trennen ist, mit den angrenzenden Gebäuden unvereinbar sei: der 50geschossige Büroturm 9 West 57th Street in New York. Früher wurden an Straßen, die in Ost-West-Richtung verlaufen, Gebäude solcher Höhe vermieden. Anders als die meisten Querstraßen in Manhattan ist die 57th Street jedoch eine ungewöhnlich breite Avenue, die durchaus 50geschossige Gebäude aufzunehmen vermag. Da es Zweck einer Stadt ist, Geld zu machen und umzusetzen, ist es töricht, zu meinen, höhere Ideale könnten diese lukrativen Giganten an ihrem Vormarsch hindern; nur Geld kann aufhalten, was es in Bewegung setzt. Der Turm 9 West 57th Street ist umstritten, wie es in den Zeitungen heißt, nicht weil er hoch ist, sondern weil er nicht vom Straßenniveau aus senkrecht aufragt (wie die Architekten jedermann zu erwarten gelehrt haben). Anlaß für die ungewohnte Form war offensichtlich die Baulinie: Da weder Rückstufungen noch eine entsprechend große »Plaza« als Ersatz dafür gewünscht waren, ließ man das Gebäude mit den ersten 19 Geschossen in einer sanften Kurve zurückschwingen und erst dann senkrecht emporwachsen. Die Straßenflucht wird somit unterbrochen, und die Seiten der Nachbargebäude bleiben teilweise sichtbar; ihre Überschneidungen mit der geschwungenen Glasfläche wirken – gelinde gesagt – unglücklich. Die Glaswand läuft über die ganze Breite des Gebäudes in eine riesige Rinne aus, die das Regenwasser ableitet und gleichzeitig ein groß-

man with a precision all the more disturbing to those who reject the man, yet this building can also be experienced *in vacuo* as the idea of monumentality, a monument in search of a hero, single-minded, undismayed, as unlikely in its time as the appearance of Brahms among the Wagnerites.

Gordon Bunshaft's Johnson Library, true to its circumstances, begins with a tactical display of reticence: placed on a beautiful wooded site, at the end of a major axis on the university campus of which it is a part, the building yields pride of place to a fountain. True, it is a fountain 80 feet in diameter, a white overflowing bowl embedded in a rolling field, but it signifies peaceful intent. The Library itself is off to one side, on a podium approached processionally by a gigantic ramp. Monolithic and calm, the form is immediately intelligible: the building consists of two thick walls tapering as they rise to support a giant roof or attic, itself accommodating the only "work" areas of ritual significance: the President's suite and the study rooms for researchers consulting Presidential papers. Like the massive side walls, the recessed end walls are also of travertine: entrance is below them and under a shelter formed by a balcony. Within, the scale is at first, deliberately and exaggeratedly, pedestrian and disappointing: a 9' high start toward a room 60' high and 80' square, reached by a monumental stair that fills most of the space. At the head of this stair the visitor sees what occasioned the building to begin with: five floors of bookstacks behind a glass wall, holding Presidential papers in thousands of red leather boxes ornamented by gold Presidential seals. Subordinate, low-ceilinged exhibition areas open off one end of this hall, as they surround the monumental stair that starts on the floor below. At each end of the main floor (a rectangle exactly twice as long as it is wide) the visitor can step out onto a balcony, from which the views are variously of the landscaped Library grounds, the long, low, adjacent building housing schools of political sciences, the campus, a stadium, and motels. Small town detritus is not enough to break a mood: this place is different from other places; people have come here because, in addition to wanting amusement, there is something important in the air. Understanding, acceptance, or rejection is sustained: scale and form signify the extraordinary, and most people find beautiful whatever removes them from their own lives. The critic may observe that the end walls, being thin and flat and plainly screens, might well have been of another material; the travertine-clad framing of the glass bookstack wall may be superfluous; and the thick, tapering side walls have no relation to the conventional column structure they conceal. But these are critics' details, and no detail outweighs the genuine achievement: this is a monument equal to a man Americans will remember for a long time. It is architecture in the service of emotion, and like many buildings whose significance is their capacity for inducing exaltation, this one serves in ways that were not foreseen. It has become a place to visit even when it is closed to the public. At night, when there is little to do in Austin, the podium is dotted with couples in quiet conversation, bicycles resting against the parapet, heads turning occasionally to contemplate the massive curved walls, shadowed and unrevealing, as problematic as the man who caused them to be built.

In the Johnson Library Bunshaft is content to write his own exegesis on the load bearing wall of antiquity, concluding that its role as sculptural mass needs no explicit structural justification. His Beinecke Library for rare books, at Yale University, doubtless because it protects intrinsically valuable works of the printer's art rather than the records of a government, uses structure and materials to suggest value, care, and expense. Like a crystal casket inside a marble box, the book storage case of this library is a glass-enclosed air-conditioned building in itself. Surrounded by an ambulatory and bathed in the warm light cast by walls of translucent Vermont marble, the interior makes it clear that something worth preserving is here enshrined. The outer marble walls, held in a structural lattice so articulated that it scarcely appears to function as a flat truss, are lifted above ground by four squat, tapered concrete columns. Small size is proper to the rare and precious, and this has been achieved by removing from the program of functions to be made manifest almost all of the strictly utilitarian office and work spaces; only a sunk plaza open to the sky reveals their underground existence. Like a Fabergé Easter egg the building titillates by being seriously frivolous, but unlike courtly amusements it is made respectable by its association with learning. Yet its architect has himself been hesitant: the closer one approaches to the books the more the language of form reverts to ordinary structuralism. At the heart of the shrine one finds the detail of a refined office building; the discrepancy is scarcely fatal, but suggests the difficulty we now have in coping with architectural events that require the superfluous embellishment, rather than the utilitarian essential. Notwithstanding, the Beinecke Library delights, as it was meant to do.

Lyndon Baines Johnson Library, University of Texas, Austin, Texas.

Beinecke Rare Book and Manuscript Library, Yale University, New Haven, Connecticut.

zügiges, auffälliges Schutzdach für den Eingang bildet. 9 West 57th Street ist einer der wenigen neueren Wolkenkratzer in New York, bei dem der Eingang weder eine lästige Unterbrechung ist, die der Architekt lieber vermieden hätte, noch ein fremdartiges, gewaltsam angefügtes Element, sondern ein unabdingbarer Bestandteil der Baugestalt. Vielleicht ist es gerade dieser Kontrast zwischen den gefälligen Größenverhältnissen auf Straßenniveau und der darüber aufragenden gläsernen Sprungschanze, der die Kritiker stört, mehr noch als der Übergang zu den Gebäuden auf beiden Seiten. Und obgleich die Fachleute darin übereinstimmen, daß der Turm eigentlich einen eigenen Block erfordert (man denke ihn sich zum Beispiel als Ersatz für das UN-Sekretariat), läuft doch die Reaktion des Laien geradezu entwaffnend der gelehrten Meinung zuwider. Der Turm läßt die Leute buchstäblich auf der Straße innehalten; die ungeheure, geschwungene Glaswand stellt ein anregendes Ereignis dar, nicht als Architektur, sondern als städtisches Schaustück, so faszinierend wie ein Brunnen.

Die Diskrepanz zwischen der Architektur im Dienst der Technik und der Architektur im Dienst eines Gehalts, für den die Technik nur Mittel zum Zweck ist, führt zu den Auseinandersetzungen unserer Tage über die Zukunft der Baukunst. Die meisten als Ausdrucksform konzipierten SOM-Gebäude dienen nichtkommerziellen Zwecken. Bauherr und Öffentlichkeit sind sich im allgemeinen darüber einig, daß solche Zwecke eine Architektur rechtfertigen, die von einem substantielleren Leitbild als reiner Nützlichkeit geprägt oder wenigstens beeinflußt wird. Die konventionelle Kritik hält es aber immer noch für nötig, jeden Ausdruck zu vermeiden (was freilich einen auszudrückenden Gehalt voraussetzt). Wenn es so etwas wie einen aristokratischen Geschmack gibt – so sehr er auch zögern mag, sich als solcher zu erklären –, ist sein hervorstechendes Merkmal zu unserer Zeit sein blasiertes Ableugnen jedes anderen Gehalts als der Form selbst: Es gibt keine Botschaft, weil es nichts gibt, das mitteilenswert wäre. So lehnt die »fortgeschrittene« Musik die emotionsgeladene Dehnung und Raffung der Zeit ab und arbeitet statt dessen mit langdauernden Pausen zwischen den Klängen, die Malerei ist womöglich nichts weiter als Farbempfindung, die Architektur nur »Haut und Skelett«. Auf der populären Ebene schrumpft die reduktionistische Ansicht schließlich zu Marshall McLuhans »Das Medium ist die Botschaft« zusammen – eine pseudotechnische Rechtfertigung der Sinnentleerung. Für Zen-Priester und christliche Mystiker mögen sich Leere und Schweigen als Folge religiöser Versenkung des Selbst in ein indifferentes Universum mit unaussprechlichem Sinn füllen – für uns führt das Leugnen des Gehalts nur zu einem leeren Kopf.

Wie schwierig ist es dann doch, Gebäude zu begreifen, die einen anderen Gehalt aufweisen als den, der in ihrer Substanz liegt! Wenn der Gehalt verständlich ist, weil er von der Gesellschaft anerkannt wird, ist es für den Architekten vielleicht leichter. So sind wir uns im allgemeinen darüber einig, daß Kirchen anders aussehen, wirken und sein sollten als Supermärkte – wenn wir überhaupt Kirchen für nötig halten. Aber Denkmäler? Haben sie eine Daseinsberechtigung? Wenn ja – wer ist des Gedenkens wert? Wie verwerflich ist ein gutes Bauwerk zu Ehren eines unwürdigen Menschen, das architektonische Größe zur Psychotherapie und vielleicht Wiedergutmachung mißbraucht? Diese Fragen sind schmerzhaft real, wenn auch die Architekten nicht häufig Gelegenheit zur Beantwortung haben. So war vorherzusehen, daß ein für einen amerikanischen Präsidenten bestimmtes Denkmal, das seine Feinde wie auch seine Freunde überdimensioniert finden, kritische Angriffe auf die Idee der Monumentalität und weniger auf den Mann selbst auslösen würde. Die Lyndon Baines Johnson Library in Austin ist auf den Mann mit einer für seine Gegner beunruhigenden Präzision abgestimmt, und doch kann man dieses Gebäude auch als Monument an sich auffassen – auf der Suche nach einem integren, standhaften Helden, der in seiner Zeit so unwahrscheinlich ist wie Brahms unter den Wagnerianern.

Getreu den Voraussetzungen vermittelt Gordon Bunshafts Johnson Library als erstes den Eindruck taktischer Zurückhaltung: Das zur University of Texas gehörende Gebäude steht zwar am Ende einer Hauptachse des Campus, überläßt jedoch die Hauptwirkung einem Brunnen. Die weiße, überströmende Brunnenschale von etwa 24 m Durchmesser liegt, Friedfertigkeit signalisierend, eingebettet in eine leicht bewegte Rasenfläche. Die Bibliothek selbst findet sich etwas abseits auf einem Podium mit einer breiten Prozessionsrampe als Zugang. Die monolithische, ruhige Gestalt ist unmittelbar verständlich: Zwei dicke Wände, die sich nach oben verjüngen, tragen ein riesiges Dach, in dem die einzigen rituell bedeutsamen »Arbeitsbereiche« untergebracht sind, die Präsidentensuite und die Studienräume für Forscher, die Dokumente aus der Amtszeit des Präsidenten einsehen wollen. Wie die Seitenwände sind auch die zurückgesetzten Querabschlüsse mit Travertin verkleidet. Darunter befinden sich die Zugänge. Im Innern sind die Größenverhältnisse zunächst absicht-

The expressive themes of Bunshaft's buildings recall classical architecture, and the means he finds most suitable for their realization are the podium and the attic. Both are used directly in the Johnson Library; the Beinecke Library transforms them, so that the ground plane is revealed to be a podium only by the hole cut into it, while the roof is implied by walls which, rooflike, are lifted above the ground. Quotations from the classics, however, are not alone responsible for the vaguely Beaux Arts aura of these and other SOM buildings. It is perhaps due more to the willingness – indeed the determination – to contain intricate and highly differentiated facilities in a shell that denies or obscures their presence, and to organize these spaces around circulation systems which, because they are big but seldom grand, are often inert.

It is not an oversight in presentation that the plans of SOM's buildings, considered as graphic compositions in themselves, are their least interesting aspect. Intention, like interest, is most sharply focused on a three dimensional form to which the plan is subordinate, but the form often lacks the animation that can come from a plan interesting in itself. That this should be so is perhaps unremarkable for offices and other commercial buildings; but it is a conspicuous difference between SOM's work (with the exception of Walter Netsch) and that of other comparable architects. Some of the problems involved in this are fundamental to the structuralist point of view; others are a matter of temperament and, therefore, of procedure. So, for example, a particular structural system is selected either because there is no other way to achieve the desired result, or because it evokes a certain character regardless of its side effects. In either case a decision regarding scale is accepted a priori; planning proceeds from it as the fitting into a container of spaces that may or may not require their own local adjustments. Thus the Johnson Library suggests on its exterior that it accommodates a gigantic room. This is in fact the case, but only for one half of the building; the other half, accommodating storage and work areas mostly inaccessible to the public and inimical to the architect's intention, is equally absorbed in the same monumental mass.

The kind of forced fit associated with bulk planning is conventionally more acceptable, if not more satisfying, when its justification is structural efficiency and logic. But when the formal determinant is an expressive intention other than that implied by structure, current sensibility tends to resist what is, after all, an assertion made by the architect about the meaning and value of his work. The nature of the profession being what it is, architects who are unable or unwilling to make such assertions are unlikely to survive as architects. Private shop talk among professionals, like folk wisdom, often recognizes the psychological factors involved; public discussion, at least as it has been largely influenced by the querulous style of English journalism, conveniently ignores the objective realities that sustain psychological patterns, preferring instead to attribute an unhappy outcome solely to the architects' natural perversity. Objective reality includes, besides everything else normally indicated by the term, the history of architecture and the history of a particular architect. It is by now a celebrated fact that modern architecture cannot cope with history – even its own. Thus shop talk grudgingly acknowledges selected pages in the various monographs of Le Corbusier or Mies, but public criticism rarely refers to the controlling influence of such specific methods and attitudes inherited from the recent past. The four methods of composition outlined by Le Corbusier in the first volume of Boesiger's monograph, for example, are still the armature on which architects hang their ideas (even though two of those methods have been found less useful in practice) and their use has distinct, predictable consequences. So, for example, the first diagram proposes the articulation of functions or spaces in shapes that can both compete and contrast with each other. Such contrasts lead to discontinuity: different treatments of facades on the same volume, or the breaking up of a volume into components ever more qualified (but still determined by some aspect of space or function, not structure). Because such qualifications tend to be costly, they are apt to be limited to small buildings and perhaps most suitably to houses. The specific advantages of the method are the increased range in scale; the heightening of interest where that is appropriate; and the possibility of a genuine response to a functional problem. The disadvantages are the competitive restlessness generated by discontinuity, especially in the urban context; and the difficulty of finding spaces or functions that can reasonably be given separate identity. Yet the alternative to an architecture determined by Miesian structural regularity has so far been keyed to this mode, whether it employs the suave curves and surfaces of early Le Corbusier or the harder shapes and materials associated with Brutalism. The expressive range the method makes possible leads to its being criticized for just the virtues said to be lacking in the structuralist approach, which is thought to offend for its repetitiveness, its often inflexible scale, and its unresponsiveness to functional distinctions.

lich, ja übertrieben fußgängermäßig und enttäuschend: Nur etwa 2,75 m hoch ist die Halle, von der eine monumentale Treppenanlage zu dem etwa 18 m hohen Hauptraum führt. Am oberen Ende der Treppe angelangt, enthüllt sich dem Besucher der Kern des Gebäudes: fünf hinter einer Glaswand liegende Archivgeschosse für Tausende von roten Lederordnern mit den Dokumenten aus der Amtszeit des Präsidenten. Die beiden Schmalseiten des Hauptgeschosses öffnen sich auf Balkone, von denen der Blick über den gepflegten Park der Bibliothek, die benachbarte Sid W. Richardson Hall, den Campus, ein Stadion und Motels schweifen kann. Das Kleinstädtische vermag die Atmosphäre nicht zu beeinträchtigen: Dieser Ort unterscheidet sich von anderen; die Leute strömen herbei, nicht nur weil sie Zerstreuung suchen, sondern weil ein Hauch von Bedeutsamkeit in der Luft liegt. Der Kritiker mag einwenden, die flachen, nur als Raumabschluß dienenden Querwände könnten auch aus einem anderen Material bestehen, die Travertinverkleidung am Rahmenwerk der Glaswand vor den Archivgeschossen sei überflüssig, und die dicken, sich verjüngenden Seitenwände hätten keine Beziehung zu der konventionellen Stützenkonstruktion, die sie verbergen. Das sind aber Details, und kein Detail kann die eigentliche Leistung, einem Mann, den die Amerikaner noch lange im Gedächtnis behalten werden, ein angemessenes Denkmal gesetzt zu haben, schmälern. Es ist Architektur im Dienst des Gefühls, und wie so viele Gebäude, deren Bedeutung darin liegt, daß sie Begeisterung wecken, zeitigt auch dieses unvorhergesehene Wirkungen. Abends, wenn in Austin nicht mehr viel los ist, sieht man hier und dort Fahrräder an der Brüstung lehnen. Auf dem Podium sitzen Paare in friedlicher Unterhaltung, und manchmal richten sich die Blicke auf die massigen, geschwungenen Wände, die verschattet und unzugänglich sind, so problematisch wie der Mann, um dessentwillen sie gebaut wurden.

Bei der Johnson Library begnügte sich Bunshaft damit, eine persönliche Exegese auf die tragende Wand der Antike zu schreiben – in der Meinung, ihre Rolle als skulpturale Masse benötige keine explizite strukturelle Rechtfertigung. Für die Beinecke Rare Book and Manuscript Library der Yale University setzte er – zweifellos weil sie äußerst wertvolle Werke der Buchdruckerkunst und keine Staatsdokumente birgt – Struktur und Materialien so ein, daß sie kostbar, erlesen und teuer wirken. Einer kristallenen Schmuckschatulle in einer marmornen Truhe gleicht das Büchermagazin dieser Bibliothek, das in sich ein eigenes glasumschlossenes und klimatisiertes Gebäude darstellt. Der von einer Empore umgebene Innenraum wird von warmem, durch Wandfelder aus durchscheinendem Vermont-Marmor sickerndem Licht erhellt. Man spürt sofort, daß hier Schätze aufbewahrt werden. Das Rahmenwerk, in dem die marmornen Außenwände sitzen, ist so gegliedert, daß seine Funktion als flaches Gittertragwerk kaum wahrnehmbar ist. Es gibt seine Lasten auf vier gedrungene, sich nach oben verjüngende Eckpfeiler aus Beton ab. Kleine Dimensionen sind dem Seltenen und Unersetzlichen angemessen; man verbannte daher fast alle zweckgebundenen Büro- und Arbeitsräume aus dem Programm der offen darzulegenden Funktionen, nur eine vertiefte Plaza unter freiem Himmel läßt auf ihre unterirdische Existenz schließen. Wie ein Osterei von Fabergé verursacht das Gebäude einen frivolen Kitzel, aber im Gegensatz zu höfischen Vergnügungen erheischt es durch sein Bündnis mit der Gelehrsamkeit zugleich Respekt. Der Architekt war jedoch nicht ganz konsequent: Je näher man den Büchern kommt, um so mehr gleitet die Formsprache in gewöhnlichen Strukturalismus ab. Im Kern des Heiligtums stößt man auf die Details eines ausgeklügelten Bürogebäudes. Die Diskrepanz ist nicht schwerwiegend, zeigt jedoch, wie schwierig es heute ist, architektonische Aufgaben zu lösen, die mehr als das nach dem Nützlichkeitsprinzip Wesentliche erfordern. Dessenungeachtet weckt die Beinecke Library freudige, erhebende Gefühle, wie es auch der Intention des Architekten entspricht, und diese Empfindungen sind nicht weniger selten als die Bücher, die sie beherbergt.

Bunshafts Kulturbauten rufen die Erinnerung an die klassische Architektur wach, und die Mittel, die ihm für die Verwirklichung dieser Bauten am geeignetsten erscheinen, sind Sockel und Attika. Beide werden bei der Johnson Library uneingeschränkt verwendet; bei der Beinecke Library sind sie so modifiziert, daß man das Erdgeschoß nur an dem eingeschnittenen Innenhof als Sockel erkennt, während die Dachzone von Wänden, die sich dachartig über den Boden erheben, gebildet wird. Der Anklang an die Beaux-Arts, den man bei diesen und bei anderen Bauwerken von SOM verspürt, ist aber nicht nur den Rückgriffen auf die Klassik zu verdanken, sondern viel eher dem Willen, ja der Entschlossenheit, hochdifferenzierte und ineinander verzahnte Nutzungsbereiche in einer einzigen Hülle, die deren Anwesenheit leugnet oder verbirgt, unterzubringen.

Daß die Grundrisse als reine Graphiken betrachtet der uninteressanteste Teil der SOM-Gebäude sind (ausgenommen die von Walter Netsch), beruht nicht etwa auf mangelhafter

The other well-known alternative available to architects is a plan module so finely grained that it allows – indeed demands – maximum maneuverability. Wright used a $2' \times 4'$ rectangle for this purpose, and achieved even greater flexibility with the hexagon. The advantage of the method (and even Wright had method) is that it encourages variety within continuity. Wright had other ways to achieve that, of course, including his occasional experiments with the 45 degree angle in plan (made feasible for his colleagues by Louis Kahn, and by James Stirling who has developed it with still greater flexibility of shape, section, and surface). It is therefore curious that the plan as such has received so little attention in recent polemics, and doubly curious that in the United States it should be an SOM partner, Walter Netsch, who has made this problem central to his work.

The term "field theory" as used by Netsch to describe his method (he would prefer to say, process) is problematic for architectural discourse in that it derives from other disciplines. Of the meanings collected around it, those associated with behavioral science are perhaps uppermost in his mind: in this context what is referred to is a method of analyzing events as the interplay of diverse "sociocultural, biomechanical, and motivational forces". Putting aside the unappetizing tautologies of behaviorism, it may also be recalled that in physics a field is "a space in which magnetic or electric lines of force are active", and more generally "the area or space under the influence of, or within the range of, some agent". These latter definitions suggest that a field is a passive subject; the former that it is an active agent. Both aspects are appropriate to its architectural employment, and to them should be added the concern of Gestalt psychology: the organically preceptual whole whose configuration cannot be reduced to, or built up from, simple "atomic" elements of sensation. In this context "field" qualities belong to the whole but not to its parts, and in an architectural plan derived from particles or modules of space the product should be a whole perceptually different from its components. What Netsch has developed is a set of components that may or may not be intended by him to meet the requirements of a Gestalt percept; he does intend them to reveal, and to generate, architectural possibilities more numerous and more satisfying than those otherwise available.

The specifics of the method are simple enough: squares of identical or varying size are overlaid and rotated. The resultant diagonals produce an interlocking second grid of octagons; to which a third or a fourth may be added when their scale and placement yield further useful subdivisions. Graphically these patterns resemble, and are direct descendants of, the complicated wall decorations of Arabian architecture and the optically disturbing window lattices of 17th century Muslim architecture in India, notably at the tomb of I'timad-ud-Daulah at Agra, and at Fatehpur-Sikri. These lattices employ interlocking patterns that are multi-axial, but because they give equal stress to two or more axes, comprehension of their pattern structure requires the observer to select one axis around which to organize the components of the others as "subordinate". Since the designers of these patterns might craftily choose to place them askew within an orthogonal architectural setting (a window frame, for instance) the observer's choice of a single axis to "read" as dominant requires an act of will, sometimes contrary to information supplied by the immediate architectural environment. The result is a kind of optical shock, a physiological derangement incomparably more subtle than any of its recent counterparts in Western op art. To press such patterns into the service of architectural planning may perhaps seem gratuitous, but there is no inherent reason why the abstract decorative arts of Asia should be less instructive to Western architects than, say, the orthogonal compositions of Mondrian and van Doesburg. Neither is it any the less plausible to rationalize the use of a plan module rather than a structural system. The only pertinent test of their value, presumably, is whether or not they make better buildings.

What is a better building? In Netsch's view it is one that contains, implicit in its plan, simultaneously coexisting possibilities for movement and development. A dense lattice contains too many possibilities: the plan is finally what survives after the architect has erased those possibilities he does not need; but their existence as an after-image is always sustained by what remains. Thus in theory the recent buildings Netsch has designed for the Chicago campus of the University of Illinois (Architecture and Art; Behavioral Sciences; Science and Engineering) might be said to contain not only themselves but also each other. In practice the observer, like the architect, is confronted with some serious problems. Foremost among them is the problem of intelligibility. These buildings require many small interior spaces, and their relation to each other must be signalled by some constant factor. On the two-dimensional paper plan all is clear because all is simultaneous; in the three-dimensional reality all is unclear because, alas, the observer can be in only one place at a time. Here in

Darstellung. Die Intention wie die Konzentration richtet sich auf die dreidimensionale Gestalt, der der Grundriß untergeordnet ist, aber der Gestalt fehlt es häufig an der Lebendigkeit, die von einem Grundriß, der als solcher ansprechend ist, ausgehen kann. Zum Teil liegt das im strukturalistischen Ansatz begründet (zum Teil ist es auch eine Sache des Temperaments und deshalb des Verfahrens). Man wählt zum Beispiel ein bestimmtes strukturelles System – ungeachtet seiner Nebenwirkungen –, entweder weil man das gewünschte Ergebnis auf keine andere Weise erzielen kann oder weil dieses System einen bestimmten Charakter heraufbeschwört. In beiden Fällen wird a priori über die Größenverhältnisse entschieden; davon geht die Planung aus, die nichts anderes zu tun hat als Räume entsprechend ihrer Nutzung in einen Behälter einzupassen. So erweckt die Johnson Library von außen den Eindruck, sie umschließe einen riesigen Innenraum. Das trifft tatsächlich zu, jedoch nur für die eine Hälfte des Gebäudes; aber auch die andere Hälfte mit den Magazinen und Arbeitsräumen, die größtenteils dem Publikum nicht zugänglich sind und der Intention des Architekten zuwiderlaufen, wird von der gleichen monumentalen Baumasse aufgenommen.

Eine bauliche Gruppierung wird mit all ihren zwangsläufigen Folgen gewöhnlich dann akzeptiert, wenn sie sich mit struktureller Effizienz und Logik rechtfertigen läßt. Ist aber die Formdeterminante offensichtlich eine andere als die von der Struktur implizierte, so neigt die öffentliche Meinung zum Widerstand, weil sie glaubt, hier vor eine subjektive Behauptung des Architekten über den Sinn und Wert seiner Arbeit gestellt zu sein. Da der Architektenberuf so ist, wie er ist, haben Architekten, die unfähig oder nicht willens sind, akzeptierbare Behauptungen aufzustellen, wenig Aussichten, sich auf die Dauer durchzusetzen. Die Fachsimpelei unter Professionellen sieht wie die Volksweisheit häufig hinter die mitspielenden psychologischen Faktoren; die öffentliche Diskussion dagegen ignoriert bequemerweise – wenigstens dort, wo sie von dem Querulantenstil des englischen Journalismus beeinflußt wurde – die den psychologischen Mustern zugrunde liegenden objektiven Realitäten und schreibt statt dessen ein mißglücktes Ergebnis einzig und allein der persönlichen Verschrobenheit des Architekten zu. Zu den objektiven Realitäten gehört neben dem, was gewöhnlich mit dem Begriff gemeint ist, die Geschichte der Architektur. Entgegen der allgemeinen Übereinkunft, die moderne Architektur habe kein Verhältnis zur Geschichte, selbst zu ihrer eigenen, ist der Einfluß, den besonders aus der jüngeren Vergangenheit überkommene Methoden und Haltungen auf sie ausüben, nicht hoch genug zu veranschlagen. So sind die vier von Le Corbusier umrissenen Kompositionsweisen im ersten Band von Boesigers Monographie noch immer die Armatur, an der die Architekten ihre Ideen aufhängen (obgleich zwei dieser Methoden sich in der Praxis als weniger brauchbar erwiesen haben). Das erste Diagramm zeigt die Gliederung von Funktionen oder Räumen in Formen, die miteinander sowohl konkurrieren als auch kontrastieren. Derartige Kontraste führen zu Kontinuitätsbrüchen, zum Beispiel zu unterschiedlichen Fassaden am gleichen Baukörper oder zur Zerteilung einer Baumasse in immer spezialisiertere Komponenten, die aber stets von irgendwelchen Raum- oder Funktionsaspekten und nicht von der Struktur bestimmt werden. Spezifische Vorteile der Methode sind ein erweiterter Maßstabsspielraum und die Möglichkeit einer angemessenen Lösung eines funktionellen Problems. Die Nachteile liegen darin, daß der Kontinuitätsbruch vor allem im Städtebau die Ruhelosigkeit einer Konkurrenz mit sich bringt und daß es schwierig ist, Räume oder Funktionen zu finden, denen in sinnvoller Weise eine eigene Identität gegeben werden kann. Noch immer gilt die beschriebene Methode – sei es in den sanften Kurven und Flächen des frühen Le Corbusier, sei es in den härteren Formen und Materialien des Brutalismus – als Alternative zu einer von struktureller Regelmäßigkeit Miesscher Provenienz regierten Architektur. Die durch sie erschlossene Ausdrucksbreite bewirkt, daß an ihr gerade die Tugenden bemängelt werden, die der strukturalistische Ansatz angeblich vermissen läßt. Dieser ist, wie man meint, unzumutbar, weil er dauernde Wiederholungen bringt, weil sein Größenmaßstab oft starr ist und weil er nicht flexibel genug ist, um funktionelle Unterschiede aufzufangen.

Die Alternative dazu ist ein Planmodul, der so fein gegittert ist, daß er größtmögliche Manövrierbarkeit gestattet, ja sogar verlangt. Wright bediente sich zu diesem Zweck eines Rechtecks von etwa 60×120 cm oder eines Hexagons, mit dem er noch größere Flexibilität erzielte. Der Vorteil der Methode liegt in der Möglichkeit von Vielfalt innerhalb von Kontinuität. Wright verfügte selbstverständlich noch über andere Mittel, um dieses Ziel zu erreichen; dazu gehören auch seine gelegentlichen Experimente mit dem 45-Grad-Winkel. Für die Architektenschaft praktikabel gemacht wurden diese Kunstgriffe von Louis Kahn und James Stirling (der ihnen eine noch größere Manipulierbarkeit der Form und Oberfläche abgewann). Angesichts dessen ist es merkwürdig, daß der Grundriß als solcher in der

fact is one generalization that can be drawn from the angles, turns, and corners generated by Netsch's geometry: like the English "picturesque" their appeal is in their irregularity; but unlike the picturesque they require not a fixed, preferred standpoint from which the whole is best seen, but rather an extended tour with a map in hand.

Where this problem refers to the interiors it may be partly resolved by a spatial element that can be perceived in its entirety; the obvious candidate is the circulation system. But it is precisely here that Netsch chooses to break corridors into short lengths with frequent turns, occasionally amplifying them into programmed multiple-use spaces too similar to serve as landmarks and too distracting to maintain the sense of direction. A stabilizing frame comparable to that found in Muslim pattern design is omitted, and the result is disorientation as a normative condition. But externally the results are more gratifying, firstly because the faceted elevations produced by the plan-pattern are accessible in amounts sufficient to suggest the underlying principle of organization; and secondly because the program of a given building usually contains some element substantially different in scale and character, thereby providing the necessary stabilizing contrast.

The cardinal advantage of a multi-axial plan geometry is its capacity to respond to exceptional situations – to qualify and particularize what might by other means be merely accommodated or obscured, or suppressed. Such amplification is humanly sympathetic: it relishes difference and seeks to enhance it. But to do so it must also depend on the availability of real occasions for complexity: what is inimical to its purpose is a situation that is genuinely simple. Where the plan deals with a multi-story building it tends to reject complexity for the vertical section, but where the architect is dealing with a one- or two-story building, particularly on an irregular site, and where it is possible to utilize the roof as a visibly articulated element, expressive possibilities are increased. Interesting examples are the pavilions of the Winnebago Children's Home in Neillsville and the Louis Jefferson Long Library at Wells College, in Aurora, New York. The library's plan is organized by nine interlocking clusters of rotated, overlapping squares, together with two or perhaps three different kinds of residual spaces between them. Because the squares are shifted within the lattice (to allow for the varying residual spaces) the basic pin-wheel plan is difficult to grasp except in diagram form. Prow-like projections and a rambling, pitched, timber roof produce five elevations which can be read as concavities – recessions that seem to invite rather than repel entrance. Awkward as some of the forms may be, the result is a building that deserves comparison with related work by Aalto and, more importantly, by Frank Lloyd Wright; the latter would have been hard put to deny the presence here of what he urged architects to seek: the "principle" with which they could generate their own effects.

Among the problems Netsch's "field theory" might be expected to solve, with greater success than has heretofore been seen, is that of relating buildings to each other on extended sites. On the Chicago Campus of the University of Illinois, where Netsch is dealing with isolated and by-passing rectangular blocks in an earlier neo-plastic layout of his own devising, the problem is largely untouched because the buildings are so dispersed. The textural continuity implied by his three most recent buildings remains unrealized. Here we

University of Illinois, Chicago Circle Campus, Chicago, Illinois.

Louis Jefferson Long Library, Wells College,
Aurora, New York.

neueren Diskussion so wenig Aufmerksamkeit erfuhr, und doppelt seltsam, daß es in den
Vereinigten Staaten ein SOM-Partner war, nämlich Walter Netsch, der diesen in den Mittelpunkt seiner Arbeit stellte.

Der von Netsch zur Beschreibung seiner Methode (er würde eher sagen: seines Arbeits-
prozesses) benutzte Begriff »Feldtheorie« ist als architektonischer Fachausdruck insofern
problematisch, als er aus anderen Disziplinen stammt. Von den Bedeutungen, die sich an
diesen Begriff geheftet haben, stehen wohl die mit der Verhaltensforschung verbundenen
im Vordergrund von Netschs Bewußtsein; in diesem Sinn ist die Feldtheorie für ihn eine
Methode, Ereignisse als in sich verflochtenes Zusammenspiel verschiedenartiger »sozio-
kultureller, biomechanischer und motivationsbestimmender Kräfte« zu analysieren. Abge-
sehen von den abstoßenden Tautologien des Behaviorismus sollte man sich ins Gedächtnis
rufen, was ein Feld physikalisch ist: »ein Raum, in dem magnetische oder elektrische Kraft-
linien wirksam sind«, und allgemeiner: »der Bereich oder Raum im Einfluß oder innerhalb
der Reichweite irgendeiner Wirkkraft«. Die letztere Definition stellt ein Feld als ein Passivum
dar; die erstere bedeutet, daß es ein aktives Agens ist. Beide Auslegungen passen durchaus auch auf den Begriff in seiner architektonischen Bedeutung. Dazu kommt noch eine
weitere aus der Gestaltpsychologie, in der ein Feld das wahrnehmbare organische Ganze,
dessen Konfiguration nicht auf einfache, »atomare« Elemente der Wahrnehmung zurück-
geführt oder aus ihnen aufgebaut werden kann, darstellt. So betrachtet sind die Eigenschaften eines »Feldes« dem Ganzen, aber nicht seinen Teilen zugehörig, und bei einem
architektonischen Plan, der aus Raumfragmenten oder -moduln hergeleitet ist, sollte das
Ergebnis ein Ganzes sein, das wahrnehmbare Unterschiede zu seinen Komponenten auf-
weist. Ob Netsch beabsichtigte, mit den von ihm entwickelten Komponenten der Gestaltpsychologie gerecht zu werden, steht nicht fest; sicher ist jedoch, daß er mit ihnen die
Absicht verfolgte, architektonische Möglichkeiten, die zahlreicher und befriedigender sind
als die bisher verfügbaren, freizulegen oder neu zu schaffen.

Die spezifischen Merkmale der Methode sind einfach: Quadrate gleicher oder verschiedener
Größe werden übereinandergelegt und gegeneinander verdreht. Die entstehenden Dia-
gonalen bringen ein zweites, verzahntes Netz von Achtecken hervor; ein drittes oder viertes
Gitter kann hinzutreten, wenn sich dadurch weitere nutzbare Unterteilungen ergeben.
Graphisch gleichen diese Muster den komplizierten Wandornamenten der arabischen Architektur und den geradezu verwirrenden Fenstergittern der mohammedanischen Architektur
des 17. Jahrhunderts in Indien, insbesondere in Agra, etwa am Grabmal von I'timad-ud-
Daulah, und in Fatehpur-Sikri. Diese Gitter weisen verschlungene multiaxiale Muster auf;
der Betrachter muß, wenn er die Musterstruktur verstehen will, in Gedanken eine Achse
herausheben und dieser die übrigen »unterordnen«. Da die Entwerfer diese Muster manchmal absichtlich schief in eine orthogonale architektonische Umfassung (zum Beispiel einen
Fensterrahmen) einsetzten, erfordert die Wahl einer Achse, die als dominierende »gelesen«
werden kann, vom Beschauer einen besonderen, gelegentlich der Information der unmittel-
baren architektonischen Umgebung zuwiderlaufenden Willensakt. Die Folge ist ein gewisser
optischer Schock, eine physiologische Störung, die weitaus subtiler ist als irgendeine ihrer
neueren Entsprechungen aus der westlichen op art. Solche Muster in den Dienst der
architektonischen Planung zu stellen, mag willkürlich erscheinen; es gibt aber keinen ein-
sichtigen Grund dafür, daß die abstrakte Ornamentik Asiens für westliche Architekten
weniger instruktiv sein sollte als zum Beispiel die orthogonalen Kompositionen Mondrians
und van Doesburgs. Deswegen ist es auch durchaus plausibel, wenn in der Praxis ein
Grundrißmodul einem strukturellen System vorgezogen wird. Der einzig stichhaltige Beweis für den Wert des Verfahrens ist vermutlich, ob es bessere Gebäude ergibt.

Was ist ein besseres Gebäude? Nach Netschs Ansicht eines, das schon in seinem Plan
Möglichkeiten für Bewegung und Entwicklung zugleich beschließt. Ein dichtes Gitter enthält zu viele Möglichkeiten. Der Plan ist schließlich das, was übrig ist, wenn der Architekt
die Möglichkeiten, die er nicht braucht, ausgeschieden hat; doch deren Existenz klingt
stets in dem, was übriggeblieben ist, noch nach. Von den neuesten Gebäuden, die Netsch
für den Chicagoer Campus der University of Illinois entworfen hat (die Architecture and
Art Laboratories, das Behavioral Sciences Building und das Science and Engineering South
Building), könnte man theoretisch sagen, sie stellten nicht nur sich selbst, sondern gleichzeitig auch einander dar. Praktisch steht der Beschauer wie der Architekt vor schwierigen
Fragen, deren ernsteste die der Überschaubarkeit ist. Auf der zweidimensionalen Zeichnung
ist alles klar, weil alles simultan vorhanden ist; in der dreidimensionalen Wirklichkeit ist
alles unklar, weil der Betrachter nicht an mehreren Orten zugleich sein kann. Hieraus läßt
sich eine Verallgemeinerung ableiten: Wie beim englischen »Pittoresken« liegt der Reiz

touch on a problem endemic to modern architecture, and one that requires an extended discussion not entirely germane to all of the buildings under review. Yet some generalizations are in order: all of them have to do with the pernicious influence of the garden city idea, and Le Corbusier's version of it in particular. By now we should need no further proof that the preoccupation with the integrity of built form renders architectural civility impossible. Buildings can be laws unto themselves, but only at the expense of the architectural community. No juxtaposition of large-scale buildings in the urban context, however skillfully they may be displayed like objects on a table, can compensate for their fundamental lack of necessary conjunction. Yet the formal integrity of the free-standing building remains the touchstone of site planning, and the greater the architect's success, the more problematic is the effect on the fabric of our cities. Thus Carlton Centre, in Johannesburg, South Africa, is no doubt as skillful a juxtaposition as may be expected of towers whose bulk is determined by non-architectural considerations, and the public space the composition yields is more coherent than most – but it is also possible to imagine similar results with an entirely different and equally arbitrary composition.

SOM's memorable achievements in site planning have been at one or another end of the scale of possibilities: either an exceptionally difficult situation involving the shape and location of a single building; or a situation of seemingly unlimited happy possibilities. In the first category may be considered two quite different buildings: the Hirshhorn Museum, on the Mall in Washington, D.C., and adjacent to the Smithsonian Institution; and the department store for Macy's in Queens, New York. In the latter case a triangular site, in the former the necessity for inserting a form of minimal resistance to its environment, yield circular buildings as the ideal solution, and in both cases the form is conspicuously successful. When scale is modest, planning problems of the second category sometimes seem to resolve themselves with form that aspires to the qualities of folk architecture, inserting buildings into the landscape with tact and reticence. Thus the Carmel Valley Manor housing in California, a residential complex for retired people comprising numerous small buildings, each with several apartments, together with related community facilities, offers a regional echo of the Spanish colonial vernacular. Beguiling in photographs, the actual effect is both more subtle and more substantial. Amenities of the site are enhanced; open but sheltered courts connect and stabilize what might have been too dispersed; patently decorative arches add continuity; and pitched roofs provide agreeable variety and interest. Indeed the entire composition achieves the kind of relaxed "ordinariness" advocated during the last several years by Robert Venturi and others, and it also employs design elements with attractive associations for the people who use the buildings – but it does this without the patronizing sarcasm that tends to make such exercises a kind of "in" joke among architects, as distinguished from the adult effort to please. The architectural smirk – its proponents prefer to call it a taste for irony – has been much admired lately; perhaps that is why this straightforward project, like the short-lived Bay Region style before it, has been so little noticed; it achieved effortlessly what now seems to require the heaving and straining of "theory".

Poise and spontaneity may be possible only in rural circumstances; the San Francisco office's attempt to accommodate to a difficult urban situation, by mediating between the demands of the street and the demands of architecture, has produced one interesting but dubious exercise in scenic design. The problem was to add a hotel tower to San Francisco's Union Square, but without disrupting the relatively uniform height of existing facades. The solution was to set the tower well back from the street, interposing a lower wing (for public rooms) conforming with adjacent buildings as it faces Union Square, but cut back from the side street at a forty-five degree angle to produce, and at the same time conceal, an entrance plaza that avoids competing with the Square itself. The result is a facade like a Hollywood stage flat; when seen from the corner it appears to have no building behind it, an effect that naturally rivets attention on itself. The arched window openings, however they were intended, are out of scale, and a disembodied facade is a somewhat cavalier gesture toward urban politesse; yet the result is not entirely unpersuasive, and one ends by wanting it to work.

An interesting counterpart to this kind of urban theater is the Mauna Kea Beach Hotel on the island of Hawaii. Merely to name the building is to state the problem, conjuring up visions of tropical fantasies, yet what distinguishes the building is that, while it is indeed architecture-at-play, it remains rational architecture of a high order. Four stories on the beach side, three inland, with a detached dining pavilion, the hotel's architectural character derives from the inward stagger of its three guest floors above a series of central courts open to the sky. Sheltered open-air corridors thus overlook thoroughly landscaped gardens, and

Carlton Centre, Johannesburg, South Africa/ Südafrika.

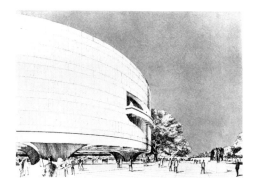

Joseph H. Hirshhorn Museum and Sculpture Garden, Washington, D.C.

Macy's Rego Park, Queens, New York, New York.

Carmel Valley Manor, Carmel Valley, California.

der Geometrie Walter Netschs in ihrer Unregelmäßigkeit, aber im Gegensatz zum Pittoresken erfordert sie keinen bevorzugten festen Standpunkt, von dem aus man das Ganze am besten überblickt, sondern eher einen langen Rundgang, bei dem man eine Übersichtskarte in der Hand hält.

Im Innern des Gebäudes kann dieses Problem teilweise mit einem Raumelement, das in seiner Gesamtheit wahrnehmbar ist, gelöst werden; dafür eignet sich am besten das Verbindungssystem. Die Flure sind jedoch bei Netsch in kurze Abschnitte mit vielen Biegungen aufgeteilt und gelegentlich zu Mehrzweckräumen erweitert, die einander zu ähnlich sind, um als Orientierungspunkte zu dienen, und so verwirrend, daß man die Richtung verliert. Auf einen Stabilisierungsrahmen wie bei den mohammedanischen Ornamenten wird verzichtet; die Folge davon ist Desorientierung als normative Kondition. Außen sind die Ergebnisse befriedigender, zum einen, weil die vom Grundrißmuster hervorgebrachten facettierten Seiten in genügend großen Flächen sichtbar sind, um das zugrunde liegende Ordnungsprinzip erkennen zu lassen, und zum anderen, weil das Programm eines Gebäudes gewöhnlich ein Element enthält, das in Maßstab und Charakter herausragt und somit einen stabilisierenden Kontrast liefert.

Der wichtigste Vorteil einer multiaxialen Grundrißgeometrie ist ihre Fähigkeit, außergewöhnlichen Situationen gerecht zu werden, also das zu bezeichnen und hervorzuheben, was mit anderen Mitteln möglicherweise nur irgendwie untergebracht oder verdunkelt oder sogar unterdrückt würde. Diese Architektur ist menschlich sympathisch: Sie hat ein Auge für die Unterschiede und versucht, sie deutlich herauszustreichen. Dazu müssen ihr aber echte Gelegenheiten offenstehen; was ihr Bemühen vereitelt, ist eine insgesamt einfache Situation. Wird das Verfahren auf vielgeschossige Gebäude angewandt, so herrscht die Tendenz, in der Vertikalen die Komplexität auszuschließen. Die günstigsten Bedingungen bieten ein- oder zweigeschossige Gebäude – besonders bei unregelmäßigem Gelände und wenn das Dach als sichtbar gegliedertes Element verwendet werden kann. Interessante Beispiele dafür sind die Pavillons des Winnebago Children's Home in Neillsville sowie die Louis Jefferson Long Library in Aurora. Das Grundrißskelett der Bibliothek besteht aus neun Paaren übereinander gelegter und gegeneinander verdrehter Quadrate. Da diese Basis-»Felder« ungleich gegeneinander verschoben sind, kann man den windmühlenartigen Grundriß außer in Diagrammform schwer erfassen. Schiffsschnabelähnliche Vorsprünge und das unregelmäßige, abfallende Holzdach ergeben fünf Gebäudeseiten, die man als Höhlungen auffassen kann, als einladende, nicht abweisende Einbuchtungen. So ungewohnt manche Formen wirken mögen – das Ergebnis ist doch ein Gebäude, das den Vergleich mit ähnlichen Werken von Aalto und, was noch wichtiger ist, von Frank Lloyd Wright aushält; Wright wäre es schwergefallen, hier das Vorhandensein dessen zu leugnen, was anzustreben er die Architekten drängte: das »Prinzip« als Voraussetzung jeder eigenständigen Leistung.

Zu den Problemen, deren erfolgreichere Lösung man von Netschs Feldtheorie erwarten könnte, gehört das der Beziehung zwischen einzelnen Gebäuden innerhalb von weitläufigen Komplexen. Auf dem Chicagoer Campus der University of Illinois, wo sich Netsch vereinzelten, frei stehenden, rechteckigen Blöcken aus einer früheren neo-plastischen Epoche seines Schaffens gegenübersah, bleibt das Problem weitgehend unberührt, weil die Bauten so weit verstreut sind. Die strukturelle Kontinuität, die seinen drei jüngsten Bauten innewohnt, ist kaum wahrnehmbar. Hier rühren wir an ein Problem, das in der modernen Architektur endemisch ist und einer ausführlichen Erörterung, die allerdings nicht für alle hier untersuchten Gebäude relevant ist, bedürfte. Einige Verallgemeinerungen sind jedoch angebracht: Sie alle unterliegen dem nachteiligen Einfluß der Gartenstadtidee und insbesondere der Fassung, die ihr Le Corbusier gegeben hat. Es ist hier kein weiterer Beweis dafür nötig, daß die Voreingenommenheit für die Integrität der Baugestalt eine architektonische Kultur unmöglich macht. Gebäude können sich selbst Gesetz sein, aber nur auf Kosten der architektonischen Gemeinschaft. Keine Nebeneinanderstellung großer Gebäude im Stadtbild, so gefällig sie auch wie Gegenstände auf einem Tisch zur Schau gestellt sein mögen, kann den grundlegenden Mangel an notwendigem Zusammenhalt wettmachen. Die formale Integrität des frei stehenden Gebäudes gilt aber nach wie vor als Prüfstein jedes städtebaulichen Entwurfs, und je größer der Erfolg des Architekten ist, um so problematischer ist die Auswirkung auf das Gefüge unserer Städte. So ist das Carlton Centre in Johannesburg zweifellos eine so geschickte Nebeneinanderstellung, wie man sie von Türmen, deren Größe von architekturfremden Erwägungen bestimmt wurde, erwarten kann, und der ausgesparte öffentliche Raum ist kohärenter als anderswo – trotzdem sind ähnliche Ergebnisse bei einer vollkommen anderen und gleich willkürlichen Komposition denkbar.

Mauna Kea Beach Hotel, Kamuela, Hawaii.

it is these corridors and bridges that lend an air of Piranesian complexity. Individual rooms, each with a balcony, are furnished lightly and almost casually; elsewhere the sense of "decor" is sustained by furnishings and decorations chosen from several countries, and constituting a highly sophisticated appraisal of "good design" as that term might be understood (and rejected) by a knowledgeable professional.

By popular agreement the climate and history of San Francisco can be held responsible for more relaxed attitudes, but whatever the reason it does seem to be the case that SOM's West Coast offices are less preoccupied with the formal justification of their work. Essays in structural calisthenics (Alcoa) are rare: the structural imperative does not have the same self-justifying persuasiveness in San Francisco that it has in Chicago. Nor is San Francisco particularly interested in forcing from high-rise structure its most operatic interludes: The Bank of America building, Egyptian in its polished, marbled grandeur, is after all an essay in the use of bay windows (curiously anticipating some aspects of the Sears Tower massing). Yet SOM's best work in the engineer's idiom is to be found nearby in Oakland: Edward Bassett's Oakland-Alameda Coliseum, based on earlier studies by Myron Goldsmith for a similar problem, is a genuinely convincing match of "pure" structural form to the actual situation and program. The arena and stadium are structures of comparable mass: their siting in relation to the highway, and the use of earth berms to reduce apparent bulk, are skillful and unaggressive; the circular concave roof suspended above an oval arena yields an intensely dynamic space, without embellishment, and difficult problems of plan and structure are resolved with unforced elegance.

In this context of low-keyed engineering on the one hand, and almost casual experiment on the other, it is perhaps surprising that the San Francisco office should have produced one of the most important of SOM's recent buildings: Edward Bassett's office for the Weyerhaeuser Company, on a rural site near Tacoma, Washington. The exurban office building, like the Beaux Arts "Palace for a Head of State", constitutes the modern "ideal" problem. Because such corporate headquarters are intended to attract employees by offering the most congenial environment, and because they stand serene in private parks, they avoid the overbearing, competitive, and increasingly ominous tone of their urban counterparts. When supplemented by collections of modern art, as is often the case, these buildings and their sites become local attractions sought out by the public. That some employees nevertheless feel trapped in paradise raises another kind of question, best left to Sunday supplement psychologists, but the fact remains that exurban corporate headquarters are architectural improvements of the environment as a result of decentralization.

The principal architectural distinction of the Weyerhaeuser building is that it is conceived as part of its site, in that metaphorical sense characteristic of Frank Lloyd Wright. This is not to say that it relies on Wrightian geometry and texture to make it seem literally an extension of the ground; but rather that its component parts are dominated by the idea of a building as an abstraction of the site's contours. Inevitably the result is formal emphasis on horizontal lines and masses, with vertical structure subordinate. At Weyerhaeuser parapets and columns alike are given minimal detailing. In this respect it makes a striking contrast with SOM's other major work in the genre, Gordon Bunshaft's office complex for the Ameri-

Bemerkenswerte Lösungen auf städtebaulichem Terrain finden sich bei SOM an beiden Enden der Skala, sowohl in Situationen, die hinsichtlich Gestalt und Plazierung eines Einzelgebäudes ungewöhnlich schwierig sind, als auch in solchen, die scheinbar unbegrenzte Möglichkeiten bieten. Der ersten Kategorie kann man zwei ganz verschiedene Gebäude zuordnen, das Hirshhorn-Museum neben der Smithsonian Institution an der Mall in Washington und das Kaufhaus Macy's in Queens. Beim letzteren führte ein dreieckiges Grundstück, beim ersteren das Verlangen nach einem Baukörper, der sich mit minimaler Resistenz in seine Umgebung einfügt, zu einem runden Gebäude, und in beiden Fällen ist die Gestalt glücklich gewählt. Städtebauliche Probleme der zweiten Kategorie scheinen sich bei bescheidenem Maßstab bisweilen mit einer Architektur zu lösen, die der Volksarchitektur nacheifert und sich gegenüber der Landschaft große Zurückhaltung auferlegt. Ein Beispiel dafür ist das Altenzentrum Carmel Valley Manor. Das Zentrum, das neben allgemeinen Einrichtungen viele kleine Häuser mit jeweils mehreren Wohnungen umfaßt, wirkt wie ein fernes Echo auf den spanischen Kolonialstil. Photographien täuschen; tatsächlich ist die Wirkung sowohl subtiler als auch substantieller. Die günstigen Gegebenheiten des Grundstücks werden hervorgehoben; offene, überdachte Höfe verbinden und stabilisieren das, was sonst vielleicht zu weit verstreut gewesen wäre; offenkundig dekorativ gemeinte Bögen tragen zur Kontinuität bei; abfallende Dächer erzeugen einen erfreulichen Abwechslungsreichtum und ziehen die Blicke auf sich. Tatsächlich strahlt die ganze Komposition jene anheimelnde »Gewöhnlichkeit« aus, der in den letzten Jahren von Robert Venturi und anderen das Wort geredet wurde – jedoch ohne den sarkastischen Unterton, der solche Experimente zu einer Art »Insider«-Scherz unter Architekten macht. Das herablassende Lächeln des Architekten – seine Träger nennen es lieber einen Hang zur Ironie – rief in letzter Zeit große Bewunderung hervor; vielleicht wurde deshalb dieses unkomplizierte Projekt (wie vor ihm der kurzlebige Bay-Region-Stil) so wenig beachtet. Es erreichte mühelos, was heute den angestrengten Aufwand an »Theorie« zu erfordern scheint.

Ausgeglichenheit und Spontaneität sind vielleicht nur in ländlicher Umwelt möglich. Das Bemühen des Büros in San Francisco, mit einer schwierigen städtischen Situation durch Vermittlung zwischen den Erfordernissen der Straße und denen der Architektur fertig zu werden, führte zu einem interessanten, aber anfechtbaren szenischen Entwurf. Aufgabe war, am Union Square in San Francisco einen Hotelturm zu errichten, ohne jedoch die verhältnismäßig einheitliche Höhe der bestehenden Fassaden zu sprengen. Man setzte den Turm weit von der Straße zurück und legte einen niedrigeren Flügel mit Gesellschaftsräumen dazwischen, der sich mit seiner zum Union Square weisenden Fassade an die Nachbargebäude anpaßt, von der Nebenstraße jedoch in einem Winkel von 45 Grad zurückweicht, so daß er eine Eingangsplaza schafft, die dem Union Square keine Konkurrenz macht. Die Fassade wirkt wie eine Bühnendekoration aus Hollywood. Blickt man seitlich darauf, so glaubt man, sie habe keinen Baukörper hinter sich - ein Effekt, der natürlich Aufmerksamkeit erregt. Die gewölbten Fensteröffnungen fallen – wie es auch beabsichtigt gewesen sein mag – im Maßstab aus dem Rahmen, und die entkörperte Fassade ist eine etwas arrogante Höflichkeitsgeste gegenüber dem Stadtraum; das Gesamtergebnis ist jedoch nicht ganz abstoßend, und nach einiger Gewöhnung wünscht man ihm guten Erfolg.

Ein interessantes Gegenstück zu dieser Art von Architektur ist das Mauna Kea Beach Hotel auf Hawaii. Das Gebäude benennen heißt bereits sein Problem umreißen. Tropische Phantasien heraufbeschwörend, stellt es echte Spielarchitektur dar, zugleich jedoch auch rationale Architektur von hohem Rang. Der Charakter des Hauptbaus wird davon bestimmt, daß sich die drei Geschosse mit den Gästeräumen über einer Reihe von zentralen, zum Himmel offenen Höfen auf beiden Gebäudelängsseiten nach oben zurückstaffeln. Überdeckte Freiluftgänge öffnen sich so auf üppig bepflanzte Gärten und verleihen zusammen mit den sie verbindenden Brücken dem Ganzen einen Hauch Piranesischer Formenfülle. Die Gästezimmer, die alle einen Balkon besitzen, sind leicht und fast zufällig eingerichtet. Die anderen Räume werden von einer »dekor«-haften Stimmung beherrscht; die hier aus den verschiedensten Ländern zusammengetragenen Möbel und Dekorationen zeugen von einer höchst differenzierten Einschätzung der »guten Gestaltung« in dem Sinn, wie sie von einem kennerischen Professionellen verstanden (und verworfen) wird.

Übereinstimmend führt man die entspanntere Haltung an der Westküste auf Klima und Geschichte zurück, doch aus welchem Grund auch immer – die SOM-Büros in San Francisco und Portland scheinen sich tatsächlich weniger um die formale Rechtfertigung ihrer Arbeit zu sorgen. Strukturelle Freiübungen (Alcoa Building) sind selten. Der strukturelle Imperativ scheint hier nicht die gleiche, sich selbst rechtfertigende Überzeugungskraft zu besitzen wie in Chicago: So ist die Hauptverwaltung der Bank of America, ägyptisch in ihrer polierten,

Bank of America Headquarters / Hauptverwaltung der Bank of America, San Francisco, California.

Oakland-Alameda County Coliseum, Oakland, California.

can Can Company, in Greenwich, Connecticut. Like Weyerhaeuser, American Can is set as a wall across its site, in the process creating an artificial lake. But where the Weyerhaeuser building is consistently and exclusively conceived as a pyramidal stack of trays or terraces, American Can presents itself as a three-story pavilion on a massive podium. The Weyer-haeuser solution is dependent on outdoor accommodations for cars; American Can's podium accommodates five floors of concealed parking. There are other major differences: at American Can executive offices are housed in a completely separate pavilion; comparable Weyerhaeuser accommodations are handled as an integral penthouse. The American Can pavilions open on interior courts. The Weyerhaeuser building, using the deep floors made possible by "office landscape" planning, is oriented entirely outward to the view. In both buildings refinements of structure serve important purposes. For American Can precast concrete double-web beams in constructivist detail produce elevations alternately over-scaled or delicate. At Weyerhaeuser round columns are arranged in a diagrid, which has the critical advantage of making successive setbacks at each floor read quite clearly, regardless of light or detail, because the unaligned columns introduce depth perspective.

Both buildings are preeminently rational solutions. Weyerhaeuser avoids all classicizing references and attempts to engage itself directly with its site, yet it may be argued that terraced car parks are not an improvement to the landscape. As with all horizontally articulated buildings, there are problems about how and where to end, and for that matter the copper-clad hipped roof of the penthouse level is a peculiarly domestic conclusion. Some of these problems are avoided at American Can by virtue of its self-containing podium, which not only leaves the landscape free of automobiles but allows an agreeably theatrical flourish: an access road that peels off into multilevel ramps vanishing into the podium. More accomplished in its handling of interior space, as well as in landscape details, the American Can complex elicits admiration but perhaps not the excitement of Weyerhaeuser's underlying idea, however incompletely realized it may be. At Weyerhaeuser some dimly remembered lesson of Wright's seems to offer an Ariadne's thread out of the intellectual labyrinth of perfect structure. Both buildings are major achievements.

The critic's conventional excuse for refraining from definitive appraisals of current work – apart from the fear of becoming a comic footnote on the pages of history – is that we are too close in time to sort out the real significance of what seems at first very good, very bad, or merely indifferent. But of course such judgments are made from moment to moment, by architects even more than critics, and the critic who advises architects to take more risks ought to be willing to take some himself. Which of the buildings reviewed here will survive? In ten years which ones will seem worth visiting; which ones will have to be included in histories of American building, either because they established a new possibility or because they seemed in their perfection to close a line of development once and for all?

Wright observed that every great thing is too much of whatever it is. If that is true, it must also apply to such problematic ventures as the Hancock tower or 9 West 57th Street: both are too much of what they are, and yet both are likely to survive in the popular imagination, growing in sentimental associations like the Eiffel Tower, which they resemble.

The Johnson and Beinecke libraries, qualitatively different, are also likely to grow in esteem because they offer experiences most architects are unwilling to grant. That the Johnson Library achieves monumentality through mass, with its concomitant historical associations, in no way invalidates the desire for monumentality. There is a kind of malnutrition, or vitamin deficiency, attributable to the modern utilitarian style: we are perishing of undernourishment but cannot bring ourselves to recognize the ailment. Those architects who do, and who try to offer a more balanced diet, find themselves accused of offering cake while the populace lacks bread. The Beinecke Library is one of those rare essays in architectural pleasure, for the public, and it has been so accepted and appreciated.

At the other end of the spectrum are those buildings really meant for architects: the BMA tower, for instance, must surely be the perfect, and the last, statement on the theme. Marine Midland, and the numerous other buildings SOM has executed in its flat style, may be as close as we can get to folk architecture (or good bread). Less dependent than is Mies' system of structural articulation on the refinement of an individual's sensibility, the style lends itself to easy adaptation. The Sears Tower would seem likely to break the spell of single-volume tower design, suggesting a flexibility more appropriate to the actual problems, even if the Sears Tower itself does not solve them all. This willingness to experiment with the plan, even more than with the structure, is carried furthest in Walter Netsch's "field theory" buildings for the University of Illinois. Though each of them seems only partly successful, the attempt to provide a rational basis for complex plan geometry is a real alternative to the

Headquarters of the Weyerhaeuser Company/ Hauptverwaltung der Weyerhaeuser Company, Tacoma, Washington.

Headquarters of the American Can Company/
Hauptverwaltung der American Can Company,
Greenwich, Connecticut.

marmornen Erhabenheit, im Grunde ein Experiment mit Erkerfenstern (merkwürdigerweise nimmt sie einige Aspekte der Baumassengruppierung des Sears Tower vorweg). Und doch entstand hier die bisher beste in der Sprache des Ingenieurs gehaltene Arbeit von SOM: Edward Bassetts Oakland-Alameda County Coliseum (basierend auf früheren Studien von Myron Goldsmith zu einer ähnlichen Aufgabe) zeigt eine wahrhaft überzeugende Anpassung der »reinen« strukturellen Gestalt an die gegebene Lage und das vorgeschriebene Programm. Das Stadion und die gesonderte Mehrzweckhalle sind als Baumassen vergleichbar und im Verhältnis zur Schnellstraße sehr geschickt plaziert; die Erdwälle, die den Maßstab reduzieren, treten nicht auffällig in Erscheinung; das kreisförmige, nach innen geneigte, die Mehrzweckhalle frei überspannende Dach ergibt einen äußerst dynamischen Raum; schwierige Entwurfs- und Konstruktionsprobleme sind mit ungezwungener Eleganz gelöst.

Angesichts der zurückhaltenden Bautechnik einerseits und des fast zufälligen Experimentierens andererseits überrascht es vielleicht, daß einer der wichtigsten neueren Bauten, die Hauptverwaltung der Weyerhaeuser Company bei Tacoma, aus dem SOM-Büro in San Francisco hervorging.

Das wichtigste architektonische Merkmal des Weyerhaeuser-Baus ist, daß er als Teil des Geländes konzipiert wurde, und zwar in jenem für Frank Lloyd Wright charakteristischen metaphorischen Sinn. Das heißt nicht, er arbeite mit Wrights Geometrie und Textur, um buchstäblich als Erweiterung des Geländes zu erscheinen, sondern vielmehr, daß seine Komposition von der Vorstellung eines Gebäudes als Abstraktion der Geländeumrisse beherrscht wird. Zwangsläufig ergibt sich daraus eine äußerst starke Betonung der Horizontalen und eine fast völlige Unterdrückung der Vertikalen. Damit steht der Bau in krassem Gegensatz zu dem anderen großen SOM-Werk dieser Art, der Hauptverwaltung der American Can Company in Greenwich. Wie der Weyerhaeuser-Bau ist der Komplex der American Can Company dammartig über eine Bodensenke gestellt, wobei hier ebenfalls ein künstlicher See aufgestaut wird. Der Weyerhaeuser-Bau ist durchgängig und ausschließlich als gestreckte Terrassenpyramide angelegt, während sich der American-Can-Komplex als eine Kombination eines dreigeschossigen und eines eingeschossigen Gebäudes auf einem massigen Sockel präsentiert. Bei Weyerhaeuser liegen die Parkplätze außerhalb des Hauses, bei der American Can Company birgt der Sockel fünf Parkgeschosse. Weitere wichtige Unterschiede: Bei der American Can Company sind die Büros für die Geschäftsleitung abgesondert (in dem eingeschossigen Gebäude), bei Weyerhaeuser integriert (in einem Penthouse). Die Gebäude der American Can Company umschließen Innenhöfe, der im Grundriß nach dem Konzept der Büro-»Landschaft« entwickelte Weyerhaeuser-Bau ist vollständig nach außen orientiert. Bei beiden Bauwerken ist die Konstruktion in raffinierter Weise in den Dienst der formalen Absichten gestellt. Beim American-Can-Komplex ergeben in konstruktivistischer Manier ausgebildete Doppelsteg-Deckenelemente Fassaden, die abwechselnd grob und elegant wirken. Beim Weyerhaeuser-Bau sind runde Stützen auf einen diagonalen Raster gestellt, der die Rückstufungen der einzelnen Geschosse unabhängig von Licht oder Detail sehr deutlich hervorhebt, weil die schräg aufeinander ausgerichteten Stützen Tiefenperspektive schaffen.

Beide Bauwerke stellen höchst rationale Lösungen dar. Der Weyerhaeuser-Bau verzichtet auf jeden klassizistischen Bezug und versucht, sich in unmittelbarer Weise mit seiner Umgebung auseinanderzusetzen; man könnte allerdings einwenden, terrassierte Parkplätze seien kein Schmuck der Landschaft. Wie bei allen horizontal gegliederten Gebäuden erhebt sich die Frage, wie und wo der Bau aufhören soll, und in dieser Hinsicht stellt das leicht angeschrägte Kupferdach des Penthousegeschosses eine eigenartig biedere Lösung dar. Einige dieser Probleme werden beim Komplex der American Can Company durch den selbständigen Sockel umgangen, der nicht nur die Landschaft von Autos frei hält, sondern auch einen an ein Bühnenbild erinnernden Anblick bietet: Die Zufahrtsstraße fächert sich in Rampen auf, die auf mehreren Ebenen im Sockel verschwinden. Der American-Can-Komplex ist in der Gestaltung des Innenraums wie auch in landschaftlichen Details geglückter und löst Bewunderung aus, aber wohl keine innere Erregung wie der Weyerhaeuser-Bau, so unvollkommen dessen Leitidee auch verwirklicht sein mag.

Welche der hier betrachteten Gebäude werden Bestand haben? Welche werden in zehn Jahren noch sehenswert sein, welche werden in die Geschichte der amerikanischen Architektur eingehen, entweder weil sie einer neuen Möglichkeit Bahn brechen oder weil sie in ihrer Vollkommenheit eine Entwicklungslinie ein für allemal abzuschließen scheinen?

Wright bemerkte einmal, alles Große sei zu viel von dem, was es ist. Wenn dies zutrifft, muß es auch für so problematische Wagnisse wie das John Hancock Center oder 9 West 57th

chic but pointless abuses of nonrectilinear planning. It is much to SOM's credit that "re-search" includes the examination of ideas, as well as technique.

The American Can and Weyerhaeuser buildings must surely be counted as likely candidates for long life, the one because it is beautiful, the other because it seems to reveal the under-lying compatibility between Wright's sense of architecture as landscaping and Mies' early clarification of Wright without benefit of romantic rhetoric. Weyerhaeuser is in some respects a Miesian diagram of certain Wright projects of the 1920's, and it may well help to focus attention on promising possibilities.

The character of architecture is determined by the kinds of problems architects are asked to solve. Like most other architects, SOM has not yet persuaded its clients that their prob-lems are sometimes improperly defined. Among such problems those created by the urban high-rise building are foremost. As the detailing and structure of the skyscraper become more sophisticated, the buildings themselves become more disturbing. It is as if we were striving to design a really beautiful electric chair: the fault is not in the style but in the thing itself.

In the 1950's immense effort was expended to convince clients and zoning boards that sky-scrapers should be set back from the building line, if that was the price to be paid for a vertical rise without setbacks. If it was possible to induce that behavior, it is scarcely sur-prising that the well established offices should now be expected to educate their clients to somewhat more desirable notions of civic responsibility. Architects will be able to persuade their clients that the street, for example, is part of the building – but only after they have persuaded themselves.

Perhaps the most urgent task confronting the architect is to ameliorate the conflict between private indifference and public well-being: in that respect the battle for modern architecture is a long way from being won. SOM's contribution has been not merely technical brilliance and a standard of professionalism second to none; it has been a champion for desirable change. Having written some of the best passages of American architectural history, it now seems fair that SOM should be expected to perform as well in the next phase.

Street gelten: Beide sind zu viel von dem, was sie sind, und doch besteht die Wahrscheinlichkeit, daß beide im Volksbewußtsein ihren Platz behalten und daß sich sentimentale Assoziationen an sie knüpfen wie an den Eiffelturm, dem sie gleichen.

Die Johnson Library und die Beinecke Library, qualitativ unterschiedlich, werden wohl ebenfalls an Wertschätzung gewinnen, weil sie Erfahrungen ermöglichen, an die sich die meisten Architekten nicht heranwagen. Daß die Johnson Library Monumentalität durch schiere Masse und deren historische Begleitassoziationen verwirklicht, würdigt ihr Verlangen nach Monumentalität in keiner Weise herab. Der moderne Utilitarismus führt sozusagen zu falscher Ernährung oder Vitaminmangel: Wir leiden an Unterernährung, können uns aber nicht dazu bringen, das Übel zu diagnostizieren. Die Architekten, die klarsehen und eine ausgewogenere Diät vorschlagen, werden beschuldigt, Kuchen anzubieten, während es dem Volk an Brot mangelt. Die Beinecke Library gehört zu den seltenen Versuchen, der Öffentlichkeit architektonisches Vergnügen zu bereiten, und sie wird in diesem Sinn anerkannt und geschätzt.

Am anderen Ende der Skala stehen die Gebäude, die im Grunde für die Architekten selbst gemeint sind: Der Turm der Business Men's Assurance Co. zum Beispiel ist sicherlich die perfekte und letztgültige Aussage zum Thema. Das Marine Midland Building in New York und die vielen anderen Gebäude, die von SOM mit ähnlich flacher Haut ausgeführt wurden, stehen möglicherweise der Volksarchitektur (oder dem gesunden Brot) so nahe, wie es nur denkbar ist. Der Sears Tower scheint den Bann des einvolumigen Turmes gebrochen zu haben, denn er weist auf eine Flexibilität, die die tatsächlich anstehenden Probleme überwinden hilft, auch wenn das Bauwerk selbst diese Probleme nicht alle löst. Die Bereitschaft, mit dem Grundriß noch mehr als mit der Struktur zu experimentieren, erreicht ihren Höhepunkt mit Walter Netschs Feldtheorie-Gebäuden für die University of Illinois. Obwohl jedes einzelne für sich nur teilweise geglückt erscheint, ist doch das Bemühen, die komplexe Grundrißgeometrie auf eine rationale Grundlage zu stellen, eine echte Alternative zu den modischen, aber sinnlosen Mißbräuchen der nichtgeradlinigen Planung.

Der American-Can-Komplex und der Weyerhaeuser-Bau haben zweifellos eine lange Zukunft vor sich, der eine, weil er schön ist, der andere, weil er zu offenbaren scheint, daß die antipodischen Architekturauffassungen von Wright und Mies van der Rohe letztlich doch miteinander vereinbar sind. Der Weyerhaeuser-Bau ist in mancher Hinsicht ein Miessches Diagramm gewisser Projekte Wrights aus den zwanziger Jahren, und er könnte durchaus dazu beitragen, daß man sich noch intensiver mit den hier beschlossenen, vielversprechenden Möglichkeiten befaßt.

Der Charakter der Architektur wird von der Beschaffenheit der Probleme bestimmt, die den Architekten zur Lösung aufgetragen sind. Wie die meisten anderen Architekturbüros hat die Firma SOM ihre Auftraggeber noch nicht davon überzeugt, daß ihre Probleme oft ungenügend definiert sind. Die vom städtischen Hochhausbau aufgeworfenen Fragen stehen hier an erster Stelle. Je mehr man die Wolkenkratzer in Detail und Struktur verfeinert, um so fragwürdiger werden die Gebäude selbst. Es ist, als bemühten wir uns, einen wirklich schönen elektrischen Stuhl zu entwerfen; der Fehler liegt nicht im Stil, sondern in der Sache selbst.

In den fünfziger Jahren wurde ungeheure Mühe darauf verwandt, Bauherren und städtischen Planungsämtern klarzumachen, daß man Wolkenkratzer von der Baulinie zurücksetzen sollte, um sie ohne Rückstufungen hochführen zu können. Wenn es möglich war, dieser Ansicht Geltung zu verschaffen, überrascht es kaum, daß man heute von den gut eingeführten Büros verlangt, sie sollten ihre Auftraggeber zu weitaus wünschenswerteren Auffassungen von bürgerlicher Verantwortung erziehen. Zweifellos werden die Architekten ihre Bauherren zu überzeugen vermögen, daß zum Beispiel die Straße Teil des Gebäudes ist – aber erst, wenn sie selbst davon überzeugt sind.

Vielleicht ist die dringlichste Aufgabe, der sich der Architekt heute gegenübergestellt sieht, die Überbrückung des Konflikts zwischen privater Gleichgültigkeit und öffentlichem Wohl. Auf diesem Gebiet ist die Schlacht für die moderne Architektur noch längst nicht geschlagen. Der SOM-Beitrag manifestierte sich sowohl in brillanter Technik und einem erstrangigen beruflichen Niveau als auch im Engagement für erstrebenswerte Veränderungen. Von der Firma SOM, die einige der besten Passagen im Buch der amerikanischen Architekturgeschichte geschrieben hat, erwartet man zu Recht auch für die Zukunft große Leistungen.

Skidmore, Owings & Merrill

Partners / Partner 1973

Gordon Bunshaft

J. Walter Severinghaus

William E. Hartmann

Walter A. Netsch

John O. Merrill, Jr.

David H. Hughes

Roy O. Allen

Edward C. Bassett

Bruce J. Graham

David A. Pugh

Myron Goldsmith

Albert Lockett

Walter H. Costa

Donald C. Smith

Marc E. Goldsmith

Fazlur R. Khan

Whitson M. Overcash

James R. DeStefano

Robert Diamant

Thomas J. Eyerman

Richard E. Lenke

Michael A. McCarthy

Leon Moed

John K. Turley

Gordon L. Wildermuth

Consulting Partner / Beratender Partner

Nathaniel A. Owings

Macy's Rego Park, Queens, New York, New York

The building has an excellent location relating to the intersection of Queens Boulevard passing to the south and the Long Island Expressway to the east, which are the two major traffic arteries serving this area.

Sales areas and parking facilities are combined in a single cylindrical building, 426' in diameter, which occupies the southern portion of an irregular site. The elegant perforated facade is formed by poured-in-place concrete which has been sandblasted to expose a coarse white aggregate. The perforations permit the natural ventilation of the garage levels which surround the inner core sales floors.

Parking is provided for 1,250 cars on five ring levels above the plaza and on the roof of the top sales floor. The arrangement provides the customer with the convenience of "curb-side parking" or a very short walk to the sales areas. Two double-helical ramps provide computer-controlled access to the parking levels. The core of the helices contains mechanical equipment areas.

There are three sales floors containing a total area of approximately 270,000 sq ft. The largest sales floor is on the ground level and extends beneath the first garage level 30'. The remaining area forms a shopper's arcade with display windows and adjoins a landscaped plaza. A basement level is provided for storage and contains trucking service facilities with access from a ramp beneath the helices.

The building has been designed to expand one sales floor and two parking levels.

Macy's Rego Park, Queens, New York, New York

Der Komplex liegt an einem verkehrsmäßig besonders begünstigten Punkt von Queens – der im Süden vorbeiführende Queens Boulevard und der diesen östlich kreuzende Long Island Expressway stellen die beiden wichtigsten Verkehrsadern dieser Gegend dar.

Verkaufsbereich und Autoabstellplätze sind in einem flachen zylinderförmigen Baukörper mit einem Durchmesser von etwa 130 m, der den breiteren südlichen Teil des unregelmäßig geschnittenen Grundstücks einnimmt, zusammengefaßt. Die durchbrochene Fassade besteht aus Sichtbeton, dessen Oberfläche durch Sandstrahlung aufgerauht wurde; die schießschartenartigen Schlitze lassen die Abgase aus den fünf sich ringartig um die inneren Verkaufsebenen legenden Parkgeschosse auf natürliche Weise abziehen.

Insgesamt stehen 1250 Autoabstellplätze zur Verfügung. Sie verteilen sich auf die bereits erwähnten Parkringe und das Dach über dem obersten Verkaufsgeschoß. Durch diese Anordnung konnten die Fußwege der motorisierten Kunden so kurz gehalten werden wie beim Parken in einer konventionellen Einkaufsstraße. Die Autoabstellplätze werden über zwei spiralförmige Rampen mit Computersteuerung erschlossen. In den Zylindern, um die sich die Rampen herumwinden, sind haustechnische Einrichtungen untergebracht.

Der dreigeschossige Verkaufsbereich beansprucht eine Fläche von etwa 25000 qm. Im Erdgeschoß ist die Verkaufsfläche um etwa 10 m unter dem Garagenring vorgezogen; ihr vorgelagert ist eine umlaufende Arkade mit Schaufenstern. Ein Kellergeschoß nimmt Lagerräume und die Anlieferung auf; die Zufahrt liegt zwischen den beiden zu den Parkgeschossen führenden Spiralrampen.

Für später ist eine Erweiterung um eine Verkaufsebene und zwei Parkgeschosse vorgesehen.

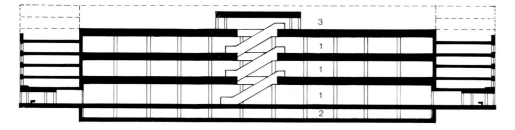

1. Section of the building. Key: 1 sales area, 2 deliveries, 3 parking facilities. The broken line indicates a possible future addition.
2. Entrance and exit ramps to and from the parking levels.

1. Schnitt durch das Gebäude. Legende: 1 Verkaufsbereich, 2 Anlieferung, 3 Autoabstellplätze. Die gestrichelte Linie deutet eine für später in Aussicht genommene Erweiterung an.
2. Blick auf die Auffahrtsrampe zu den Autoabstellplätzen.

3. View of the department store from across Queens Boulevard.
4. Plans (ground floor, typical floor). Key: 1 Queens Boulevard, 2 55th Avenue, 3 Justice Avenue, 4 56th Avenue, 5 sales area, 6 arcade, 7 entrance ramp, 8 exit ramp, 9 down and up ramps to and from service basement, 10 garage ring.
5. Close-up of the building.

3. Blick über den Queens Boulevard auf das Kaufhaus.
4. Grundrisse (Erdgeschoß, Normalgeschoß). Legende: 1 Queens Boulevard, 2 55th Avenue, 3 Justice Avenue, 4 56th Avenue, 5 Verkaufsfläche, 6 Arkade, 7 Auffahrtsrampe, 8 Abfahrtsrampe, 9 Auf- und Abfahrt zum Anlieferungsgeschoß, 10 Garagenring.
5. Detailansicht des Kaufhauses.

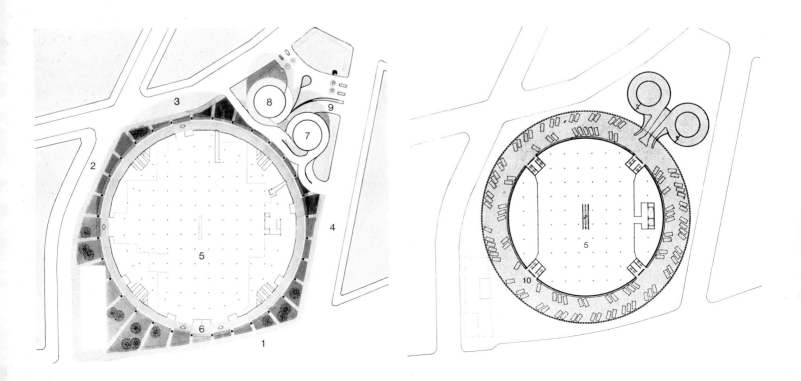

Publishing House and Printing Plant of the Newspaper "The Republic", Columbus, Indiana

The new building for the newspaper, which celebrated its centenary in 1972, is situated in the center of the town, directly opposite the historic Bartholomew County Courthouse. It represents an important part of the redevelopment plan for the town center, also prepared by Skidmore, Owings & Merrill, which provides among other facilities for an enclosed shopping mall extending over two blocks.

The ground floor covers an area of 256′×96′. On the west side are a cafeteria, the staff offices, the management offices as well as the accounting department. To the east of these is a lobby which extends across the building from one long side to the other. Adjacent to the south side of the lobby is the editorial department, on the north side the advertising department. Also on the north side are the composing and printing plants. At the eastern end of the ground floor is the delivery zone. In the basement below the printing plant and delivery zone, covering an area of 96′×96′, are the paper store, the paper feed to the printing machine as well as mechanical installations. The paper rolls are delivered by means of an elevator outside the building which, when not in use, is covered by a slab flush with the ground.

While the internal columns in the ground floor are on a grid of 32′×32′, those along the facades are spaced at 10′8″ so as to permit an integration of facade and bearing structure and thereby to convey an impression of extreme lightness. An independent foundation below the printing machine ensures that machine vibrations are not transferred to the building. Measures have also been taken to prevent noise disturbance from the printing process. The noise level of 90 decibles experienced in the printing section is reduced by special glass walls so that, in the other rooms, no more than a slight humming noise can be heard which does not rise beyond the general noise level.

To expose the newspaper operation as much as possible to the outside, the building is almost wholly glazed.

Verlags- und Druckereigebäude der Zeitung »The Republic«, Columbus, Indiana

Der Neubau der im Jahr 1972 100 Jahre alt gewordenen Zeitung liegt im Zentrum der Stadt, direkt gegenüber dem historischen Bartholomew County Courthouse. Er stellt einen wichtigen Bestandteil des ebenfalls von Skidmore, Owings & Merrill entwickelten Sanierungsplans für die Innenstadt dar, der unter anderem auch eine überdachte, sich über zwei Baublöcke erstreckende Einkaufsstraße vorsieht.

Das Erdgeschoß bedeckt eine Fläche von etwa 78×29 m. Auf der westlichen Querseite sind eine Cafeteria, das Personalbüro, die Räume der Geschäftsleitung sowie die Buchhaltung untergebracht. Nach Osten folgt die von einer Gebäudelängsseite bis zur anderen durchlaufende Lobby. Auf der Südseite schließt sich dieser die Redaktion, auf der Nordseite die Anzeigenabteilung an. Auf der Nordseite sind weiterhin die Setzerei und die Druckerei untergebracht. Den östlichen Abschluß der Raumfolge des Erdgeschosses bildet die Auslieferung. Das etwa 29×29 m große Untergeschoß unter der Druckerei und der Auslieferung beherbergt das Papierlager, die Papierzufuhr zur Druckmaschine sowie haustechnische Anlagen. Die Anlieferung der Papierrollen erfolgt über einen außerhalb des Gebäudes liegenden Aufzug, der bei Nichtbetrieb durch eine mit der Erdoberfläche abschließenden Platte verdeckt wird.

Während die inneren Stützen des Erdgeschosses einem Raster von etwa 9,60×9,60 m folgen, wurde für die äußeren ein Abstand von nur etwa 3,20 m gewählt, um eine Integration von Fassade und Tragwerk zu ermöglichen und dadurch dem Bau eine extreme Leichtigkeit zu geben. Ein unabhängiges Fundament unter der Druckmaschine sorgt dafür, daß keine Maschinenvibrationen auf das Gebäude übertragen werden. Einer akustischen Belästigung durch den Druckvorgang ist ebenfalls vorgebeugt: Spezielle Glaswände reduzieren die 90 Phon, die in der Druckerei herrschen, in den übrigen Räumen auf ein leichtes, im Allgemeingeräusch untergehendes Summen.

Um den Zeitungsbetrieb nach außen so weit wie möglich sichtbar zu machen, wurde der Bau fast vollständig verglast.

1. Plan. Key: 1 lobby, 2 cafeteria, 3 staff office, 4 management offices, 5 accounting department, 6 editor's office, 7 advertising department, 8 composing plant, 9 printing plant, 10 deliveries, 11 elevator to basement.
2. Cafeteria. On the rear wall, the sign of the company which used to be mounted on the old building of the newspaper.

1. Grundriß. Legende: 1 Lobby, 2 Cafeteria, 3 Personalbüro, 4 Geschäftsleitung, 5 Buchhaltung, 6 Redaktion, 7 Anzeigenabteilung, 8 Setzerei, 9 Druckerei, 10 Auslieferung, 11 Fahrstuhl zum Untergeschoß.
2. Blick in die Cafeteria. An der Rückwand wurde das am ehemaligen Gebäude der Zeitung angebrachte Firmenzeichen aufgehängt.

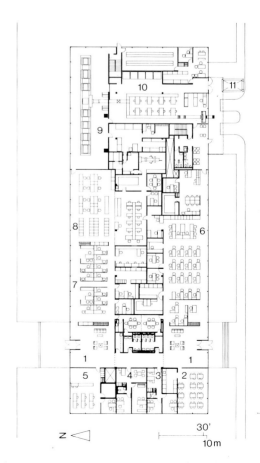

30′
10 m

3. West side of the building. Here are cafeteria, staff office, management office and accounting.
4. North side of the building. In the foreground, the printing plant. Through the large glass walls, the newspaper making process is fully exposed to the passer-by.
5. Bartholomew County Courthouse, seen from the printing plant.

3. Westseite des Gebäudes. Hier befinden sich die Cafeteria, das Personalbüro, die Räume der Geschäftsleitung sowie die Buchhaltung.
4. Nordseite des Gebäudes. Im Vordergrund die Druckerei. Durch die großen Glaswände erhält der Passant vollen Einblick in den Zeitungsbetrieb.
5. Blick von der Druckerei auf das Bartholomew County Courthouse.

Philip Morris Cigarette Manufacturing Plant, Richmond, Virginia. Under construction

The site on which the factory is being erected covers an area of 125 acres. A large oval reflecting pool and extensive landscaping with formally and informally arranged groups of trees will help to give the site a park-like character.

The plant itself has a total area of 1,700,000 sq ft. All buildings are of steel frame construction clad with precast concrete panels.

The cigarette making and packing plant proper, covering an area of 212′ × 1,000′, must be regarded as one of the largest of its kind in the world. The first floor is divided into five compartments and is spanned by trusses 23′ high without intermediate columns. This entire area is exclusively reserved for cigarette making and packing; ancillary spaces not directly concerned with the manufacturing process – air conditioning plant, toilets, lounges, etc. – are accommodated in tower-like structures 96′ high which provide vertical accents, to the otherwise predominantly horizontal mass. These towers serve not only the main building but also two parallel buildings, one for the administration, the other for workshops and the manufacture of filters. The spaces between the main building and these ancillary buildings are landscaped luxuriant gardens.

On the south side of this central core area is a large, square building for the primary processing of the tobacco. Another building on the west side serves as a warehouse, with unloading and loading facilities for supplies and finished goods.

All buildings except the warehouse are fully air-conditioned.

Zigarettenfabrik Philip Morris, Richmond, Virginia. Im Bau

Das Gelände, auf dem die Fabrik errichtet werden soll, umfaßt eine Fläche von fast 51 ha. Ein großer ovaler Teich und ausgedehnte, teils streng geometrisch, teils in freier Form angeordnete Baumgruppen werden dazu beitragen, ihm einen parkartigen Charakter zu verleihen.

Die Fabrikanlage selbst ist etwa 158000 qm groß. Alle Gebäude sind Stahlskelettkonstruktionen mit außenliegenden Verkleidungselementen aus Beton.

Mit einer Breite von etwa 65 m und einer Länge von etwa 305 m dürfte der Bau, in dem die Zigaretten gefertigt und versandfertig verpackt werden, zu den größten seiner Art in der Welt zählen. Das Erdgeschoß ist in fünf gleich große Abschnitte unterteilt und wird von einem 6,50 m hohen Trägerrost stützenfrei überspannt. In der Halle befinden sich keinerlei Nebenräume, die gesamte Fläche steht ausschließlich den Fertigungsanlagen zur Verfügung. Die nicht zur Fabrikation gehörenden Nebeneinrichtungen – Klimazentralen, Umkleideräume für das Personal und so weiter – wurden in außenstehenden, etwa 29 m hohen Türmen, die innerhalb der sonst vorherrschenden horizontalen Linien willkommene vertikale Akzente setzen, untergebracht. Die Türme bedienen nicht nur die große Halle, sondern zugleich zwei Parallelbauten, von denen der eine die Verwaltung, der andere Werkstätten und eine Halle zur Herstellung von Filtern aufnimmt. Die nicht von den Flügeln beanspruchten Flächen in der Zone zwischen der großen Halle und den sie begleitenden Bauten werden von üppig bepflanzten Gärten eingenommen.

Im Süden schließt an diesen zentralen Kernbereich eine große quadratische Halle für die Vorbereitung des Tabaks an. In einer weiteren, im Westen liegenden Halle befinden sich An- und Auslieferung.

Bis auf das Warenhaus sind alle Bauten vollklimatisiert.

1. Site plan. Key: 1 tobacco processing, 2 cigarette making and packing, 3 filter manufacture, 4 workshops, 5 supply warehouse, 6 finished goods warehouse, 7 administration, 8 power plant.

1. Lageplan. Legende: 1 Tabakvorbereitung, 2 Zigarettenfertigung, 3 Filterfertigung, 4 Werkstätten, 5 Anlieferung, 6 Auslieferung, 7 Verwaltung, 8 Energiezentrale.

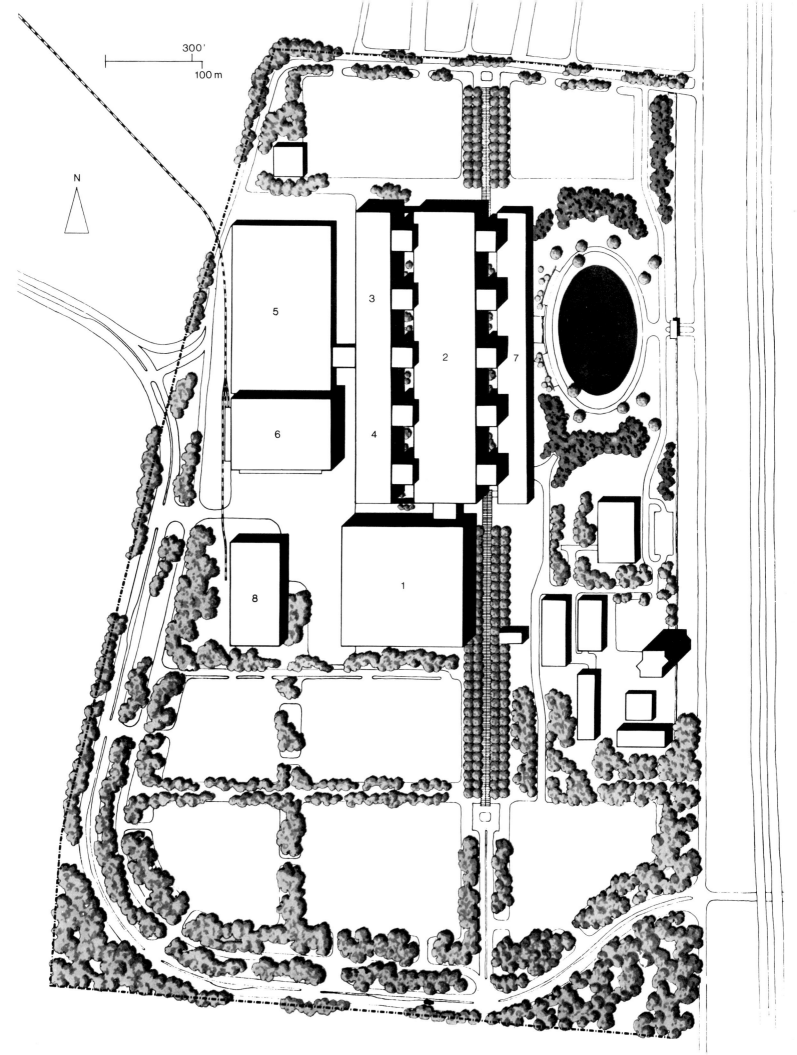

300'

100 m

N

2. View from northeast (model).
3. Cross-section through the central complex. On the left, the administration building; in the center, the cigarette making and packing plant; on the right, the workshops and filter manufacturing room.

2. Ansicht von Nordosten (Modell).
3. Querschnitt durch den Kernbereich. Links die Verwaltung, in der Mitte die Zigarettenfertigung, rechts die Werkstätten und die Filterfertigung.

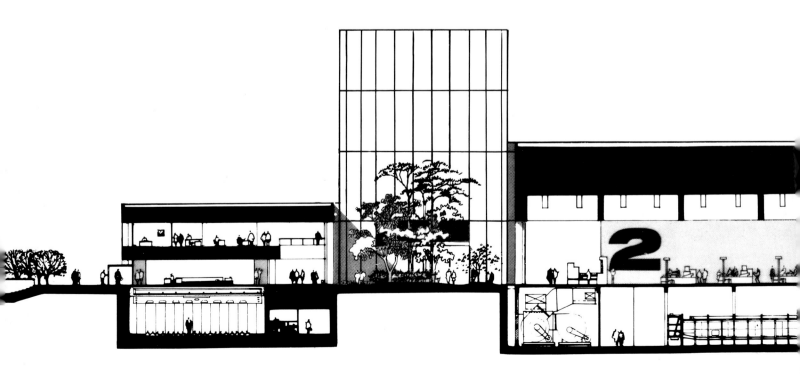

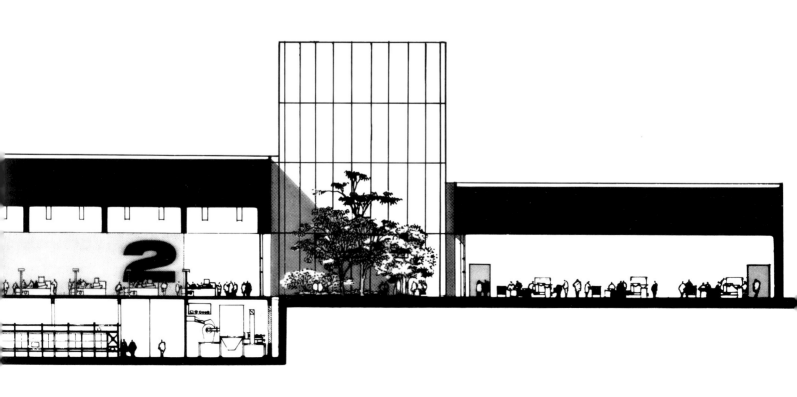

Central Engineering Building of the Armstrong Cork Company, Lancaster, Pennsylvania

The building, accommodating some 200 staff members of the development section of the internationally known manufacturer of building materials, is situated at the edge of the company's land surrounded by a large lawn.

The upper level is a column-free space about 11'6" high with a narrow core and a few floor-to-ceiling glass partitions. In addition to some conference rooms and offices and a small reference library of technical books, this floor accommodates four large drafting rooms for engineers and architects. The ground floor, only about 9' high and divided by columns, contains entrance lobby, administrative offices, cafeteria, archives and a drafting room for designers. On the basement level are service rooms and display rooms for the company's products.

The externally exposed, black painted steel framework clearly reveals the structural system. At the roof for instance, a clear distinction is made between the short sides where the main girders, spanning about 117', emerge into the open, and the long sides with their secondary beams above the non-bearing cladding. A view of the short sides also provides an instant appreciation of the closer column spacing at ground floor level which permitted to size the intermediate ceiling about three times less deep than the roof. The structural system is also clearly emphasized by the deep setback (about 8') of the floor-to-ceiling glass walls and by the white painted undersides of suspended ceiling and roof.

Technisches Zentrum der Armstrong Cork Company, Lancaster, Pennsylvania

Der Bau, in dem die etwa 200 Angestellte umfassende Entwicklungsabteilung des international bekannten Baustoffherstellers untergebracht ist, liegt am Rande des Firmengeländes, umgeben von einer großen Rasenfläche.

Das Obergeschoß ist ein etwa 3,50 m hoher, stützenfreier Raum mit einem schmalen Kernbereich und wenigen vom Boden bis zur Decke reichenden Glastrennwänden. Es beherbergt neben einigen Konferenz- und Büroräumen sowie einer kleinen technischen Handbibliothek vier Zeichensäle für Ingenieure und Architekten. Das nicht stützenfreie Erdgeschoß ist nur etwa 2,75 m hoch und nimmt Eingangshalle, Verwaltungsräume, Cafeteria, Registratur und einen Zeichensaal für Designer auf. Im Untergeschoß liegen technische Anlagen und Musterräume mit Firmenprodukten.

Das im Außenbereich unverkleidete, schwarz gestrichene Stahlskelett bringt die statischen Verhältnisse des Gebäudes klar zum Ausdruck: So wird in der Dachzone deutlich zwischen den Schmalseiten, an denen die etwa 35,60 m weit spannenden Hauptträger zutage treten, und den Längsseiten mit ihren Nebenträgern und der nichttragenden Verkleidung darunter unterschieden; auch läßt sich an den Schmalseiten auf den ersten Blick die engere Stützenstellung im Erdgeschoß, die eine gegenüber dem Dach etwa um das Dreifache niedrigere Zwischendecke erlaubte, ablesen. Unterstrichen wird die strukturelle Klarheit durch die etwa 2,40 m zurückgesetzten, vom Boden bis zur Decke reichenden Glasfassaden sowie durch die weißen Unterseiten der Zwischendecke und des Daches.

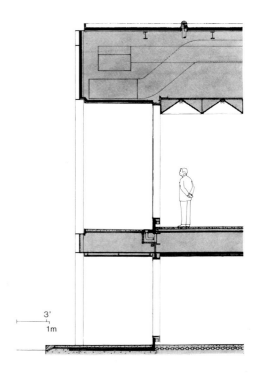

3'
1m

1. Facade section. The roof, which spans the entire width of the building, is about three times as high as the intermediate ceiling which is supported by columns on a grid of 16'8" × 29'2".
2. Corner of the building. The black painted steel structure is clearly distinguishable from the recessed glass walls.

1. Fassadenschnitt. Das über die gesamte Breite spannende Dach hat ungefähr die dreifache Höhe der in einem Raster von etwa 5,10 × 8,90 m unterstützten Zwischendecke.
2. Gebäudeecke. Das schwarz gestrichene Stahlskelett hebt sich kräftig von den zurückgesetzten Fassaden ab.

B

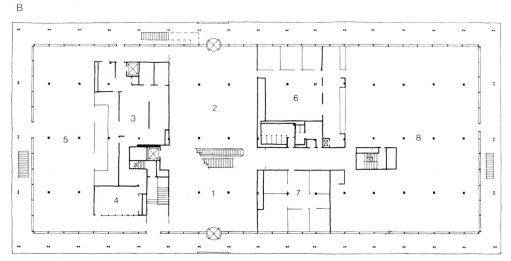

A

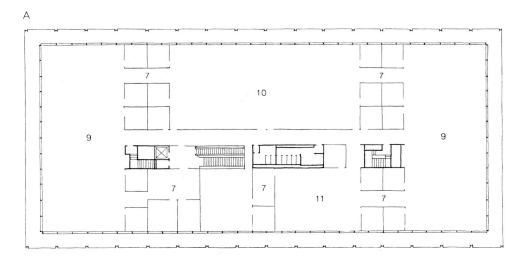

3. One of the short sides of the building. The intermediate columns at the ground floor show clearly in this view.

4. Plans (A ground floor, B upper floor). Key: 1 entrance lobby, 2 central cloakroom, 3 kitchen, 4 dining room, 5 cafeteria, 6 reference library, 7 offices and conference rooms, 8 designers, 9 project engineers, 10 specialities engineers, 11 architects and engineers.

5. Part of the long facade. The steel framework is externally exposed and painted black.

3. Eine der Schmalseiten des Gebäudes. Die engere Stützenstellung im Erdgeschoß ist klar zum Ausdruck gebracht.

4. Grundrisse (A Erdgeschoß, B Obergeschoß). Legende: 1 Eingangshalle, 2 Zentralgarderobe, 3 Küche, 4 Speiseraum, 5 Cafeteria, 6 Nachschlagewerke, 7 Büros und Konferenzräume, 8 Designer, 9 Projektingenieure, 10 Sonderingenieure, 11 Architekten und Ingenieure.

5. Ausschnitt aus der Längsseite. Die Stahlkonstruktion ist außen unverkleidet und schwarz gestrichen.

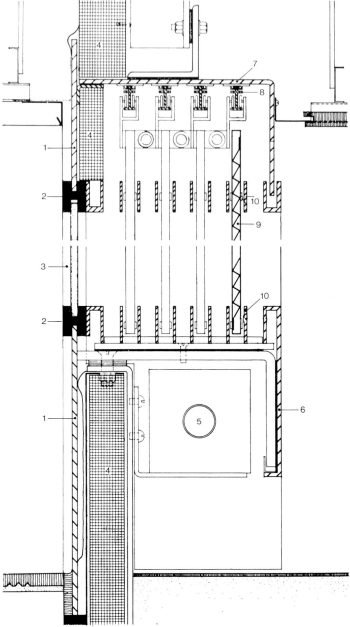

6, 7. Apart from the deep setback of the glass, sun protection is also provided by internally mounted steel sunshades, 25″ wide, which run on plastic rails above the radiators.

8. Detail of outer wall. Key: 1 steel plate, 2 plastic frame, 3 glass, 4 rigid insulation, 5 radiator, 6 radiator cover, 7 holding rail for metal sunshades, 8 track, 9 metal sunshade, 10 guide rail.

6, 7. Dem Sonnenschutz dienen – neben dem tiefen Decken- und Dachvorsprung und getöntem Glas – innenliegende, etwa 63,5 cm breite Metallgittertafeln, die über den Konvektoren in Kunststoffschienen laufen.

8. Detailschnitt durch die Außenwand. Legende: 1 Stahltafel, 2 Kunststoffrahmen, 3 Glas, 4 Dämmplatte, 5 Radiator, 6 Radiatorverkleidung, 7 Halteschiene für die Metallgittertafeln, 8 Laufschiene, 9 Metallgittertafel, 10 Führungsschiene.

9, 10. The prismatic panels of the upper floor ceiling, each carrying two unconcealed fluorescent lamps, emphasize the basic building module of 50″ × 50″. Fresh air enters through perforations in the panels, return air escapes through slots adjacent to the light fixtures. The space is divided by module-wide glass partitions, held at top and bottom only. Compared with a level ceiling, the prismatic panels have the advantage of providing a better dispersal of the light, a more effective sound absorption, and a more accentuated faceting of the space.

9, 10. Die Decke im Obergeschoß markiert mit ihren prismatischen Feldern, in denen jeweils zwei unverkleidete Leuchtstoffröhren sitzen, den Grundraster des Gebäudes von etwa 1,27 × 1,27 m. Die Zuluft wird durch Perforationen der schrägen Feldbegrenzungen eingeführt, die Abluft entweicht durch Schlitze neben den Leuchten. Zur Unterteilung des Raumes dienen geschoßhohe, nur oben und unten gehaltene Glastafeln in Modulbreite. Gegenüber einer glatten Decke hat die Prismendecke den Vorteil der besseren Lichtverteilung, der höheren Schallschluckung sowie der akzentuierteren Raumgliederung.

Headquarters of the Boots Pure Drug Company, Nottingham, England

This building, in which about 1,300 people work, is situated on a former storage site in an industrial estate 10 minutes by car from the town center. The move had been decided despite the fact that, in recent years, a number of new buildings had been erected at the old location in the town center.

Because of the large site it was possible, in designing the building, to assign a predominant role to such considerations as economical construction methods and efficient organization of work. The result was a low-rise, two-story building with an interior court, covering an area of 480′×288′. About one-half of the lower floor is below natural ground level and another quarter is concealed behind a sloped in-filling of excavated soil so that the upper floor is the only one visible. Its structural steel frame consists of cruciform columns and of truss girders bridging bays of 96′ side length. Surrounding the interior court at upper floor level is a continuous open-plan office area. At one of the short ends of the building, this area is flanked by a group of individual offices for executives, conference and other ancillary rooms as well as two minor open-plan office spaces. The lower floor has a reinforced concrete structure with mushroom-type columns spaced at 24′. This close spacing was acceptable as there was little need for flexibility for the facilities to be accommodated here.

Key elements in the open-plan offices are free-standing natural oak carrels with 5′8″ high walls which, like the building itself, conform to a module of 6′×6′.

The steel framework is painted black, forming a contrast to the bronze anodized aluminum window frames and to the grey granite used for the cladding of the base.

Hauptverwaltung der Boots Pure Drug Company, Nottingham, England

Das Gebäude, in dem etwa 1300 Menschen arbeiten, liegt in einem etwa 10 Autominuten vom Stadtzentrum entfernten Industriegebiet auf einem ehemaligen Lagerplatz. Man hatte sich zum Umzug hierher entschlossen, obwohl man am alten Standort im Stadtzentrum in den letzten Jahren noch eine Reihe neuer Gebäude errichtet hatte.

Der große Bauplatz erlaubte es, bei der Wahl der Gebäudeform bauökonomische und betriebsorganisatorische Gesichtspunkte in den Vordergrund zu stellen. So entstand ein in der Grundfläche etwa 146×88 m messender, einen Innenhof einschließender Flachbau mit zwei Geschossen. Die Hälfte des unteren Geschosses liegt unterhalb des regulären Erdniveaus, etwa ein weiteres Viertel wurde mit der ausgehobenen Erde schräg anlaufend abgedeckt, so daß von außen nur das obere Geschoß in Erscheinung tritt. Dieses ist eine Stahlkonstruktion mit Kreuzstützen und Fachwerkbindern; der Stützenabstand beträgt etwa 29,30 m. Der den Innenhof umgebende Bereich des Obergeschosses wird von einem durchgehenden Bürogroßraum eingenommen; diesem vorgelagert sind auf der tieferen der beiden Schmalseiten Einzelbüros für die Direktion, Konferenz- und sonstige Nebenräume sowie zwei kleinere Großraumbüros. Das untere Geschoß ist eine Stahlbetonkonstruktion. Die Decke wird von pilzförmigen Stützen getragen, die in einem Abstand von etwa 7,32 m stehen. Der kleinere Stützenabstand war möglich, weil hier nur Räume mit geringeren Ansprüchen an Flexibilität untergebracht wurden.

Die Möblierung der Großräume besteht aus frei stehenden Eichenholzcarrels mit etwa 1,73 m hohen Trennwänden. Sie basiert wie das Gebäude selbst auf einem Raster von etwa 1,83×1,83 m.

Das Stahlskelett wurde schwarz gestrichen. Dazu kontrastieren Fensterrahmen aus bronzefarben anodisiertem Aluminium und Sockelverkleidungen aus grauem Granit.

1. The steel framework of the upper floor is clearly distinguishable from the glass wall and from the upper part of the lower floor, visible below.

1. Das Stahltragwerk des Obergeschosses ist von der Glasfassade und der darunter sichtbaren Oberkante des Untergeschosses klar abgesetzt.

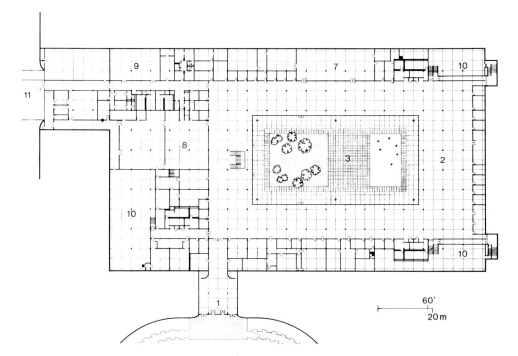

2. General view of the building. Only the upper floor seems to emerge from the ground.

3. Plans (lower floor, upper floor). Key: 1 entrance lobby, 2 open-plan office, 3 open court, 4 dining room, 5 conference room, 6 individual offices, 7 data processing, 8 mail room, 9 stores, 10 mechanical equipment, 11 loading ramp.

2. Gesamtansicht des Gebäudes. Von außen tritt nur das obere der beiden Geschosse in Erscheinung.

3. Grundrisse (Untergeschoß, Obergeschoß). Legende: 1 Eingangshalle, 2 Großraumbüro, 3 Hof, 4 Cafeteria, 5 Konferenzraum, 6 Einzelbüros, 7 Datenverarbeitungszentrale, 8 Postraum, 9 Lager, 10 technische Anlagen, 11 Anlieferung.

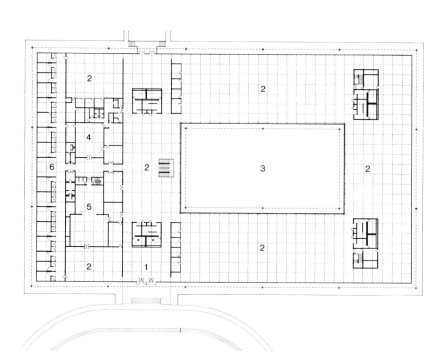

4. Interior court, seen from the main stairs.
5. The open-plan offices are furnished with free-standing natural oak carrels with 5'8'' high walls. They conform to the same module as the building.
6. Corner of the building. The foundations of the outer steel columns are independent of the lower floor.

4. Blick von der Haupttreppe in den Hof.
5. Die Möblierung der Großräume besteht aus frei stehenden Eichenholzcarrels mit etwa 1,73 m hohen Trennwänden. Sie basiert auf dem gleichen Raster wie das Gebäude.
6. Gebäudeecke. Die äußeren Stahlstützen sind unabhängig vom Untergeschoß fundiert.

Training Center of the Eastman Kodak Company, Henrietta, New York

This group of buildings is designed to promote the advanced training of the technical and commercial members of the staff. It is located on an attractive rural site of 400 acres and has a total floor space of about 350,000 sq ft. It can accommodate 200 trainees at a time and has a permanent staff of 300.

The program specified a high degree of flexibility, with the possibility of altering one area without disturbing an adjacent area. The group consists of four buildings specially adapted for distinct functions; their building materials – weathering steel, brown brick and bronze tinted glass – as well as their size are designed to merge unobtrusively with the landscape.

Three of the buildings – laboratory, seminar and reception – are connected by service towers so as to form a single group while the fourth – a dining pavilion which is also formally distinguished by its curved walls – is self-contained though linked with the other buildings by a pedestrian subway.

The laboratory building has external corridors surrounding a central modular space which permits complete flexibility of use. Underfloor ducts connect the workplaces with a central core containing the service piping. The laboratory furniture conforms to the same module of 3′×3′.

The seminar building contains external classroom zones with movable partitions governed by a module of 6′×6′, and a central zone with permanently equipped lecture rooms. The four tiered seminar rooms on top are equipped with turntables which rotate the front walls. One lecture room on the lower level has a complete audio-visual equipment.

In the reception building are the administrative offices as well as the common rooms and studies of the teaching staff, and a library. The only fixed point in an otherwise open plan is a core with stairs, service rooms and installation shafts.

The main floor of the dining pavilion is spanned by a steel truss roof without intermediate columns. Roof structure and supporting brick walls are separated by small steel hinges.

Ausbildungszentrum der Eastman Kodak Company, Henrietta, New York

Der Komplex dient der Weiterbildung von technischen und kaufmännischen Mitarbeitern der Firma. Er liegt auf einem etwa 162 ha großen, landschaftlich sehr reizvollen Gelände und enthält eine Nutzfläche von etwa 32500 qm. Einem ständigen Stab von 300 Personen stehen 200 Auszubildende gegenüber.

Im Bauprogramm war ein hohes Maß an Flexibilität für die einzelnen Bereiche gefordert worden, ebenso die Möglichkeit, Änderungen innerhalb eines Bereichs ohne Beeinträchtigung eines benachbarten vornehmen zu können. Die Hauptbereiche verteilen sich auf vier den jeweiligen Bedingungen besonders angepaßte Einzelbauten,die sich mit ihren Materialien – wetterfester Stahl, braune Ziegelsteine und bronzefarben getöntes Glas –, aber auch mit ihren Dimensionen unauffällig in die Landschaft einfügen.

Laboratoriums-, Seminar- und Empfangsbau sind über Servicetürme zu einer Gruppe zusammengeschlossen, während der durch seine gekurvten Wände auch formal besonders hervorgehobene Kantinenbau einen autonomen, mit den übrigen Bauten nur durch einen Fußgängertunnel verbundenen Pavillon bildet.

Die auf einem Raster von etwa 91,5×91,5 cm frei unterteilbaren Laboratorien werden über außenliegende Korridore erschlossen. Unterflurleitungen stellen die Verbindung der Arbeitsplätze mit dem in der Gebäudelängsachse angeordneten Installationskern her. Die Laboreinrichtung ist maßlich auf den Ausbauraster abgestimmt.

Der Seminarbau gliedert sich in äußere Klassenraumzonen, deren Wände auf einem Raster von etwa 1,83×1,83 m versetzt werden können, und eine innere Zone mit fest eingerichteten Vortragsräumen. Die oberen vier Vortragsräume besitzen drehbare Frontwände, der eine der unteren ist voll mit audiovisuellen Geräten ausgestattet.

Der Empfangsbau enthält neben der Verwaltung Aufenthalts- und Arbeitsräume für das Lehrpersonal und eine Bibliothek. Einziger Fixpunkt im offenen Grundriß ist ein Kern mit Treppen, Nebenräumen und Installationsschächten.

Der Kantinenbau bietet im Hauptgeschoß eine von Fachwerkträgern stützenfrei überspannte Fläche. Die Dachkonstruktion und die sie tragenden Ziegelsteinwände sind durch kleine Stahlgelenke voneinander getrennt.

1. Laboratory building, seen from northeast. In the background, right, part of the dining pavilion. 2. Plan (2nd floor) and section. Key: 1 reception building, 2 seminar building, 3 laboratory building, 4 dining pavilion.

1. Blick von Nordosten auf den Laboratoriumsbau. Rechts hinten ein Stück des Kantinenbaus. 2. Grundriß (1. Obergeschoß) und Schnitt. Legende: 1 Empfangsbau, 2 Seminarbau, 3 Laboratoriumsbau, 4 Kantinenbau.

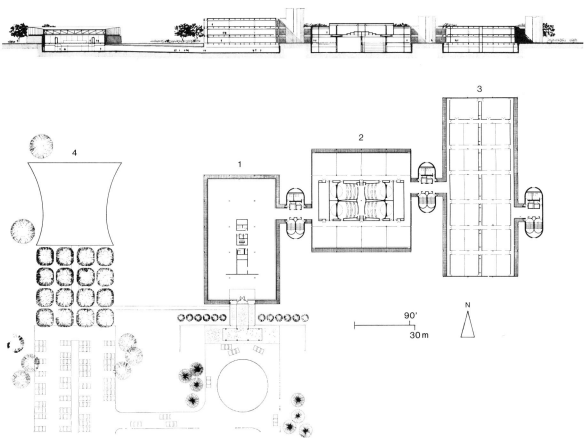

3. Seminar and reception buildings, seen from southeast.
4. Service tower between the laboratory and seminar buildings.
5. South side of the dining pavilion.
6. Seminar and laboratory buildings, seen from the forecourt of the reception building.

3. Blick von Südosten auf Seminar- und Empfangsbau.
4. Der Serviceturm zwischen Laboratoriums- und Seminarbau.
5. Der Kantinenbau von Süden.
6. Blick vom Vorplatz des Empfangsbaus auf Seminar- und Laboratoriumsbau.

Boise Cascade Home Office, Boise, Idaho

The building is situated in the central business district of the city. To promote close contacts between departments and facilitate changes in organization, the company had insisted on an owner-occupied building with open-plan office accommodation. This resulted in a fairly compact volume of low profile, in keeping with the existing scale of the central business district. The building accommodates the 1,200 members of the headquarters staff whose number is not expected to rise so that extensions need not be envisaged within a foreseeable future.

The building covers an area of 260′×260′ and encloses, above ground, a court with an area of about 106′×106′. The basement provides space for a computer center, mechanical equipments as well as a dispatching and receiving area accessible by a ramp. The ground floor is a pedestrian precinct open to the street, with the court serving as an entry loggia open on all four sides. Each of the five upper floors has a floor area of 56,000 sq ft. At the four corners are cores with toilets, fire exit stairs, storerooms and mains shafts; the intermediate space along the four sides is occupied by column-free open-plan spaces, used as offices on the 2nd, 3rd, 4th, and 6th floor while the 5th floor contains a cafeteria seating 250 persons as well as a fully equipped audio-visual center. Each floor is connected by bridges with the elevator core in the center of the court.

The building is planned on a 5′2″ module and has a one-story concrete basement structure supporting a steel frame structure for the upper floors. The columns along the outer walls and facing the court have a spacing of 36′2″ while the main girders have a span of 72′4″. The facade is painted steel cladding with bronze tinted glass. The plastic skylights above the court are supported by an aluminum space frame.

Boise Cascade Home Office, Boise, Idaho

Das Gebäude liegt im zentralen Geschäftsviertel der Stadt. Zur Begünstigung innerbetrieblicher Kontakte und organisatorischer Umstellungen hatte der als Alleinnutzer auftretende Bauherr weiträumige Großraumbüros gefordert; so ergab sich eine verhältnismäßig niedrige und kompakte Baumasse, die den bestehenden Maßstab der Innenstadt nicht sprengte. Die Kapazität ist auf 1200 Angestellte bemessen; man geht davon aus, daß in absehbarer Zeit keine Bauerweiterung erfolgen muß, da hier nur die Zentrale des Unternehmens untergebracht ist.

Der Bau nimmt eine Grundfläche von etwa 79×79 m ein und umschließt oberhalb der Erde einen gedeckten, etwa 32,50×32,50 m großen Hof. Im Untergeschoß befinden sich die elektronische Datenanlage, haustechnische Anlagen sowie eine durch eine Rampe erschlossene Anlieferungs- und Versandstelle. Das Erdgeschoß ist als offener Fußgängerbereich ausgebildet; Eingangsfoyer ist der Hof, der sich nach allen vier Seiten öffnet. Die jeweils etwa 5200 qm großen Nutzflächen der fünf Obergeschosse sind durch vier in den Gebäudeecken liegende Kerne mit Toiletten, Nottreppen, Abstellräumen und Leitungsschächten in jeweils vier stützenfreie Großräume geteilt. Die ersten drei Obergeschosse enthalten Büros, im 4. Obergeschoß sind eine Cafeteria mit 250 Plätzen sowie ein audiovisuell voll ausgestattetes Auditorium untergebracht, das 5. enthält wiederum Büros. Mit der Aufzugsanlage im Zentrum des Innenhofes stehen die einzelnen Stockwerke durch Brücken in Verbindung.

Das Gebäude ist auf einem Raster von etwa 1,57×1,57 m aufgebaut. Während der Unterbau aus Beton gegossen wurde, wählte man als Tragwerk für den Oberbau ein Stahlskelett; die Stützen an den Außenwänden und am Innenhof haben einen Abstand von etwa 11 m, die Hauptträger spannen etwa 22 m weit. Die Fassadenmaterialien sind gestrichener Stahl und bronzefarben getöntes Glas. Als Auflager der Kunststoff-Oberlichter über dem Innenhof dient ein Raumfachwerk aus Aluminium.

1. General view from the south. The compact building occupies an entire street block. The ground floor is designed as a pedestrian precinct, open to the street.
2. Site plan. The covered court serves as an entry loggia. In its center are four elevator towers, connected by bridges with the upper floors.

1. Gesamtansicht von Süden. Der kompakte Bau nimmt einen ganzen Straßenblock ein. Das Erdgeschoß ist als offener Fußgängerbereich ausgebildet.
2. Lageplan. Der überdeckte Hof dient als Eingangsfoyer. Im Zentrum vier Aufzugstürme, die mit den Obergeschossen durch Brücken verbunden sind.

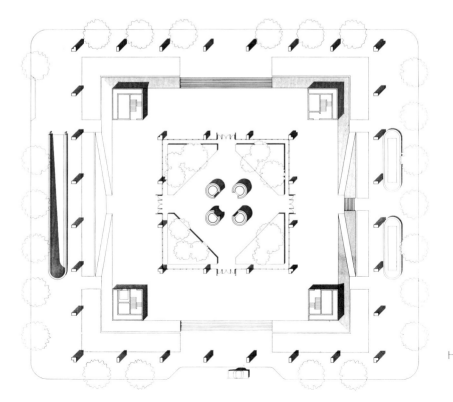

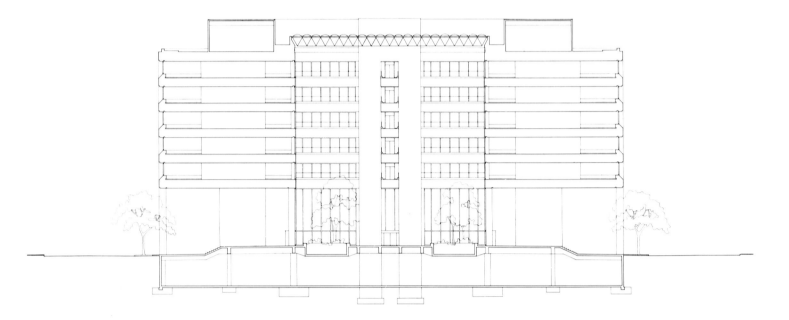

3. Plan of typical floor, and section.

3. Grundriß (Normalgeschoß) und Schnitt.

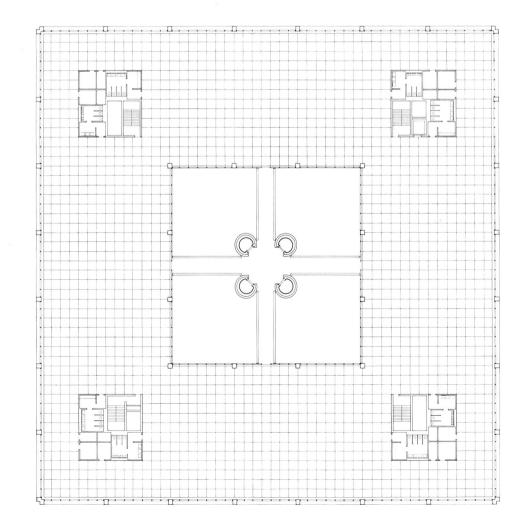

4, 5. Views of the court. The four circular elevator towers form a lively contrast to the strictly orthogonal shapes of the main building.

4, 5. Blicke in den Hof. Die vier runden Aufzugstürme bilden einen lebendigen Kontrast zu den übrigen, streng orthogonalen Formen.

Administrative and Research Headquarters of the Emhart Corporation, Bloomfield, Connecticut

The building occupies a site of 100 acres, has a total floor area of about 160,000 sq ft, and can accommodate 400 persons. The site adjoins that of the Connecticut General Life Insurance building, completed by Skidmore, Owings & Merrill in 1957. The two neighbors form a striking contrast. Connecticut General has non-fireproof steel structures with metal and glass curtain walls dominating the design, and surface parking, whereas Emhart is an early example of the use of exposed structural concrete with the more complex sculptural forms which that material permits, and the parking is virtually invisible both from within the building and from the approach.

The owner wished to have all his working departments on one level and this led to planning the office space around the upper part of a higher pilot laboratory. Because of the terrain it was possible to put the laboratory and its service access at grade and carry the surrounding office floor on concrete trees so that it rides majestically across the spine of the ridge which is the principal feature of the site. Beneath this horizontal umbrella is the parking, some open and some in a basement garage beneath an entrance court. This court leads to a lobby in the very center of the building giving access to the main floor from below by a stairway. Suspended from the concrete soffit is a cafeteria which rides over the parking and affords a dramatic view of the adjacent valley.

The predominant element of the design is the concrete structure. The cantilevered trees, spaced 42' apart, consist of ribbed columns whose ribs are extended to produce a vaulted design for the soffit. At the corners of the square trees are fireproofed steel columns on the inside and precast concrete columns on the perimeter, the latter being separated by hinges from the steel roof.

The low white concrete structure, accentuated by the dark recessed glass wall behind, dominates the top of the hill and the concealment of the parking was a pivotal step in the handling of this recurrent contemporary problem.

Verwaltungs- und Forschungszentrum der Emhart Corporation, Bloomfield, Connecticut

Der Bau liegt auf einem etwa 40 ha großen Grundstück in unmittelbarer Nachbarschaft des im Jahre 1957 fertiggestellten und ebenfalls von Skidmore, Owings & Merrill stammenden Verwaltungskomplexes der Connecticut Life Insurance Co. Er bietet auf einer Nutzfläche von etwa 15000 qm Arbeitsplätze für 400 Mitarbeiter. Zwischen ihm und seinem Nachbarn herrscht ein bemerkenswerter Kontrast: Während für die Anlage der Connecticut Life Insurance Co. nichtfeuergeschützte Stahltragwerke, betont flache Vorhangfassaden und frei auf dem Gelände liegende Parkplätze charakteristisch sind, zeichnet sich das Emhart-Gebäude durch skulptural behandelte Tragelemente aus Sichtbeton und in den Baukomplex integrierte Autoabstellplätze aus, wobei letzteres als entscheidender Vorstoß zur Lösung dieses immer wiederkehrenden Problems unserer Zeit gewertet werden muß.

Die Organisation des Gebäudes wurde vor allem von dem Wunsch des Bauherrn, alle Büros auf einer Ebene zu haben, bestimmt. Fixpunkt des komplexen Raumgefüges ist ein von außen nicht erkennbarer Kern mit technischen Räumen im Erdgeschoß und Laboratorien in den beiden Obergeschossen; diesem vorgelagert ist ein ebenso langer, aber weniger breiter eingeschossiger Garagensockel. Die Verwaltungsräume liegen im 2. Obergeschoß, das die Silhouette des Gebäudes bestimmt. Sie umschließen sowohl die Laboratorien als auch einen über dem Garagensockel endenden Innenhof, an dem sich der Hauptzugang zum Gebäude befindet. Die Cafeteria bildet zusammen mit ihrer Küche einen eigenen, unter dem Bürogeschoß hängenden Bauteil. Zum Parken stehen zusätzlich zur Garage die freien Erdgeschoßflächen zur Verfügung.

Vorherrschendes Strukturelement ist das einem Raster von etwa 12,80 × 12,80 m folgende Betontragwerk, auf dem die äußere Zone des Gebäudes ruht. Es besteht aus profilierten Stützen und von diesen allseits auskragenden, auf der Unterseite ebenfalls profilierten Deckenplatten. Die Lasten des Daches werden über die Eckpunkte der Deckenplatten abgetragen – außen durch Betonstützen mit akzentuierten oberen Gelenken, innen durch ummantelte Stahlstützen.

Zurückgesetzte dunkle Glaswände lassen das weiße Betontragwerk des flachen, majestätisch über einer geländebestimmenden Hügelkuppe thronenden Baukörpers mit großer Deutlichkeit hervortreten.

1. A view of the court from the zone facing the main entrance.
2. Site plan. Top, right: Part of the building of the Connecticut General Life Insurance Co.

1. Blick von der Zone vor dem Haupteingang in den Hof.
2. Lageplan. Oben rechts im Anschnitt das Verwaltungsgebäude der Connecticut General Life Insurance Co.

Pages 76–77:
3. General view of the building from the south. The main floor with the administrative offices rides majestically across the flat ridge.

Seiten 76–77:
3. Gesamtansicht des Gebäudes von Süden. Majestätisch thront das Hauptgeschoß mit den Verwaltungsräumen über der flachen Hügelkuppe.

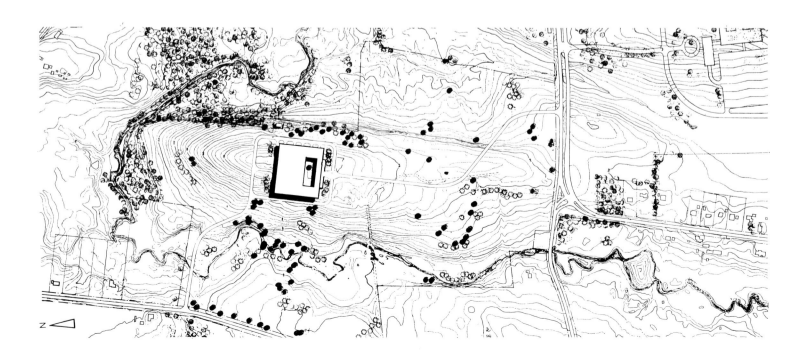

N

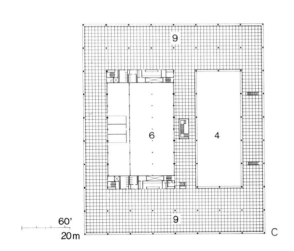

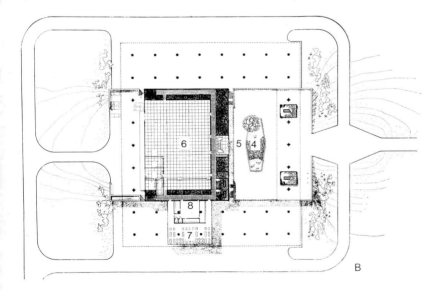

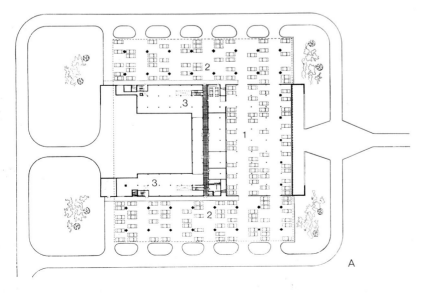

4. Plans (A ground level, B entrance floor, C main
floor) and section across the court looking toward
main entrance. Key: 1 garage, 2 parking, 3 service rooms, 4 court, 5 main entrance, 6 laboratory,
7 cafeteria, 8 kitchen, 9 office area.
5. Corner of cantilevered main floor.

4. Grundrisse (A Erdgeschoß, B Eingangsgeschoß, C Hauptgeschoß) und Schnitt durch den
Hof in Richtung auf den Haupteingang. Legende: 1 Garage, 2 Autoabstellplätze, 3 technische Räume, 4 Hof, 5 Haupteingang, 6 Labo-
ratorium, 7 Cafeteria, 8 Küche, 9 Bürofläche.
5. Ecke des auskragenden Hauptgeschosses.

Headquarters of the General Reinsurance Company, Greenwich, Connecticut.
Under construction

The plot is situated directly adjacent to Greenwich harbor. To enable the greatest possible number of staff to enjoy the fine view, it was decided to give the building a long and narrow shape, parallel to the water's edge.

The parking garage, accommodating some 450 cars, is on two basement levels; one of these is completely below ground, while the other is contained below two grassplanted terraces which are sloped at the edges. The terraces are interrupted by a wide passage which, even from the road, provides a view of the bay. It is at this passage that the main entrances with lobbies for visitors and guests are situated. The upper part of the building comprises three floors which are divided into three units by pairs of recessed service cores. These contain stairs, elevators, toilets and miscellaneous storage areas and – in the top part which over-towers the main block by nearly 17′ – the elevator machinery, heating and air-conditioning plant. The areas in the three units separated by the cores cover about 145′ × 85′ each and are interrupted by only four columns. At terrace level, the two units at the ends contain cafeteria and other areas with direct access to the outsides; all the other areas – totalling some 165,000 sq ft – contain offices. The ceilings which, like the other parts of the bearing structure, consist of concrete have a waffle pattern governed by a 5′ × 5′ module. They are left exposed, and their recessed spaces contain the light fixtures. The bronze tinted windows, set back by one module, extend from floor to ceiling so that the framework structure is clearly visible.

It is planned to landscape the site with more than eighty new trees.

Hauptverwaltung der General Reinsurance Company, Greenwich, Connecticut. Im Bau

Das Grundstück liegt direkt am Hafen von Greenwich. Um möglichst viele Angestellte des Unternehmens in den Genuß des schönen Ausblicks zu bringen, entschied man sich für einen schmalen, parallel zum Ufer verlaufenden Riegel.

Der Sockel, in dem etwa 450 Wagen abgestellt werden können, umfaßt zwei Stockwerke – das eine im Erdboden verborgen, das andere zwei an den Rändern abgeschrägte Terrassen bildend, zwischen die eine breite Passage gelegt ist. An der Passage, die schon von der Straße aus einen Blick auf das Wasser gestattet, liegen die Haupteingänge mit Wartehallen für Besucher und Gäste. Der obere Teil des Komplexes ist dreigeschossig und durch zurückgesetzte Festpunktpaare in drei Abschnitte gegliedert. Die Festpunkte enthalten im unteren Teil Treppen, Aufzüge, Toiletten und kleinere Abstellräume, im oberen, die Haupt-baukörper um etwa 6 m überragenden Teil Aufzugsmaschinen, Klima- und Heizzentralen. Die Räume in den drei zwischen den Festpunkten liegenden Abschnitten haben eine Ausdehnung von etwa 44 × 26 m, wobei jeweils nur vier Stützen die durchgehenden Flächen unterteilen. In den beiden äußeren Abschnitten sind auf der Terrassenebene Cafeterias mit direktem Zugang ins Freie untergebracht; die übrigen Räume – zusammen etwa 15300 qm groß – enthalten die Büros. Die Decken, die wie die anderen Teile des Tragwerkes aus Beton bestehen, sind in einem Raster von etwa 1,52 × 1,52 m kassettiert. Sie sind unverkleidet und nehmen in den offenen Feldern die Beleuchtung auf. Die um eine Kassettenreihe von der Außenkante zurückgesetzten Außenwände aus bronzefarben getöntem Glas reichen vom Boden bis zur Decke und lassen so das Tragwerk klar hervortreten.

Es ist geplant, auf dem Grundstück mehr als 80 Bäume neu anzupflanzen.

1. Facade detail (model). The glass walls are set back by one row of waffle ceiling units from the outer edge of the building so that the framework structure is clearly visible.

1. Fassadenausschnitt (Modell). Die Glaswände sind um eine Kassettenreihe von der Außenkante des Gebäudes zurückgesetzt und lassen so das Tragwerk klar hervortreten.

2. General view from the west (model).
3. Plan (typical floor). Key: 1 office area, 2 core,
3 passage, 4 terrace, 5 water.

2. Gesamtansicht von Westen (Modell).
3. Grundriß (Normalgeschoß). Legende: 1 Bürofläche, 2 Festpunkt, 3 Passage, 4 Terrasse,
5 Wasser.

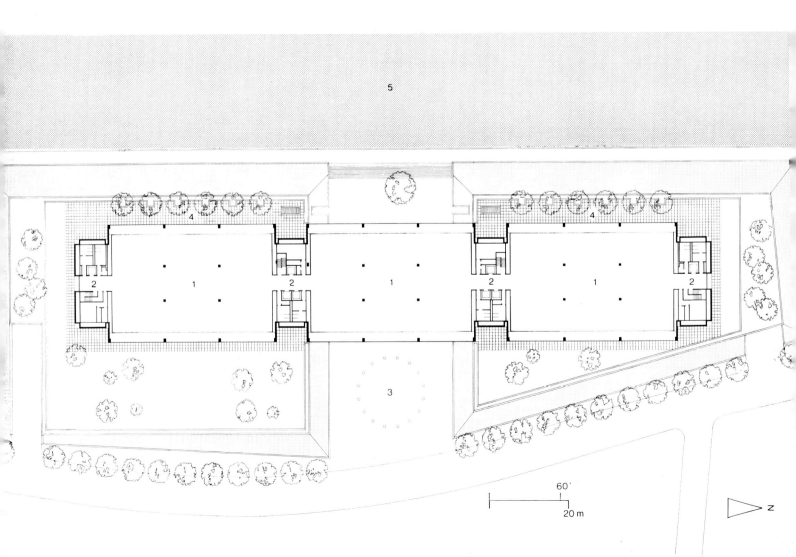

4. Cross-section at the passage.
5. Model, seen from above.

4. Querschnitt im Bereich der Passage.
5. Dachaufsicht (Modell).

Headquarters of the American Can Company, Greenwich, Connecticut

The buildings have been placed on an estate of 175 acres in such a way that they remain concealed from the residential area in the southeast. They comprise a podium with garage accommodation for 1,700 cars and ancillary facilities, a general administration building, and a smaller single-story building for the executive offices.

The podium bridges a small ravine, acting as a dam and thereby creating a lake on the upstream side from which the flow of water to a swampy bird sanctuary along the southwest border of the estate can be regulated. The cafeteria is on the top floor of the podium, with a terrace overlooking the lake.

The main building above the podium covers an area of 525′×255′ and contains, on its three levels, a total office floor area of 558,422 sq ft. The inside areas are mainly used as open-plan offices, with individual offices along the periphery. The structural bays measure 30′×60′. The structure consists of a poured-in-place reinforced concrete framework with twin girders, supporting precast double-web ceiling beams placed longitudinally. The tubes suspended between the webs, which have the treble function of carrying the light fixtures, acting as sound absorbers and serving as air ducts, represent a variation of an idea used first at the headquarters of the American Republic Insurance Company, Des Moines (pages 112–119). But while in Des Moines, the air is diffused and returned at the bottom of the tube, the openings are, in the present building, on top of the tube on either side of the light fixture.

The smaller executive building has but one story, covering an area of 165′×165′. Because of the larger bays of 60′×60′, the girders are here of one piece, and are prestressed. In contrast to the main building, the roof structure is concealed inside behind a continuous suspended ceiling.

Hauptverwaltung der American Can Company, Greenwich, Connecticut

Der Gebäudekomplex wurde so auf dem etwa 70 ha großen Gelände plaziert, daß er nicht von dem im Südosten angrenzenden Wohnviertel gesehen werden kann. Er besteht aus einem Sockel, in dem Parkplätze für 1 700 Wagen und Nebenräume untergebracht sind, einem allgemeinen Verwaltungsgebäude und einem kleineren Pavillon für die Geschäftsleitung.

Der Sockel legt sich als Damm über ein kleines Tal und staut oberhalb der Baugruppe einen See auf, mit dessen Hilfe der Wasserzufluß zu einem an der Südwestgrenze des Grundstückes liegenden Sumpfgelände – einem Vogelschutzgebiet – reguliert werden kann. Die Cafeteria im obersten Geschoß des Sockels öffnet sich mit einer Terrasse auf die Wasserfläche.

Das allgemeine Verwaltungsgebäude hat bei einer Grundfläche von etwa 160×78 m und drei Geschossen eine Bürofläche von fast 52000 qm. Während die Innenflächen weitgehend als Großräume genutzt werden, befinden sich an den Außenwänden Einzelbüros. Das Tragwerk ist auf einem Raster von etwa 9,15×18,30 m aufgebaut. Es besteht aus einem Ortbetonskelett mit zweigeteilten Trägern und darauf in Längsrichtung aufliegenden, vorgefertigten Doppelsteg-Deckenelementen. Die zwischen den Stegen hängenden Rohre, die gleichzeitig als Beleuchtungsträger, Schallschlucker und Luftkanal fungieren, variieren eine zum ersten Mal im Verwaltungsgebäude der American Republic Insurance Company, Des Moines (Seiten 112–119), verwirklichte Idee. Während dort die Luft auf der Unterseite des Rohres ausgeblasen und angesaugt wird, geschieht dies hier auf der Oberseite beiderseits der Leuchte.

Das kleinere Gebäude für die Geschäftsleitung ist eingeschossig und hat eine Grundfläche von etwa 50×50 m. Wegen des größeren Stützenrasters von etwa 18,30×18,30 m wurden hier die Träger einteilig ausgeführt und vorgespannt. Im Gegensatz zum allgemeinen Verwaltungsgebäude isl im Innern die Dachkonstruktion hinter einer durchgehenden abgehängten Decke verborgen.

1. Site plan. Key: 1 general administration building, 2 executive offices.
2. View of the general administration building from southeast, with the highway in the foreground.

1. Lageplan. Legende: 1 allgemeines Verwaltungsgebäude, 2 Pavillon für die Geschäftsleitung.
2. Blick von Südosten auf das allgemeine Verwaltungsgebäude. Im Vordergrund die Durchgangsstraße.

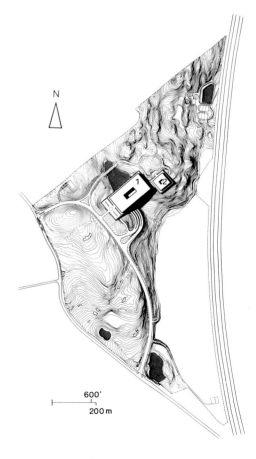

600′
200 m

3. View of the buildings from the west, with visitors' parking in the foreground.
4. View of the buildings from the south. Each floor of the garage has its own access ramp.
5. Cross-section and longitudinal section of the main building.

3. Blick von Westen auf die Baugruppe. Im Vordergrund der Besucherparkplatz.
4. Blick von Süden auf die Baugruppe. Zu jedem Garagengeschoß führt eine eigene Rampe.
5. Querschnitt und Längsschnitt durch den Hauptbau.

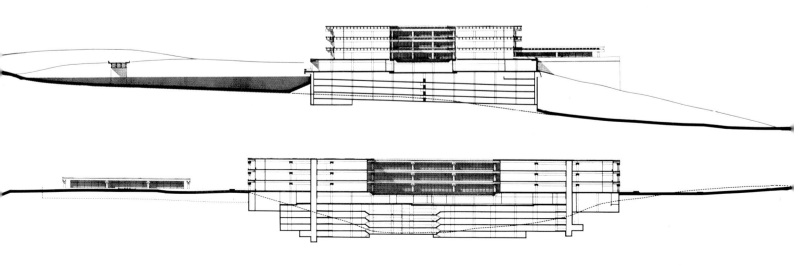

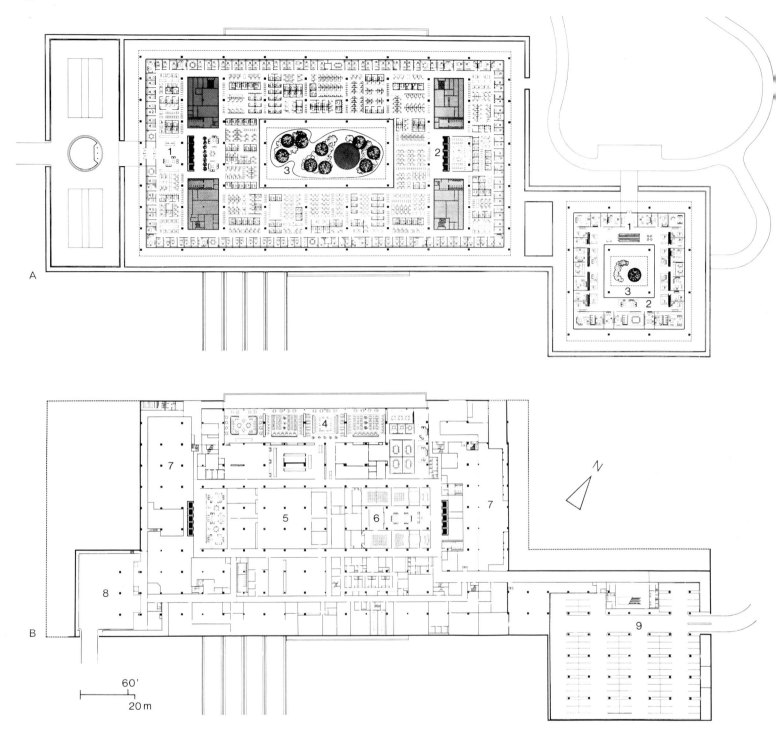

6. Plans (A top floor of podium, B ground floor).
Key: 1 entrance lobby, 2 offices, 3 central court,
4 cafeteria, 5 data processing center, 6 training
center, 7 mechanical equipment, 8 loading dock,
9 executive garage.

Pages 88–89:
7. View from the north. On the left, the single-
story executive building; on the right, the general
administration building.

6. Grundrisse (A oberstes Sockelgeschoß, B Erdgeschoß). Legende: 1 Eingangshalle, 2 Büros,
3 Innenhof, 4 Cafeteria, 5 Datenverarbeitungszentrale, 6 Lehrzentrum, 7 technische Räume,
8 Anlieferung, 9 Garage der Geschäftsleitung.

Seiten 88–89:
7. Ansicht von Norden. Links das eingeschossige
Gebäude der Geschäftsleitung, rechts das allgemeine Verwaltungsgebäude.

8. Central court in the executive building. The tree was brought in by helicopter.
9. Corner of the executive building. The caps of the tensioning cables in the main girders are of stainless steel.

8. Innenhof im Gebäude der Geschäftsleitung. Der Baum wurde von einem Hubschrauber heruntergelassen.
9. Ecke des Gebäudes der Geschäftsleitung. Die Köpfe der Spannkabel in den Hauptträgern bestehen aus Edelstahl.

10. The executive building, seen from the north, with the entrance to its garage on the left.
11. Waiting area in the executive building.

10. Blick von Norden auf das Gebäude der Geschäftsleitung. Links die Zufahrt der dazugehörigen Garage.
11. Warteplatz im Gebäude der Geschäftsleitung.

12. View from the cafeteria over the artificial lake toward the bridge carrying the access road to the executive building.
13. General administration building, seen from across the lake.
14. Corner of the general administration building. The bearing structure consists of a framework of poured-in-place sandblasted reinforced concrete and precast double-web floor units.

12. Blick von der Cafeteria im obersten Sockelgeschoß auf den künstlichen See und die Brücke der Straße, die zum Gebäude der Geschäftsleitung führt.
13. Blick über den See auf das allgemeine Verwaltungsgebäude.
14. Ecke des allgemeinen Verwaltungsgebäudes. Das Tragwerk besteht aus einem gesandstrahlten Ortbetonskelett und vorgefertigten Doppelsteg-Deckenelementen.

Headquarters of the Weyerhaeuser Company, Tacoma, Washington

The building occupies a site about midway between Tacoma and the Seattle-Tacoma Airport. The dominant feature of the site is a shallow valley, running north to south.
The building is placed like a dam across the valley and its five floors are stepped back on the long sides so that each successive floor is narrower than the one below. In the three lower floors are the general offices. The next floor is level with the ridges on either side of the valley and contains the main entrances, a cafeteria, a small lecture room and employees' lounge. On the narrowest 5th floor are the executive offices.
The architects' guiding idea had been to create a building which would "literally tend to disappear – becoming one with the landscape". All the roof surfaces are gently sloped and are, except for the 5th floor, covered with ivy. The windows are hardly apparent as they are deeply recessed behind the roof edges and are, moreover, not interrupted by any vertical dividers which might impair the visual merger between interior and exterior.
Even in the design of the offices, the architects were guided by the principle of undefined boundaries. There are no full-height interior partitions and the different departments merge imperceptibly. The endeavor to create open office landscapes is also emphasized by the placing of the columns which is governed by a diamond-shaped grid turned at an angle to the basic rectangle of the building.
The structure of the building is a concrete-clad steel frame. Much of the interior woodwork was produced in the workshops of the company which is one of the leading manufacturers of wood products.
The landscape architects were Sasaki, Walker Associates.

Hauptverwaltung der Weyerhaeuser Company, Tacoma, Washington

Das Grundstück, auf dem das Gebäude errichtet wurde, liegt etwa auf halbem Wege zwischen Tacoma und dem Seattle-Tacoma Airport. Beherrschendes Element ist eine in nord-südlicher Richtung verlaufende Bodensenke.
Das Gebäude ist wie ein Damm quer über diese Senke gesetzt, wobei die fünf Geschosse an beiden Längsseiten von unten nach oben zurückgestuft sind. Die unteren drei Geschosse enthalten die Normalbüros. Das nächste Geschoß, das mit weitausholenden Dächern, unter denen Besucher ihre Fahrzeuge parken können, an das obere Niveau des Geländes anbindet, ist das »Forum« des Gebäudes; hier befinden sich die Haupteingänge, eine Cafeteria sowie ein kleiner Vortragsraum. Das oberste, schmalste Geschoß schließlich beherbergt die Räume der Geschäftsleitung.
Die Leitidee der Architekten war, einen Bau zu schaffen, der »buchstäblich dahin tendiert, zu verschwinden – eins zu werden mit der Landschaft«. So sind alle Dachflächen leicht angeschrägt und mit Ausnahme der obersten über dem 5. Geschoß mit Efeu bepflanzt. Außerdem wurden die Verglasungen so ausgeführt, daß sie kaum noch in Erscheinung treten: Zum einen liegen sie weit hinter den Vorderkanten der Dächer, zum anderen gibt es keine senkrechten Sprossen, die die optische Verschmelzung zwischen Innen- und Außenraum stören könnten.
Auch bei der Gestaltung der Büros ließen sich die Architekten vom Prinzip der Grenzverwischung leiten. Es gibt keine raumhohen Trennwände; die verschiedenen Abteilungen fließen kontinuierlich ineinander. Unterstrichen wird das Bemühen, offene Büro-»Landschaften« herzustellen, dadurch, daß die Stützen nicht auf das übliche orthogonale, sondern auf ein diagonales Raster gestellt wurden.
Das Tragwerk des Gebäudes besteht aus Stahl, der mit Beton umkleidet ist. Ein großer Teil der Holzeinbauten stammt aus eigenen Werkstätten der Firma, die ja zu den größten Unternehmen der Holzindustrie gehört.
Die Grünplanung lag in Händen der Landschaftsarchitekten Sasaki, Walker Associates.

1. Site plan. The building is placed like a dam across a valley, and both its long sides are stepped back from bottom to top floor.

1. Lageplan. Das Gebäude ist wie ein Damm quer über eine Bodensenke gesetzt und an beiden Längsseiten von unten nach oben zurückgestuft.

Pages 96–97:
2. View of the eastern main entrance at 4th-floor level.

Seiten 96–97:
2. Blick auf den östlichen Haupteingang im 4. Geschoß.

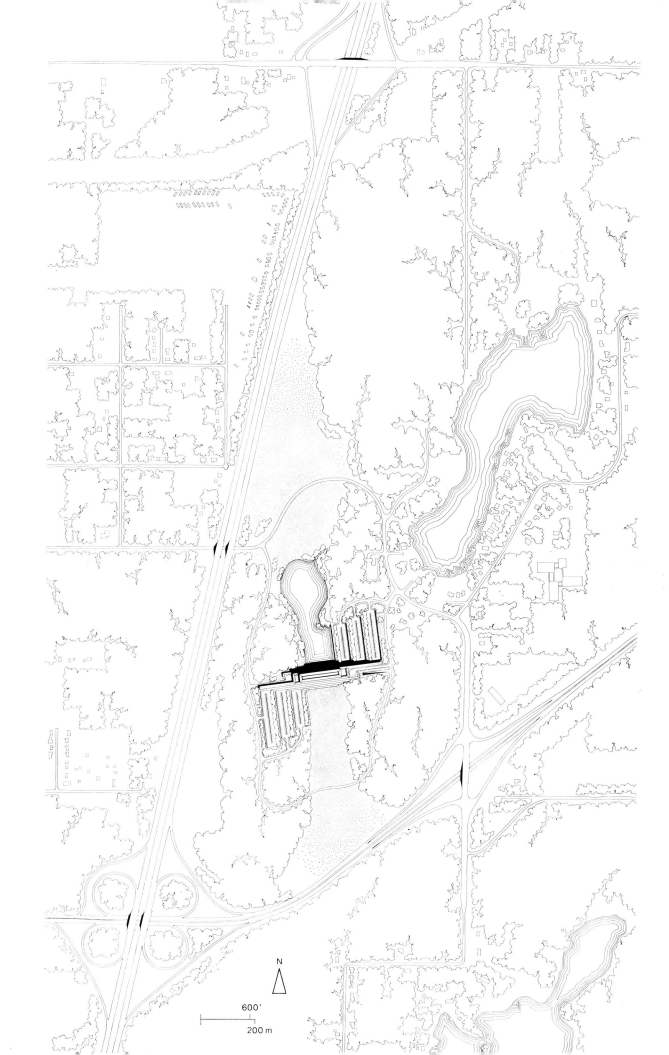

N

600'
200 m

3, 4. General view of the building. On the north side, the valley has been converted into a small lake.

5. Plans (A ground floor, B 2nd floor, C 3rd floor, D 4th floor, E 5th floor) and sections. Key: 1 office area, 2 service core, 3 mechanical equipment, 4 incoming goods, 5 car parks, 6 main entrance, 7 elevator lobby, 8 lounge, 9 cafeteria, 10 lecture room.

3, 4. Gesamtansichten des Gebäudes. Auf der Nordseite wurde in der Bodensenke ein kleiner See geschaffen.

5. Grundrisse (A Erdgeschoß, B 1. Obergeschoß, C 2. Obergeschoß, D 3. Obergeschoß, E 4. Obergeschoß) und Schnitte. Legende: 1 Bürofläche, 2 Kern, 3 technische Anlagen, 4 Anlieferung, 5 Parkplätze, 6 Haupteingang, 7 Aufzugsvorraum, 8 Lounge, 9 Cafeteria, 10 Vortragsraum.

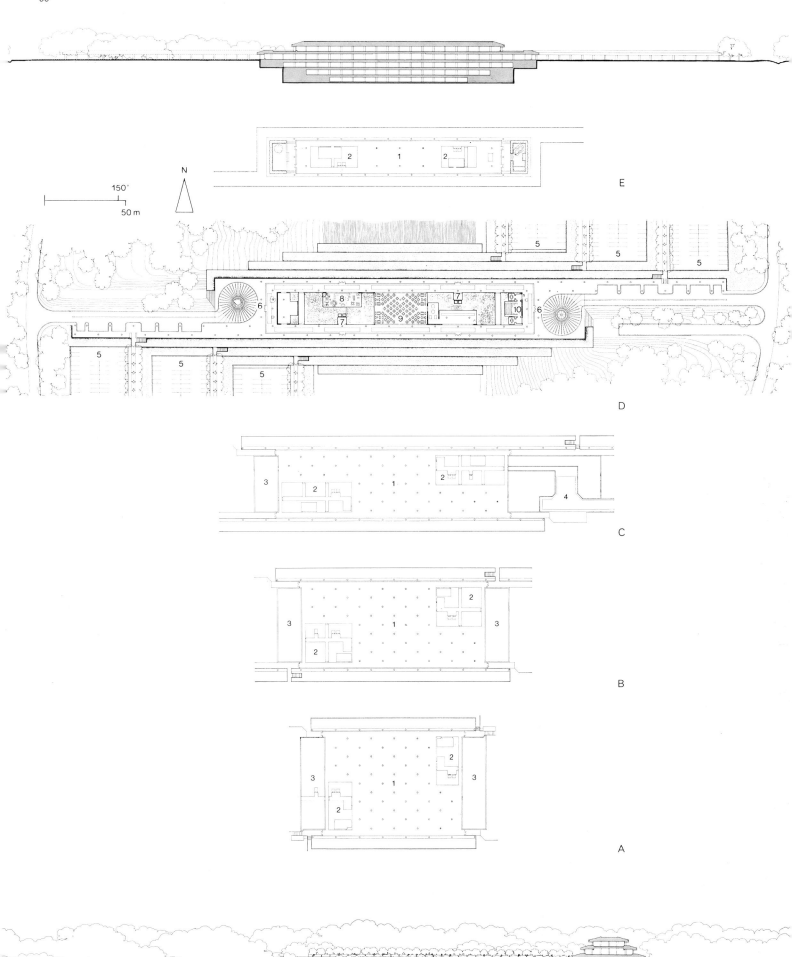

150'

50 m

N

E

5

5

5

6

8

7

9

7

10

6

5

5

5

D

3

2

1

2

4

C

3

2

1

2

3

2

B

3

2

1

2

3

2

A

6, 7. Like the three lower floors, the 5th floor with the executive offices is designed as an "office landscape".

6, 7. Das 5. Geschoß, in dem die Geschäftsleitung untergebracht ist, wurde ebenso wie die anderen Geschosse als Büro-»Landschaft« eingerichtet.

8. View of one of the two long side corridors on the 4th floor.

8. Blick in eine der beiden langen Wandelhallen des 4. Geschosses.

9. Conversation group at one end of the central expanse on the 5th floor. The tapestry is by Helena Hernmarck.

9. Sitzplatz am Ende des mittleren Raumes im 5. Geschoß. Der Wandteppich stammt von Helena Hernmarck.

10. Office of the company's president in the central expanse on the 5th floor.

10. Büro des Präsidenten der Gesellschaft im mittleren Raum des 5. Geschosses.

11. The cafeteria on the 4th floor.
12. Cashier's station and condiment stands. On
the left, the access to the cafeteria.

11. Die Cafeteria im 4. Geschoß.
12. Kassen und Besteckstände. Links der Durchgang zur Cafeteria.

Banque Lambert, Brussels

The building faces the Avenue Marnix which is part of the inner ring of boulevards surrounding the town center and is opposite the Royal Palace. It has nine stories above two basements.

The basements occupy the whole site and contain the bank vault, an employees' cafeteria, mechanical equipment and a garage for 120 cars. The ground floor is recessed from the facades above and contains the entrance lobbies and banking hall. Above the ground floor are seven typical office floors which can be flexibly subdivided as open areas or private offices. The top floor is again set back and contains the apartment of the Lambert family as well as a suite of rooms for conference and entertaining. The plan of the typical floors, which cover an area of 100′×240′, is based on a module of 4′6″×4′6″. A central service core contains elevators, stairs, toilets and mechanical shafts.

The bearing structure of the building is of reinforced concrete. The ribbed floor slabs are supported at the inside by columns along the lines of the walls of the central core and, at the outer perimeter, by cross-shaped precast concrete units which form the facades outside the glass walls. These units are one module wide and one story high, with half units top and bottom. The vertical legs join half-way between floors where the load is transmitted through polished steel ball-and-socket hinge joints cast integrally with the crosses. At the ground floor ceiling, the perimeter loads are transmitted by a floor beam to columns set back from the facades and spaced 31′6″ apart.

Banque Lambert, Brüssel

Der Bau liegt gegenüber dem Palais du Roi an der Avenue Marnix, die zu dem die Innenstadt umgebenden Boulevardring gehört. Er besteht aus einem zweigeschossigen Sockel und einem neungeschossigen Oberbau.

Der Sockel nimmt die gesamte Fläche des Grundstücks ein. Er enthält Banktresore, eine Cafeteria für die Angestellten, technische Anlagen sowie Abstellplätze für 120 Wagen. Auf dem Sockel liegen neben einem kleineren abgeschirmten Parkplatz das zurückgesetzte Eingangsgeschoß mit Bankräumen für den Publikumsverkehr. Es folgen sieben Normalgeschosse mit flexibel unterteilbaren Flächen für Bürosäle und Einzelbüros. Den oberen Abschluß des Gebäudes bildet ein wiederum zurückgesetztes Penthouse, in dem die Wohnung der Familie Lambert sowie Konferenz- und Gesellschaftsräume untergebracht sind. Der Grundriß der etwa 31×73 m großen Normalgeschosse ist auf einem Raster von etwa 1,37×1,37 m aufgebaut. Eine zentrale Kernzone nimmt Aufzüge, Treppen, Toiletten und Leitungsschächte auf.

Für das Tragwerk des Gebäudes wurde eine Stahlbetonkonstruktion gewählt. Die Rippendecken der Normalgeschosse geben ihre Lasten zum einen auf innere, in den Linien der Längsbegrenzungen des Kernes angeordnete Stützen ab, zum anderen auf frei vor die Glasaußenwände gesetzte, wabenförmig durchbrochene Wände aus Fertigteilelementen. Die Elemente sind modulbreit und bis auf die oberen und unteren Abschlußstücke geschoßhoch. Sie treffen sich mit ihren senkrechten Stegen jeweils in Geschoßmitte auf anbetonierten Anschlußstücken aus poliertem Edelstahl. Eine kräftiger ausgebildete Decke fängt die Lasten der Außenwände über dem Erdgeschoß ab und gibt sie an zurückgesetzte, im Abstand von etwa 9,60 m stehende Stützen weiter.

1. The vertical legs of the load-bearing cross-shaped facade units join at polished steel hinge joints embedded in the concrete.
2. Southwest corner of the plaza with Henry Moore's sculpture "Locking Piece".

1. Die tragenden, kreuzförmig ausgebildeten Außenwandelemente treffen sich mit ihren senkrechten Stegen auf anbetonierten Anschlußstücken aus poliertem Edelstahl.
2. Die Südwestecke des Vorplatzes mit der Skulptur »Locking Piece« von Henry Moore.

3. Plans (A entrance floor, B typical floor, C penthouse floor) and section. Key: 1 entrance lobby, 2 banking hall, 3 offices open to the public, 4 typical offices, 5 ballroom, 6 executive dining room, 7 drawing room, 8 gallery, 9 library, 10 bedroom, 11 guest room, 12 private dining room, 13 kitchen, 14 servants' lounge.

3. Grundrisse (A Eingangsgeschoß, B Normalgeschoß, C Penthouse) und Schnitt. Legende: 1 Eingangshalle, 2 Schalterhalle, 3 Büros mit Publikumsverkehr, 4 Normalbüros, 5 Ballraum, 6 Direktionsspeiseraum, 7 Salon, 8 Galerie, 9 Bibliothek, 10 Schlafraum, 11 Gästeraum, 12 privater Speiseraum, 13 Küche, 14 Personalaufenthaltsraum.

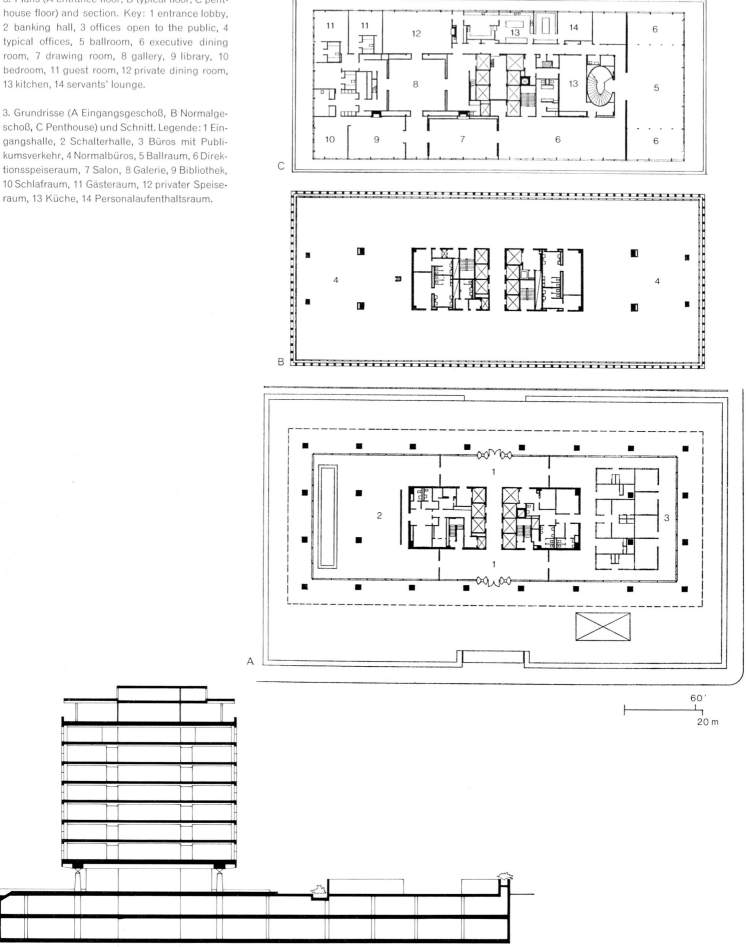

60'

20 m

4. General view of the building from northwest, with the Avenue Marnix in the foreground.

4. Gesamtansicht des Gebäudes von Nordwesten. Im Vordergrund die Avenue Marnix.

5. Baron Lambert's office.
6. Executive dining room in the penthouse.
7. Baron Lambert's library, with drawing room and executive dining room in the background.
8. Gallery in the center of the penthouse apartment. In the foreground a sculpture by Giacometti; next to the passage a Baga figure; in the room between drawing room and library a sculpture by Ipousteguy. Daylight enters through plastic domes in the roof. Floor slabs are of travertine; the walls are plastered.

5. Das Arbeitszimmer von Baron Lambert.
6. Direktionsspeiseraum im Penthouse.
7. Die Bibliothek von Baron Lambert mit Blick in den Salon und den großen Direktionsspeiseraum.
8. Die Galerie im Zentrum der Wohnung. Im Vordergrund eine Skulptur von Giacometti, neben dem Durchgang eine Baga-Figur, im Verbindungsraum zwischen Salon und Bibliothek eine Skulptur von Ipousteguy. Der Raum erhält durch Plastikkuppeln Oberlicht. Die Bodenplatten bestehen aus Travertin, die Wände sind verputzt.

Headquarters of the American Republic Insurance Company, Des Moines, Iowa

The building is located on a narrow site sloping from north to south on the periphery of the central business district, and can accommodate 650 people. It consists of a six-story office tower above an enclosed podium which projects to the south around an entrance courtyard. Podium and tower are independent both structurally and visually, merely sharing a common central core which stiffens the entire structure. To emphasize the suspension of the upper block the one-story space between it and the podium is enclosed with continuous glass and contains the cafeteria and a lounge opening on to a terrace overlooking the entrance court.
The load-bearing walls on the east and west of the tower are of poured-in-place reinforced concrete with a selected granite aggregate which is sandblasted. They are about 180′ long and taper from 4′ at the bottom to 21″ at the top as the loads diminish. The wall loads are transmitted to four concrete columns on either side, which are totally free of the podium, by story-high steel hinges painted black which punctuate the cafeteria level. The floors of the tower are of prestressed precast tees with a span of 98′ and these are smooth-finished in contrast to the rough texture of the sandblasted walls. The north and south walls are of floor to ceiling gray glass deeply recessed.
The ceiling system represents a complete integration of structural and mechanical elements. Between the structural tees are tubes covered with acoustical material which alternate as supply and return air ducts: above the tubes are placed very high intensity fluorescent lights which are fully concealed from the observer. The result is a uniform distribution of indirect light, conditioned air and sound absorption within the framework of the exposed structure.
All the details are carefully attuned to the basic structural concept. The architectural effect is handsomely complemented by works of art by contemporary artists, including a specially commissioned stabile by Alexander Calder in the entrance court and a Corbusier tapestry in the chairman's office on the top floor.

Hauptverwaltung der American Republic Insurance Company, Des Moines, Iowa

Das Gebäude liegt am Rand der Innenstadt von Des Moines auf einem langgestreckten, von Norden nach Süden abfallenden Gelände. Es bietet etwa 650 Arbeitsplätze und gliedert sich in einen sechsgeschossigen Turm sowie ein flaches Podium, dessen Wände im Süden einen Eingangshof umschließen. Podium und Turm bilden visuell und konstruktiv unabhängige, nur durch einen aussteifenden Festpunkt verbundene Bauteile. Um die Trennung beider Teile zu betonen, ist das dazwischenliegende Geschoß, das die Cafeteria und eine Lounge aufnimmt, rundum verglast, wobei sich die Lounge auf eine den Innenhof umgebende Dachterrasse öffnet.
Die tragenden Längswände des Turmes bestehen aus rauh gesandstrahltem Sichtbeton mit Granit als Zuschlagstoff. Sie sind etwa 55 m lang und verjüngen sich entsprechend der abnehmenden statischen Beanspruchung von etwa 1,22 m an der Basis auf etwa 53 cm an der Spitze. Ihre Lasten geben sie auf je vier, frei vor dem Podium stehende Betonstützen ab; als Auflager dienen schwarze gestrichene Stahlgelenke, die die volle Höhe des Cafeteria-Geschosses einnehmen. Die fast 30 m spannenden Turmdecken sind aus T-förmigen Spannbetonelementen zusammengesetzt; im Kontrast zu den rauhen Wänden haben sie eine glatte Oberfläche. Die grau getönten Glaswände auf der Nord- und der Südseite des Turmes sind geschoßhoch und weit zurückgesetzt.
Ein besonderes Augenmerk verdient die Integration verschiedenster Funktionen in den Metallrohren, die in den nach unten sichtbar gelassenen Tragelementen der Turmdecken hängen. Sie bilden einmal eine Abschirmung gegen die darüber montierten Leuchtstofflampen; dann wirken sie mit ihrer perforierten Oberfläche und dem auf der Innenseite angebrachten Schallschluckmantel als Akustikelemente. Schließlich sind sie alternierend Zuluftverteiler und Abluftsammler.
Alle Details sind sorgfältig auf das konstruktive Konzept abgestimmt. Eine glückliche Ergänzung findet die Architektur in einer Reihe von Werken bekannter zeitgenössischer Künstler, von denen die im Eingangshof aufgestellte (eigens in Auftrag gegebene) Plastik von Alexander Calder und ein im Büro des Präsidenten hängender Wandteppich von Le Corbusier die wichtigsten sind.

1. Corner of the building. The walls and columns of sandblasted exposed concrete, the smooth prestressed concrete members, the black painted steel hinges and the aluminum-framed windows create a lively contrast.

1. Gebäudeecke. Die Wände und Stützen aus rauh gesandstrahltem Sichtbeton, die glatten Spannbetonelemente, die schwarz gestrichenen Stahlgelenke sowie die in Aluminiumrahmen gefaßten Glasflächen stehen zueinander in einem lebhaften Kontrast.

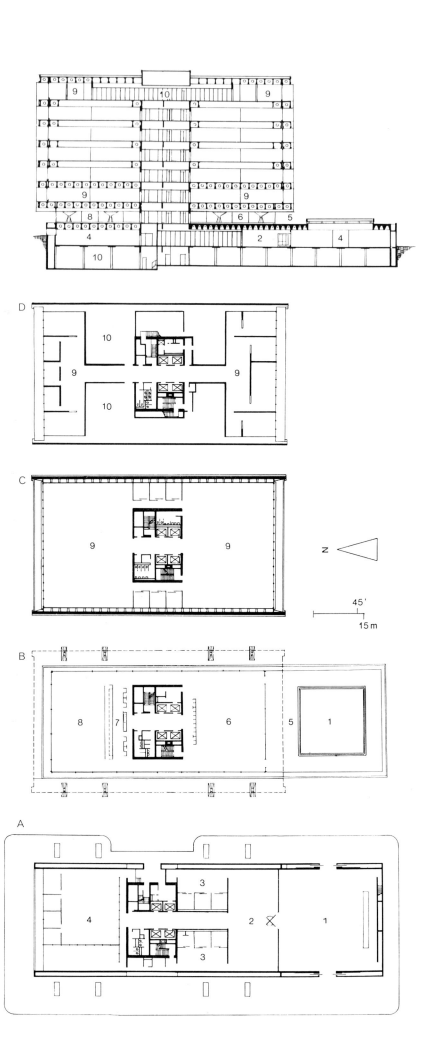

2. Plans (A ground floor, B mezzanine, C typical floor, D executive floor) and longitudinal section. Key: 1 entrance court, 2 lobby, 3 visitors' offices, 4 computer area, 5 terrace, 6 lounge, 7 food service, 8 cafeteria, 9 offices, 10 mechanical equipment.
3, 4. Views from northeast. As the load-bearing walls taper towards the upper floors while the perimeter partitions remain in the same vertical alignment, the intermediate space available for the ducting decreases from top to bottom in keeping with the technical requirements – the air-conditioning plant being installed on the top floor.

2. Grundrisse (A Erdgeschoß, B Zwischengeschoß, C Normalgeschoß, D Dachgeschoß) und Längsschnitt. Legende: 1 Eingangshof, 2 Eingangshalle, 3 Kundenbüros, 4 Datenverarbeitungszentrale, 5 Terrasse, 6 Lounge, 7 Speisenausgabe, 8 Cafeteria, 9 Büros, 10 technische Räume.
3, 4. Ansichten von Norden. Da die tragenden Wände in ihrer Dicke nach oben abnehmen, die davorgesetzten Verkleidungen jedoch auf der Raumseite senkrecht hochlaufen, verjüngt sich entsprechend den lufttechnischen Erfordernissen – die Klimazentrale befindet sich im Dachgeschoß – der vertikale Installationsraum zwischen Verkleidung und Wand von oben nach unten.

Pages 116–117:
5. Employees' lounge. In the background, two of the black painted steel hinges.

Seiten 116–117:
5. Die Lounge vor der Cafeteria. Im Hintergrund zwei der schwarz gestrichenen Stahlgelenke.

6. West-side access to entrance court.
7. Entrance court, seen from the lobby.
8. Office area. The metal tubes suspended between the stems of the T-beams have the multiple function of diffusing the light of the fluorescent light fixtures mounted above them, acting as sound-absorbing elements with perforated cover and inside fiberglass insulation, and serving alternately as ducts for supply and return air.

6. Westlicher Zugang zum Eingangshof.
7. Blick von der Eingangshalle in den Hof.
8. Großraumbüro. Die zwischen die Stege der Deckenelemente gehängten Metallrohre bilden einmal eine Abschirmung gegen die darüber montierten Leuchtstofflampen. Dann wirken sie mit ihrer perforierten Oberfläche und dem auf der Innenseite befindlichen Fiberglasmantel als Akustikelemente. Schließlich sind sie alternierend Zuluftverteiler und Abluftsammler.

9. Detail section of a structural floor in the office tower. Key: 1 prestressed concrete T-beam, 2 stiffener, 3 flooring, 4 carpeting, 5 air duct, also serving as sound-absorber, 6 fluorescent light fixture.

10. Cross-section of air duct/acoustic unit. Key: 1 hanger rod, 2 perforated aluminum tube, 3 sound-absorbing coating, 4 cover, 5 air supply or return diffuser, 6 base of fluorescent light fixture, 7 fluorescent light fixture.

11. Air supply or return diffuser. Key: 1 aperture leading to air duct, 2 aperture leading to office space.

9. Detailschnitt durch eine Decke im Büroturm. Legende: 1 T-Element aus vorgespanntem Beton, 2 Aussteifungsglied, 3 Estrich, 4 Teppichboden, 5 Akustik/Luft-Rohr, 6 Leuchtstofflampe.

10. Schnitt durch ein Akustik/Luft-Rohr. Legende: 1 Hängestab, 2 perforiertes Aluminiumrohr, 3 Schallschluckmantel, 4 Abdeckung, 5 Ausblas-/Ansaug-Schiene, 6 Sockel der Leuchtstofflampe, 7 Leuchtstofflampe.

11. Ausblas-/Ansaug-Schiene. Legende: 1 Öffnung zum Luftkanal, 2 Öffnung zum Raum.

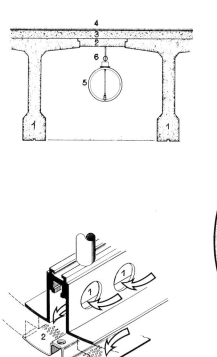

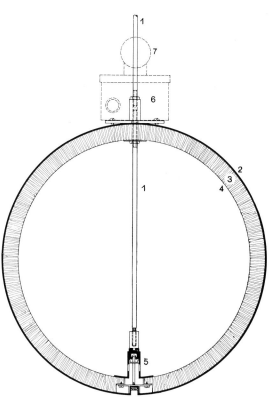

Headquarters of the Business Men's Assurance Co. of America, Kansas City, Missouri

The building is situated outside the city on a hill at the edge of a park. In addition to the 19-story tower, both a lower tower and a one- or two-story structure had been considered. The lower tower, however, would have had an unfavorable proportion with relation to the hill while the low-rise structure would have had to occupy nearly all of the 7-acre site to provide equivalent area.

The tower stands on a large platform. Below this platform are parking facilities, mechanical and other ancillary rooms as well as a cafeteria. The bearing structure is a frame of continuously welded high-strength steel with a column spacing of 36′ × 36′. Because of the frequent tornadoes experienced in this region, wind bracing had to be particularly strong, allowing for a maximum sway of about 5″ at the top. Cladding is of white Georgia marble.

The interior is developed on a 6′ × 6′ module. The window walls of grey, heat-absorbent glass, set back by one module, are held in black anodized aluminum frames. Behind every other window mullion is an air-conditioning duct leading to induction units on typical floors and low sill diffusers on the two top floors.

Hauptverwaltung der Business Men's Assurance Co. of America, Kansas City, Missouri

Das Gebäude liegt etwas außerhalb der Stadt auf einer an einen Park grenzenden Anhöhe. Neben dem 19geschossigen Turm standen sowohl ein niedrigerer Turm als auch eine ein- oder zweigeschossige Anlage zur Diskussion. Bei dem niedrigeren Turm hätte sich jedoch eine ungünstige Proportion zwischen Hügel und Gebäude ergeben, und bei dem Flachbau wäre man bei Einhaltung des Raumprogramms gezwungen gewesen, das etwa 2,84 ha große Grundstück fast vollständig zu überbauen.

Der Turm steht auf einer großen Plattform, unter der Parkplätze, technische und andere Nebenräume sowie eine Cafeteria untergebracht sind. Sein Tragwerk ist ein biegesteif verschweißtes Stahlskelett mit einem Stützenraster von etwa 11 × 11 m. Angesichts der häufig über diesem Gebiet wütenden Tornados wurde einer ausreichenden Steifigkeit des Skeletts besondere Beachtung geschenkt: Die maximale Schwingung an der Spitze beträgt etwa 13 cm. Für die Verkleidung wählte man weißen Marmor aus Georgia.

Der Ausbau basiert auf einem Raster von etwa 1,83 × 1,83 m. Die um eine Ausbauachse zurückgesetzten Außenwände aus grauem hitzeabsorbierenden Glas werden in schwarz anodisierten Aluminiumrahmen gehalten. Hinter jeder zweiten senkrechten Fenstersprosse liegt ein Klimakanal; zur Luftverteilung dienen brüstungshohe Induktionsgeräte in den Normalgeschossen sowie Unterflurgeräte in den beiden obersten Geschossen.

1. The building is situated on a hill adjacent to a park outside the city.

1. Der Bau liegt etwas außerhalb der Stadt auf einer an einen Park grenzenden Anhöhe.

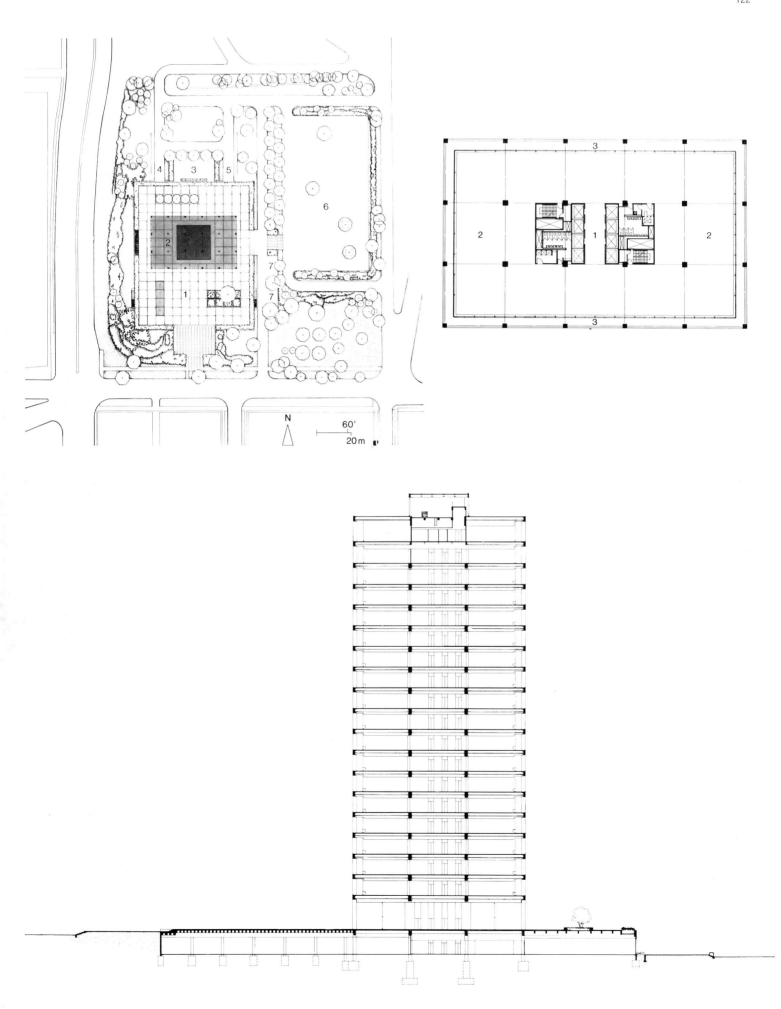

2. Site plan. Key: 1 terrace, 2 tower, 3 cafeteria terrace, 4 garage entrance drive, 5 supplies, 6 staff parking, 7 visitors' parking.
3. Plan (ground floor). Key: 1 elevator lobby, 2 office space, 3 surrounding gallery.
4. Section.
5. South side of the building. The structural frame, clad in white marble, is impressively distinguished from the recessed walls of grey, heat-absorbent glass.

2. Lageplan. Legende: 1 Terrasse, 2 Turm, 3 Garten vor der Cafeteria, 4 Garagenzufahrt, 5 Anlieferung, 6 Angestelltenparkplätze, 7 Gästeparkplätze.
3. Grundriß (Erdgeschoß). Legende: 1 Aufzugshalle, 2 Bürofläche, 3 umlaufende Galerie.
4. Schnitt.
5. Südseite des Gebäudes. Das mit weißem Marmor verkleidete Tragwerk hebt sich eindrucksvoll von den zurückgesetzten Außenwänden aus grauem hitzeabsorbierenden Glas ab.

Tenneco Building, Houston, Texas

The building, headquarters of the Tennessee Gas Transmission Co. and the Tennessee Bank and Trust Co., stands in the center of a square block in the central business district of Houston. It covers an area of 195′4″ × 195′4″ with a total effective floor area of 907, 190 sq ft, including some 845,320 sq ft on the 28 typical floors.

The comparatively low ground floor core is set back about 42′8″ on all sides from the outside of the building so that, despite the high plot ratio, a spacious plaza has been created. The plaza is flanked by car ramps on two opposite sides and by five semi-circular drive-in tellers' booths on one of the two other sides. The two-story bank premises above the ground floor are likewise set back from the outside of the building, though by about 15′2″ only. On the 28 typical floors, office space which can be partitioned at will is available on a module of 5′6″ × 5′6″ over a depth of 48′ between the centrally placed core and the window walls. As the orientation of the building is such that each of the four sides is liable to be exposed to the sun at some time during the day, the window walls of the typical floors are set back by 6′ from the spandrel line. Further protection against the hot southern sun is provided by sun screens suspended from the edge beams. The deep set-back of the first three floors is repeated at the top of the building where the lower part of the mechanical floor is also deeply recessed.

The bearing structure of the tower consists of a concrete-clad steel framework and steel floor units. The two-story bank premises above the ground floor are suspended from the nethermost typical floor by means of bars in the curtain wall. The cladding is "amber grey" anodized aluminum which has also been used for the window frames. The window panes are grey tinted.

Tenneco Building, Houston, Texas

Das Gebäude, das die Tennessee Gas Transmission Co. und die Tennessee Bank and Trust Co. beherbergt, liegt auf einem quadratischen Grundstück im Zentrum der Stadt. Es überdeckt ein Areal von etwa 59,60 × 59,60 m und bietet eine Gesamtnutzfläche von fast 85000 qm, wovon etwa 78000 qm auf die 28 Normalgeschosse entfallen.

Das verhältnismäßig niedrige Erdgeschoß ist um etwa 13 m allseitig von der Gebäudeaußenkante zurückgesetzt. So konnte trotz der weitgehenden Überbauung des Grundstücks eine geräumige Plaza geschaffen werden. Die Plaza wird an zwei gegenüberliegenden Seiten von Autorampen begrenzt, an einer der beiden übrigen von fünf halbrunden Autoschaltern. Die zweigeschossige Bankhalle über dem Erdgeschoß ist ebenfalls hinter die Gebäudeflucht zurückgesetzt, allerdings nur um etwa 4,62 m. In den 28 Normalgeschossen stehen zwischen dem zentral angeordneten Erschließungskern und den äußeren Glaswänden etwa 14,60 m tiefe, auf einem Raster von etwa 1,68 × 1,68 m frei unterteilbare Flächen zur Verfügung. Da das Gebäude so orientiert ist, daß alle vier Seiten zu den verschiedenen Zeiten des Tages Sonne erhalten, bleibt die Glashaut in den Normalgeschossen ringsum fast 2 m hinter den Vorderkanten der Außenstützen zurück; einen zusätzlichen Schutz vor der heißen südlichen Sonne bieten unter den Randbalken installierte Sonnenbrecher. Wie die Basis hat auch die obere, technische Einrichtungen beherbergende Abschlußzone des Gebäudes eine differenzierte Gliederung erfahren.

Das Tragwerk des Turmes besteht aus einem betonummantelten Stahlskelett und Stahlzellendecken. Die peripheren Lasten der zweigeschossigen Bankhalle über dem Erdgeschoß werden durch Zugstangen in den Sprossen der Glaswand aufgenommen. Das Turmtragwerk ist außen mit Tafeln aus »ambergrau« anodisiertem Aluminium verkleidet. Aus dem gleichen Material wurden auch die Fensterrahmen gefertigt. Die Glasscheiben sind grau getönt.

1. The ground floor and the bank premises above it are set back so as to widen the plaza.
2. The lower parts of the external columns are reinforced. In the foreground, the semi-circular drive-in tellers' booths.
3. General view of the building.

1. Das Erdgeschoß und die darüberliegende Bankhalle sind zurückgesetzt, um den Fußgängerplatz zu erweitern.
2. In der unteren Zone sind die Außenstützen verstärkt. Im Vordergrund die halbrunden Autoschalter.
3. Gesamtansicht des Gebäudes.

4. Corner of the building. The plaza is paved with Texas red granite.
5. Section of the facade at typical floor level. Because of Houston's southern climate, the glass wall is set back 6′ from the spandrel line, and sun screens are suspended from the edge beams.
6. With its dark cladding and agreeable proportions, the building has a distinguished appearance.
7. Plans (ground floor, typical floor). Key: 1 plaza, 2 lobby, 3 drive-in tellers' booths, 4 car ramp, 5 office area, capable of being partitioned at will.

4. Gebäudeecke. Die Plaza wurde mit roten texanischen Granitplatten belegt.
5. Fassadenschnitt im Bereich der Normalgeschosse. Wegen des südlichen Klimas von Houston ist die Glashaut fast 2 m hinter die Vorderkanten der Außenstützen gesetzt; zusätzlich wurden Sonnenbrecher unter die Randbalken gehängt.
6. Die dunkle Verkleidung und die ausgewogenen Proportionen geben dem Gebäude eine vornehme Note.
7. Grundrisse (Erdgeschoß, Normalgeschoß). Legende: 1 Plaza, 2 Eingangshalle, 3 Autoschalter, 4 Autorampe, 5 unterteilbare Bürofläche.

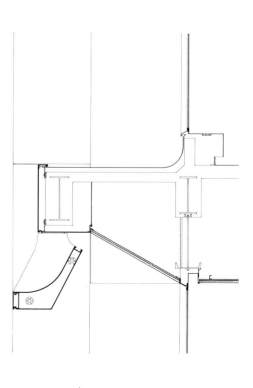

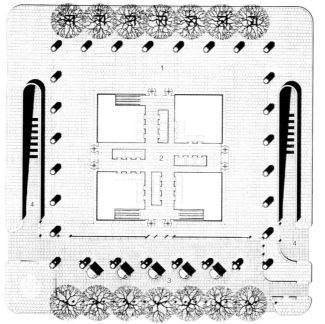

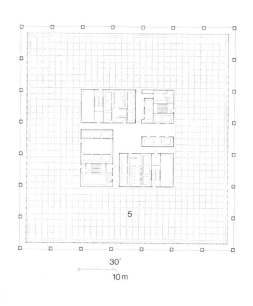

30'
10 m

Carlton Centre, Johannesburg, South Africa

Carlton Centre, designed jointly by Skidmore, Owings & Merrill and W. Rhodes-Harrison, Hoffe and Partners was the first major redevelopment of a portion of downtown Johannesburg, and has served as a catalyst for other developments.

Four small city blocks, characteristic of the basic city structure which dates back to the time when it was little more than a miners' camp, were incorporated into one "superblock" by closing portions of two intersecting streets. Parts of two other blocks were also developed concurrently on the south side of Main Street. A 50-story office building, a 600-room luxury hotel, and a department store, the main architectural elements of the complex, are grouped around a large circular court which penetrates the two shopping levels below the plaza. Much of the street level is therefore left open for pedestrians, landscaped areas, open courts and entrances to the shopping levels.

South of Main Street, a large rectangular structure contains a department store and shops at street level and on two levels below the street, 6 floors of parking and at the top a column-free exhibition hall. The two lower shopping levels are joined beneath Main Street to the major shopping concourses below the plaza. 140 retail shops, restaurants and banks are thus connected by covered malls, providing shoppers with a traffic-free, all-weather shopping complex connected vertically by escalators and elevators to the major buildings as well as to parking spaces for more than 2,000 cars both below and above street level. A service level immediately below the shopping concourse is reserved exclusively for the delivery of goods.

The entire complex is designed in poured-in-place reinforced concrete and all structures above grade have an integral finish of local gray granite exposed by sandblasting. The total area of the project is approximately 3,500,000 sq ft.

Carlton Centre, Johannesburg, Südafrika

Charakteristisch für die Innenstadt von Johannesburg, deren Grundstruktur noch aus der Zeit stammt, in der hier nur ein Bergbaulager stand, sind kleine, von schmalen Straßen durchzogene Blöcke. Das Carlton Centre, ein Gemeinschaftswerk von Skidmore, Owings & Merrill und W. Rhodes-Harrison, Hoffe and Partners setzte mit seinen an New York oder Chicago gemahnenden Dimensionen in diesem engmaschigen Gewebe das Zeichen für eine neue städtebauliche Entwicklung. Es beansprucht nicht weniger als fünf Blöcke und bietet eine Gesamtgeschoßfläche von etwa 325000 qm.

Auf dem Straßenniveau wurden vier der ehemaligen Blöcke zu einer durchgehenden Plaza zusammengeschlossen. Über dieser erheben sich ein Kaufhaus, ein 50geschossiges Bürohaus sowie ein Hotel mit 600 Betten. Der fünfte Block jenseits der den Komplex durchquerenden Main Street wurde voll überbaut; das im Grundriß quadratische Gebäude enthält im Erdgeschoß die Hauptzugangsebene eines weiteren Kaufhauses sowie verschiedene Einzelhandelsgeschäfte, in den folgenden sechs Obergeschossen Parkplätze und im Dachgeschoß eine große stützenfreie Ausstellungshalle. In den beiden ersten Untergeschossen, die das gesamte Grundstück einnehmen und wegen des von Norden nach Süden abfallenden Geländes einmal abgetreppt sind, befinden sich neben weiteren Verkaufsflächen der beiden Kaufhäuser etwa 140 Einzelhandelsgeschäfte sowie Restaurants und Bankfilialen. Ein großer runder sowie ein kleinerer rechteckiger Hof stellen eine optische Verbindung zur Plazaebene her und unterstützen so das Bemühen, hier einen kommunikativen Kristallisationspunkt für die Stadt zu schaffen. Die übrigen Untergeschosse nehmen nur noch den Raum unter dem neu geschaffenen Großblock ein; das erste dient der Anlieferung, die restlichen vier enthalten Parkplätze.

Alle Betonteile des Komplexes bestehen aus Ortbeton; der Zuschlagstoff in den sichtbaren Flächen ist durch Sandstrahlung nachbehandelter grauer Granit.

1. Carlton Centre, viewed from the southeast. In the left foreground, the Carlton Exhibition Centre; beyond it the Carlton Hotel; in the background the 50-story office tower.

1. Gesamtansicht des Komplexes von Südosten. Links im Vordergrund das Carlton Exhibition Centre, dahinter das Carlton Hotel, rechts neben dem Hotel der 50geschossige Büroturm.

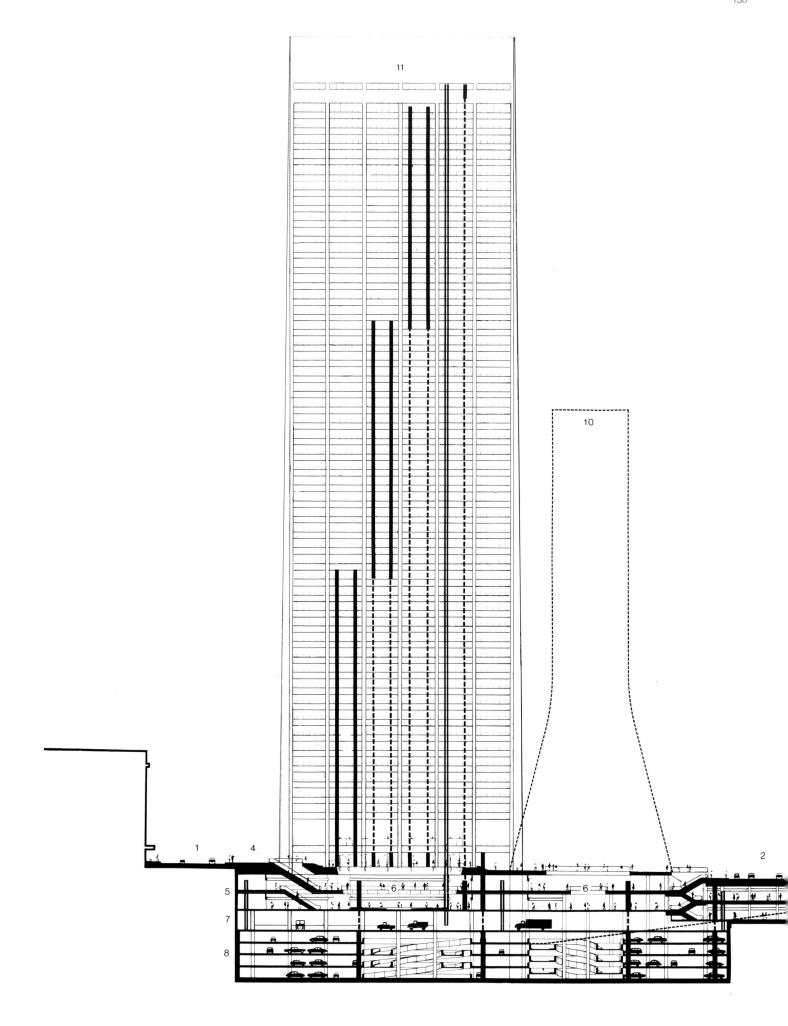

131

2. Section. Key: 1 Commissioner Street, 2 Main Street, 3 Marshall Street, 4 plaza, 5 shops, 6 court, 7 delivery level, 8 parking, 9 exhibition hall, 10 hotel, 11 office tower.
3. Plans (A first basement, B plaza level). Key: 1 Commissioner Street, 2 Main Street, 3 Marshall Street, 4 Kruis Street, 5 Von Wielligh Street, 6 plaza, 7 court, 8 department store, 9 retail shops, 10 hotel, 11 office tower.

2. Schnitt. Legende: 1 Commissioner Street, 2 Main Street, 3 Marshall Street, 4 Plaza, 5 Läden, 6 Hof, 7 Anlieferung, 8 Parkplätze, 9 Ausstellungshalle, 10 Hotel, 11 Bürohaus.
3. Grundrisse (A 1. Untergeschoß, B Plazageschoß). Legende: 1 Commissioner Street, 2 Main Street, 3 Marshall Street, 4 Kruis Street, 5 Von Wielligh Street, 6 Plaza, 7 Hof, 8 Kaufhaus, 9 Einzelhandelsgeschäfte, 10 Hotel, 11 Bürohaus.

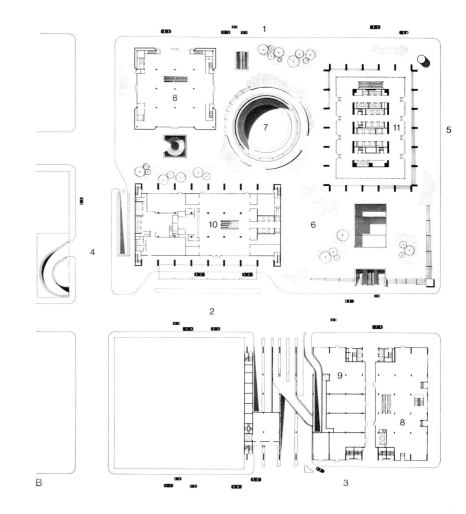

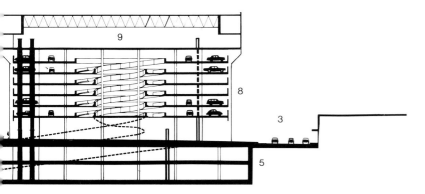

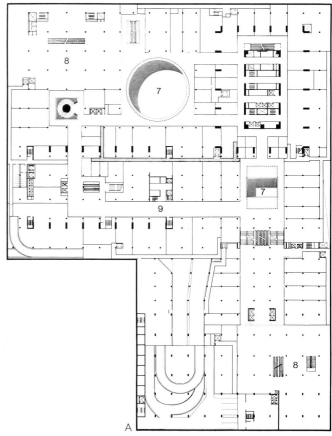

4. The large circular court is a central feature of the plaza. It provides a visual link between the shopping levels and the street. Ice-skating in the winter and a large fountain in the summer are added attractions.
5. The Carlton Exhibition Centre, with shops at the ground floor and two basement levels, six levels of parking and an exhibition hall at the top.
6. Office building and the hotel. The lower portions of the hotel becomes wider to accommodate special suites, function rooms, a ballroom, restaurants and other public areas.

4. Der große runde Hof im Zentrum der Plaza. Er bindet die beiden ersten Untergeschosse eng an den Straßenraum. Im Winter dient das Brunnenbecken als vielbesuchte Schlittschuhbahn.
5. Das Carlton Exhibition Centre enthält im Erdgeschoß Läden, in den folgenden sechs Obergeschossen Parkplätze und im Dachgeschoß eine Ausstellungshalle.
6. Blick auf Bürohaus und Hotel. Der Hotelturm verbreitert sich im unteren Drittel, um auch die großflächigeren allgemeinen Räume aufnehmen zu können.

Bank of America Headquarters, San Francisco, California

The complex – a joint venture of Skidmore, Owings & Merrill and Wurster, Bernardi and Emmons with Pietro Belluschi as consulting architect – consists of a 52-story tower, a pavilion with ground floor and galleries on two levels, and a four-level base.

The tower was placed at the extreme southwest corner and the pavilion at the extreme northeast corner of the site, leaving about 50 per cent of the site free for a large plaza along California Street on the north side.

The level immediately below the plaza contains a pedestrian concourse with entrances from three streets. Here are a cafeteria, an auditorium with 220 seats, as well as shops. Below that level are truck delivery and pick-up facilities and a three-level basement garage for 420 cars.

The pavilion, containing the San Francisco main office branch of the bank, is supported by four robust corner columns. The two gallery levels and the ground floor, accessible from Montgomery Street on the east side, offer a total floor area of 30,000 sq ft.

The tower, covering an area of 143′×243′ in the plan, contains a total floor area of 1,600,000 sq ft. The bank occupies about one-third of the office space, the remainder being available for tenancy by other firms. To improve the sculptural quality of the 779′ high tower, a bay window design has been adopted for the facades, and the upper floors are distinguished by irregular setbacks. The facades are composed of polished granite of a reddish color, and of bronze tinted glass. While, on the standard floors, the windows point outwards and the columns are merged with the inside window posts, giving the appearance of a smooth skin which does not conceal the plastic shape of the building, the windows of the banking hall on the 2nd and 3rd floor point inwards so as to emphasize the columns and to preserve formal continuity with the recessed main lobby on the ground floor.

Hauptverwaltung der Bank of America, San Francisco, California

Der Komplex – ein Gemeinschaftswerk von Skidmore, Owings & Merrill und Wurster, Bernardi and Emmons mit Pietro Belluschi als architektonischem Berater – besteht aus einem 52geschossigen Hochhaus, einem Pavillon mit einem Haupt- und zwei Galeriegeschossen sowie einem viergeschossigen Unterbau.

Das Hochhaus wurde in die äußerste Südwestecke, der Pavillon in die äußerste Nordostecke des Grundstücks gesetzt; dadurch entstand an der im Norden vorbeiführenden California Street ein etwa 50% des Baugrundes einnehmender freier Platz.

Das darunterliegende Geschoß beherbergt eine von drei Straßen zugängliche Fußgängerebene mit einer Cafeteria, einem 220 Personen fassenden Auditorium und Läden. Unter der Fußgängerebene liegen die Anlieferung und eine Tiefgarage für 420 Wagen.

Der die Stadtfiliale der Bank aufnehmende Pavillon wird von vier kräftigen Eckstützen getragen. Die beiden Galeriegeschosse und das von der Montgomery Street aus, die das Grundstück im Osten begrenzt, erschlossene Hauptgeschoß bieten zusammen eine Fläche von etwa 2800 qm.

Das im Grundriß etwa 43,50×74 m messende Hochhaus hat eine Gesamtfläche von etwa 149000 qm. Ungefähr ein Drittel davon wird von der Bank beansprucht, der Rest ist vermietet. Um den etwa 237 m hohen Turm zu gliedern, wurden die Fassaden erkerförmig aufgefaltet und die oberen Geschosse unregelmäßig zurückgestuft. Die Fassaden bestehen aus poliertem, rötlichem Granit und bronzefarben getöntem Glas. Während in den Normalgeschossen die Fensterspitzen nach außen weisen und die Stützen in den Fassadenkehlen untergehen, so daß sich hier eine glattflächige, den plastischen Gebäudeumriß nicht übertönende Haut ergibt, sind in der das 1. und 2. Obergeschoß einnehmenden Bankhalle die Fenster nach innen gefaltet, um die Stützen zu betonen und dadurch eine formale Kongruenz zur weit zurückgesetzten Eingangshalle herzustellen.

1. Section. On the left, the glass pavilion with the San Francisco main office branch of the bank.
2. The tower, seen from the north. The facade is enlivened by a bay window pattern and the upper floors by irregular setbacks.

1. Schnitt. Links der die Stadtfiliale der Bank aufnehmende Glaspavillon.
2. Blick von Norden auf das Hochhaus. Die Fassaden wurden erkerförmig aufgefaltet und die oberen Geschosse unregelmäßig zurückgestuft.

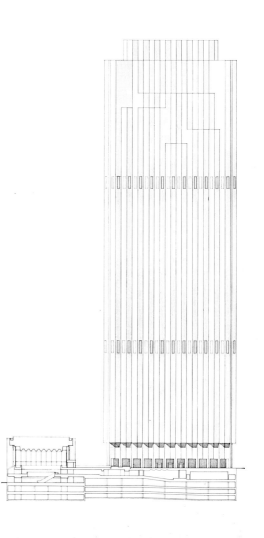

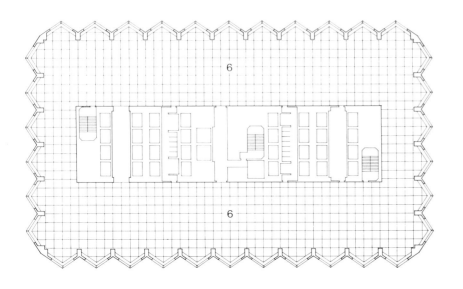

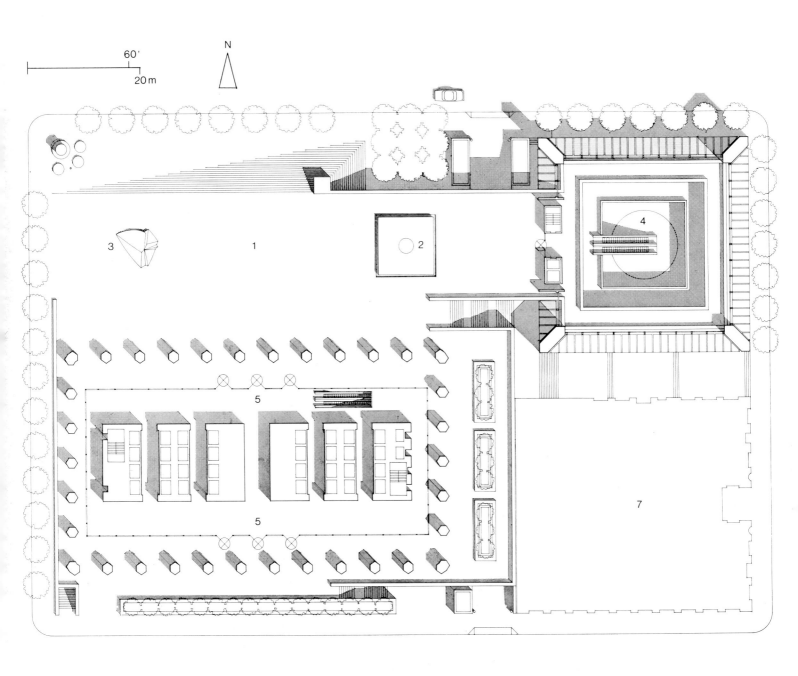

3. Plans (plaza level, standard office floor). Key: 1 plaza, 2 fountain, 3 sculpture, 4 pavilion, 5 main lobby of office tower, 6 office space, 7 California Commercial Union Building.

3. Grundrisse (Plazageschoß, Normalgeschoß des Hochhauses). Legende: 1 Plaza, 2 Brunnen, 3 Skulptur, 4 Pavillon, 5 Eingangshalle des Hochhauses, 6 Bürofläche, 7 California Commercial Union Building.

4. Office with view across the San Francisco Bay.
5. Interior of the two-story banking hall in the tower.

4. Büroraum mit Ausblick auf die Bucht von San Francisco.
5. Blick in die zweigeschossige Bankhalle im Hochhaus.

6. Plaza, adjoining California Street.
7. Interior of the pavilion. Northeast corner of the building, seen from the upper gallery.
8. The pavilion, seen from the west.

6. Die an der California Street gelegene Plaza.
7. Der Innenraum des Pavillons. Blick von der oberen Galerie auf die Nordostecke des Gebäudes.
8. Blick von Westen auf den Pavillon.

Marine Midland Center, Buffalo, New York. Under construction

The site earmarked for this office block, designed for rental, covers two street blocks in the central business district. The phase I project includes a 40-story tower, bridging Main Street and covering an area of 120' × 160', as well as an L-shaped ancillary building which flanks the tower on the south and west sides, with the south wing likewise bridging the street. Total floor area is about 1,400,000 sq ft. Some 82 per cent of the office space is available to the principal tenants (Marine Midland Bank) for their own purposes or for sub-letting.

The two basements contain a garage accommodating 550 cars, which is wholly owned and operated by the City of Buffalo, as well as the bank's computer center and storage and mechanical areas. At the level of Main Street is a spacious plaza, enlivened by regularly spaced flower boxes with honey locust trees and by a large sculpture piece. Pedestrian access to the tower is from lobbies on either side of Main Street. Primary access to the ancillary building is placed at the intersection of its two wings. The ground floor of its south wing contains a branch bank; in the west wing are a restaurant and shops; from the entrance lobbies on either side of Main Street, escalators lead to a two-story high main lobby which is also the bottom landing for most of the elevators serving the upper floors of the tower. A bridge, approximately 90' wide, connects the lobby with the south wing of the ancillary building which, at that level, contains an auditorium and a cafeteria. The executive dining rooms are on the top floor of the tower.

The buildings are clad in chamfered precast concrete panels, 4" in thickness, finished with washed silicate gravel. The window ribbons have bronze tinted glass panes with dark anodized aluminum frames.

Marine Midland Center, Buffalo, New York. Im Bau

Das Grundstück, auf dem dieses Mietobjekt errichtet werden soll, liegt im Zentrum der Stadt und erstreckt sich über zwei Straßenblocks. Die erste Baustufe umfaßt ein die Main Street überspannendes 40geschossiges Hochhaus mit einer Grundfläche von 36,60 × 48,80 m sowie ein viergeschossiges Nebengebäude, das sich in L-Form um dieses herumlegt und mit seinem Südflügel ebenfalls über die Straße hinwegsetzt. Der Komplex bietet eine Gesamtfläche von etwa 130000 qm. Etwa 82% der Bürofläche stehen dem Hauptmieter, der Marine Midland Bank, für Eigennutzung oder Untervermietung zur Verfügung.

In den beiden Untergeschossen sind eine der Stadt Buffalo gehörende und von ihr unterhaltene Garage mit 550 Autoabstellplätzen, das Computerzentrum der Bank sowie haustechnische Anlagen untergebracht. Auf dem Niveau der Main Street findet sich eine weiträumige Plaza. Sie wird durch regelmäßig gesetzte Kübel, in die Christusdorn gepflanzt ist, und eine große Plastik belebt. Die Erschließung des Hochhauses erfolgt über zwei beiderseits der Main Street liegende Eingangshallen, der Hauptzugang zum Nebengebäude befindet sich am Knotenpunkt seiner beiden Flügel. Der südliche Flügel des Nebengebäudes nimmt im Erdgeschoß die Schalterhalle der Bank, der westliche Flügel ein Restaurant und Läden auf. Von den Eingangshallen beiderseits der Main Street gelangt man aufwärts in eine zweigeschossige Lobby, dem Ausgangspunkt für die Mehrzahl der die oberen Geschosse des Hochhauses bedienenden Aufzüge. Eine etwa 27,50 m breite Brücke verbindet die Lobby mit dem südlichen Flügel des Nebengebäudes, der auf dieser Ebene ein Auditorium und eine Cafeteria beherbergt. Eine weitere Cafeteria für die Geschäftsleitung der Bank befindet sich im obersten Turmgeschoß.

Die Fassaden werden von kräftig hervortretenden und im Brüstungsbereich abgeschrägten Waschbetonverkleidungen mit einer Dicke von etwa 10 cm sowie Fensterbändern mit Scheiben aus bronzefarben getöntem Glas und Rahmen aus dunkel anodisiertem Aluminium gebildet.

1. The group of buildings, seen from the north (model).

1. Ansicht des Komplexes von Norden (Modell).

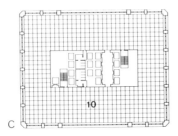

C

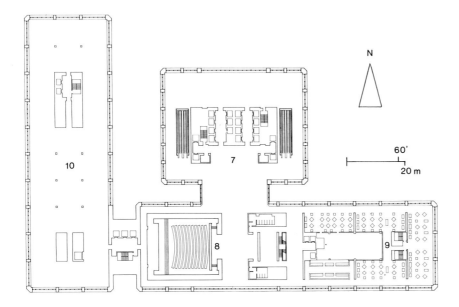

N

60'
20 m

B

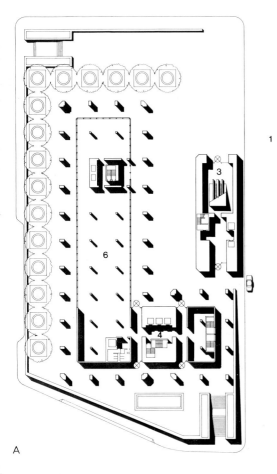

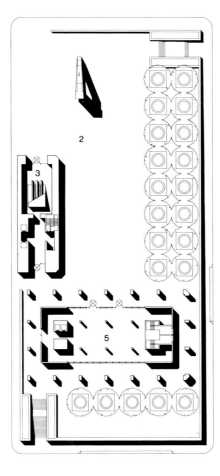

1

2

A

2. Plans (A ground floor, B 2nd floor, C typical floor of the tower). Key: 1 Main Street, 2 plaza, 3 tower entrance lobby, 4 lobby of ancillary building, 5 banking area, 6 restaurant and shops, 7 main lobby of tower, 8 auditorium, 9 cafeteria, 10 office space.
3. View from above on the northern part of the plaza (model).

2. Grundrisse (A Erdgeschoß, B 1. Obergeschoß, C Normalgeschoß des Hochhauses). Legende: 1 Main Street, 2 Plaza, 3 Eingangshalle des Hochhauses, 4 Eingangshalle des Nebengebäudes, 5 Bankschalterhalle, 6 Restaurant und Läden, 7 Lobby des Hochhauses, 8 Auditorium, 9 Cafeteria, 10 Bürofläche.
3. Blick von oben auf den nördlichen Teil der Plaza (Modell).

Marine Midland Building, New York, New York

The Marine Midland Building was the first New York office building designed by Skidmore, Owings & Merrill as a commercial building for general rental, which has somewhat different demands from those of a corporate headquarters. It occupies a small site in the Wall Street area in the immediate vicinity of the Chase Manhattan Bank, completed in 1961.

As it was desired to leave as much open space as possible facing Broadway and Cedar Street without, however, voluntarily foregoing the maximum permissible plot ratio on this very costly site, the setback from the two other streets had to be reduced to the minimum permitted by the 1961 zoning ordinance. The building was therefore given the same trapezoidal shape as the site itself which entailed, however, hardly any disadvantages compared with a rectangular plan as the odd angles could be absorbed in the likewise trapezoidal central core so that the number of critical points could be reduced to a minimum.

The major tenant, for whom the building is named, is the Marine Midland Grace Trust Company (now the Marine Midland Bank). This bank occupies the two basements which cover the entire site, as well as the first ten floors above street level. The main banking hall is placed on the 2nd floor while the ground floor had to be reserved for general facilities available to all the tenants, particularly the main lobby.

The bearing structure of the tower is a welded steel frame, with approximately 30′ × 30′ bays. Because of the irregular angles, the architects opted for a smooth facade clad with a uniform skin of mat-black anodized aluminum and bronze tinted glass, emphasizing the structure as a whole while repressing the individual elements.

The sculpture on the plaza facing Broadway, a red painted rhombohedron 28′ high, was designed by Isamu Noguchi in collaboration with Skidmore, Owings & Merrill.

Marine Midland Building, New York, New York

Das Marine Midland Building ist im Gegensatz zu allen früheren von Skidmore, Owings & Merrill entworfenen New Yorker Bürobauten nicht als repräsentativer Sitz einer Firma, sondern als normales Mietobjekt mit entsprechend niedrigerem Anspruch konzipiert worden. Es liegt auf einem kleinen Grundstück im Wallstreet-Viertel, in unmittelbarer Nachbarschaft der 1961 fertiggestellten Chase Manhattan Bank.

Da man bestrebt war, am Broadway und an der Cedar Street möglichst große Freiräume zu schaffen, wegen der sehr hohen Grundstückskosten jedoch keine freiwillige Unterschreitung der höchstzulässigen Bebauungsdichte in Kauf nehmen konnte, mußte man an den beiden übrigen Seiten so dicht an die Straßenkanten herangehen, wie es die New Yorker Baubestimmungen von 1961 erlauben. Auf diese Weise ergab sich ein die Grundstücksgestalt wiederholender trapezförmiger Grundriß, der jedoch für die Inneneinrichtung gegenüber einem rechtwinkligen Grundriß kaum Nachteile bringt, weil auch der Kern einen trapezförmigen Umriß hat und dadurch die Zahl der kritischen Punkte auf ein Minimum reduziert ist.

Der Hauptmieter des Gebäudes, der ihm auch den Namen gab, ist die Marine Midland Grace Trust Company (jetzt die Marine Midland Bank). Sie beansprucht die beiden das gesamte Gelände einnehmenden Untergeschosse sowie die ersten zehn Turmgeschosse. Die Bankhalle liegt im 1. Obergeschoß, weil das Erdgeschoß zum größten Teil für allgemeine, der Gesamtheit der Mieter zur Verfügung stehende Einrichtungen freigehalten werden mußte.

Das Tragwerk des Turmes ist ein geschweißtes Stahlskelett; der Regelabstand der Stützen beträgt in beiden Richtungen etwa 9,15 m. Wegen des schiefwinkligen Umrisses wählte man eine glatte, wie eine durchgehende Haut wirkende Fassade aus mattschwarz anodisiertem Aluminium und bronzefarben getöntem Glas, die die Gesamtform unterstreicht und das Einzelelement zurückdrängt.

Die Skulptur auf der Plaza am Broadway, ein roter Rhomboeder mit einer Höhe von über 8,50 m, wurde von Isamu Noguchi in Zusammenarbeit mit Skidmore, Owings & Merrill entworfen.

1. Site plan. Key: 1 Broadway, 2 Cedar Street, 3 Liberty Street, 4 Nassau Street, 5 Pine Street, 6 William Street, 7 Marine Midland Building, 8 Chase Manhattan Bank.
2. Northwest side of the building, with Isamu Noguchi's sculpture in the foreground.

1. Lageplan. Legende: 1 Broadway, 2 Cedar Street, 3 Liberty Street, 4 Nassau Street, 5 Pine Street, 6 William Street, 7 Marine Midland Building, 8 Chase Manhattan Bank.
2. Nordwestseite des Gebäudes. Im Vordergrund die Skulptur von Isamu Noguchi.

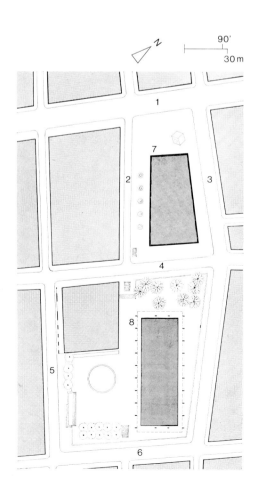

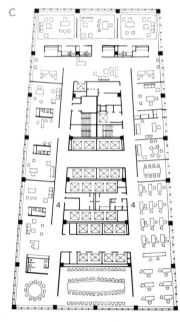

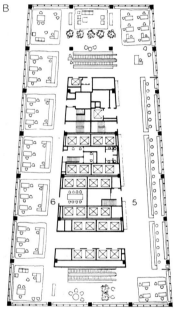

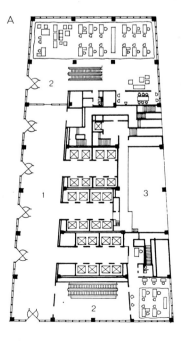

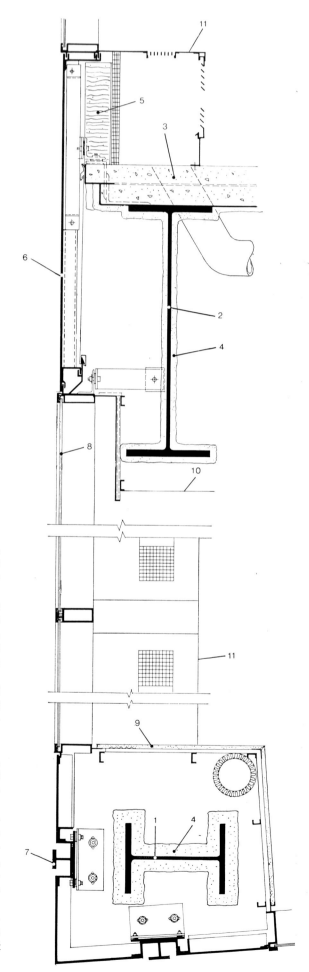

3. Plans (A ground floor, B 2nd floor, C 3rd floor).
Key: 1 entrance lobby, 2 bank premises, 3 truck
dock, 4 offices, 5 banking hall, 6 officers' platform.

4. Facade detail. Key: 1 corner column, 2 edge
beam, 3 steel deck floor with concrete cover, 4
fire proofing, 5 concrete block, 6 aluminum panel,
7 guide rail for window washing rig, 8 glass, 9
metal lath and plaster, 10 suspended ceiling, 11
cladding of induction unit.

5. The smooth facade of mat-black anodized
aluminum and bronze tinted glass has the effect
of emphasizing the shape as a whole and sub-
ordinating the individual elements.

3. Grundrisse (A Erdgeschoß, B 1. Obergeschoß,
C 2. Obergeschoß). Legende: 1 Eingangshalle, 2
Bankhalle, 3 Anlieferung, 4 Büros, 5 Bankschal-
ter, 6 Beratungsplätze.

4. Fassadendetail. Legende: 1 Eckstütze, 2 Randträger, 3 Stahlzellendecke mit Aufbeton, 4 Feuer-
schutz, 5 Betonblock, 6 Aluminiumtafel, 7 Führungsschiene des Fassadenreinigungsgerätes,
8 Glas, 9 Putz auf Rippenstreckmetall, 10 abgehängte Decke, 11 Verkleidung des Induktionsge-
rätes.

5. Die glatte Fassade aus mattschwarz anodisiertem Aluminium und bronzefarben getöntem
Glas unterstreicht die Gesamtform und drängt
das Einzelelement zurück.

140

6. View of the building from west with the Chase Manhattan Bank in the background.
7, 8. Banking hall on the 2nd floor.

6. Blick von Westen auf das Gebäude. Im Hintergrund die Chase Manhattan Bank.
7, 8. Die Bankhalle im 1. Obergeschoß.

U.S. Steel Building, One Liberty Plaza, New York, New York

The building is situated between Broadway, Liberty, Church and Cortlandt Streets. To the west is the World Trade Center; to the east, the Marine Midland Building which was also designed by SOM.
U.S. Steel, joint owner with Galbreath-Ruffin Corporation, requested a tower clearly expressing the steel structure and utilizing the latest technology commensurate with a prestige rental office building. To achieve an exemplary building SOM understook a major research program along with the design of the building. The main emphasis of this research was structural but it also encompassed other aspects, integration of lighting and air-conditioning, elevatoring (this led to the split core). Nine prototype structural schemes, all based on a column-free plan, were analysed for cost, leading to the choice of the scheme built. The scheme selected uses the fireproofed flanges to protect the unfireproofed web, providing a significant saving in cladding. An additional cost advantage of the selected scheme is the 6'3" deep girders which give a 50% column connection allowing a major part of the wind stress to be taken by the exterior frame.
A special zoning resolution was adopted to permit consolidating the total allowable floor area on the larger block leaving the other block for a park. This park is a tree filled plaza similar in design to the plaza around the building. The site slopes approximately 10' down from Broadway to Church Street. The plaza with large steps at each end for seating was established at a mid-point on this slope permitting the lobby entrances to be at the center of the building.
The building has a gross floor area of about 2,130,000 sq ft, including about 128,000 sq ft in the two stories below the plaza. From the first level below the plaza, connected with the lobby by escalator, pedestrian passages lead to subway stations and to the World Trade Center. This pedestrian connection is part of a comprehensive pedestrian circulation system in the new Special Greenwich Street Development district.

U.S. Steel Building, One Liberty Plaza, New York, New York

Das Gebäude liegt zwischen Broadway, Liberty Street, Church Street und Cortlandt Street. Unmittelbare Nachbarn sind das World Trade Center und das ebenfalls von Skidmore, Owings & Merrill entworfene Marine Midland Building.
Die vom Bauherrn und Teileigentümer, der U.S. Steel, gestellten Bedingungen waren ein außen klar und kräftig in Erscheinung tretendes Stahlskelett sowie ein höchsten Ansprüchen gerecht werdender Ausbau. Um zu einer für die Verwendung von Stahl bei Bürobauten wegweisenden Lösung zu gelangen, erhielten die Architekten die Möglichkeit zu einer über den Rahmen eines normalen Entwurfs hinausgehenden Studie. Das Schwergewicht dieser Studie lag zwar auf konstruktiven Aspekten, darüber hinaus wurden jedoch auch viele andere Fragen behandelt, so die der Erschließung (was zur Aufgliederung des Kernbereichs in einzelne Kerngruppen führte), der Klimatechnik und der Beleuchtung. Es wurden neun Prototypen mit einer jeweils etwa 13,70 m tiefen stützenfreien Bürofläche untersucht. Die beiden Typen mit dem geringsten Stahlverbrauch erwiesen sich gegenüber dem konstruktiv weniger effizienten, dafür aber einfacheren Typ, der schließlich realisiert wurde, als kostenmäßig nicht konkurrenzfähig, da die Materialersparnis die teilweise durch einen schwierigeren Brandschutz sich ergebenden höheren Erstellungskosten nicht aufwiegen konnte. Bei dem ausgewählten Typ sind die Randträger fast 1,91 m hoch, wodurch sich eine lange Verbindung zwischen ihnen und den Außenstützen und damit eine hohe Stabilität des Skeletts ergibt. Die Stege konnten außen ungeschützt bleiben, weil die vorgezogenen Verkleidungen der Flansche bei einem Brand als Hitzeschild wirken.
Das Grundstück umfaßt zwei Blocks. Durch eine Ausnahmegenehmigung war es möglich, die für beide Blocks erlaubte Nutzfläche auf dem größeren Block zu konzentrieren und den kleineren Block in eine mit Bäumen bepflanzte Plaza umzuwandeln. Um trotz des Höhenunterschiedes von etwa 3 m zwischen Broadway und Church Street ebene und in Gebäudemitte auf die Querstraßen auslaufende Grundflächen zu erhalten, wurden diese auf der einen Seite in das Gelände eingeschnitten und auf der anderen Seite darüber angehoben.
Der Komplex bietet eine Gesamtfläche von etwa 198 000 qm, davon entfallen etwa 11 900 qm auf zwei Untergeschosse. Vom 1. Untergeschoß, das mit dem Eingangsgeschoß durch Rolltreppen verbunden ist, führen Fußgängerpassagen zur U-Bahn und zum benachbarten World Trade Center.

1. Spandrel section. The spandrel girders are 6'3" high providing a 50% column connection which is used for resting the wind load.
2. Tower, seen from the World Trade Center.

1. Fassadendetail. Die Randträger sind fast 1,91 m hoch, wodurch sich eine 50%ige Verbindung zwischen ihnen und den Außenstützen und damit eine hohe Stabilität des Skeletts ergibt.
2. Ansicht des Turmes vom World Trade Center aus.

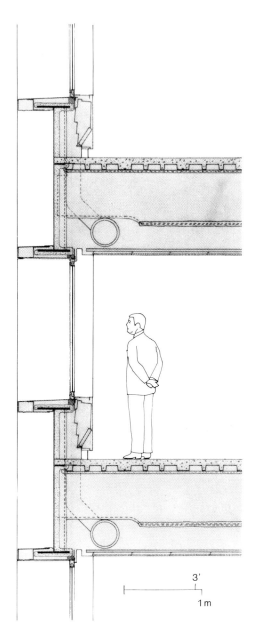

3'
1 m

Pages 152–153:
3. The first floor above street level is higher than the lobby floor and the typical floors.

Seiten 152–153:
3. Gegenüber dem Eingangsgeschoß und den Normalgeschossen ist das 1. Obergeschoß durch eine größere Höhe abgehoben.

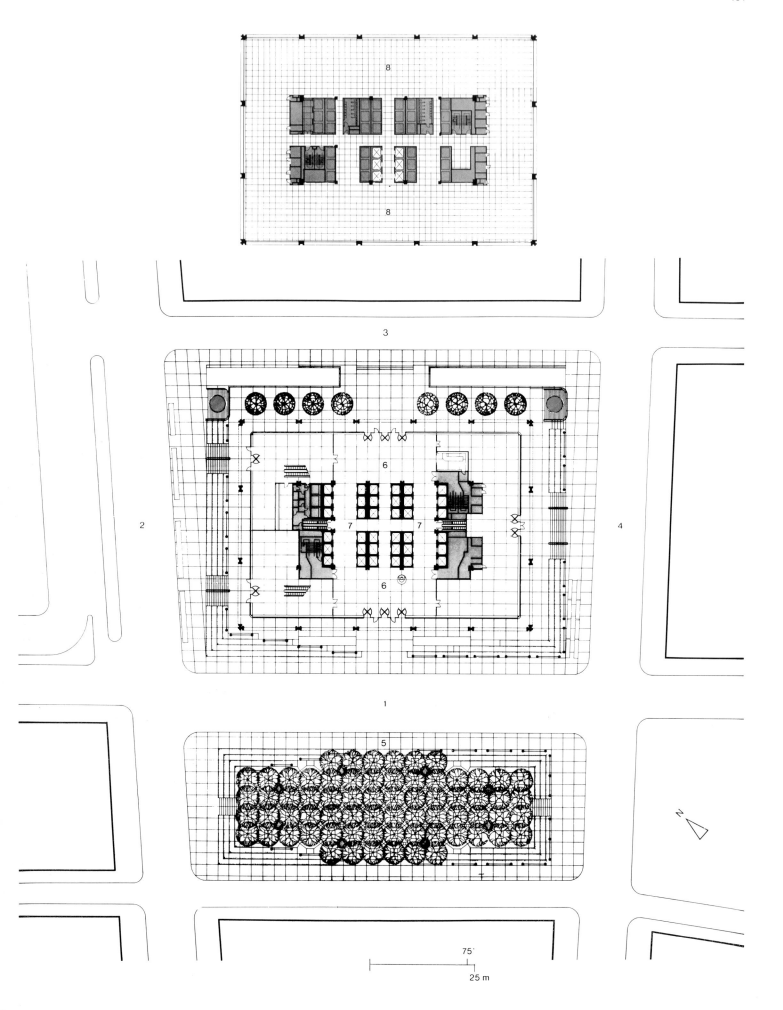

8

8

3

2

6

7   7

6

4

1

5

75'

25 m

155

4. Plans (ground floor, typical floor). Key: 1 Liberty Street, 2 Church Street, 3 Cortlandt Street, 4 Broadway, 5 plaza with trees, 6 lobby, 7 elevator lobby, 8 office area.
5. South side of the building, seen across the plaza.
6. Southwest corner.

4. Grundrisse (Erdgeschoß, Normalgeschoß). Legende: 1 Liberty Street, 2 Church Street, 3 Cortlandt Street, 4 Broadway, 5 baumbestandene Plaza, 6 Eingangshalle, 7 Aufzugshalle, 8 Bürofläche.
5. Blick über die baumbestandene Plaza auf die südliche Längsseite des Gebäudes.
6. Südwestecke.

7. South elevation. Trinity Church in foreground.
8. View of the building across Broadway. In the foreground, the plaza of the Marine Midland Building.

7. Südseite des Gebäudes. Im Vordergrund die Trinity Church.
8. Blick über den Broadway auf das Gebäude. Im Vordergrund die Plaza des Marine Midland Building.

Alcoa Building, San Francisco, California

The building is set astride a three-level public garage designed by Wurster, Bernardi and Emmons and DeMars and Reay at the southern end of the Golden Gateway Center, a residential and commercial redevelopment in the vicinity of the waterfront. The floor area on the 24 typical office floors totals 400,000 sq ft.
The garage roof with the entrance lobby is two stories above street level and has become a handsomely landscaped plaza with a large fountain and four sunken gardens. Connection with street level is provided by four open flights of stairs and a set of escalators placed in a protected position next to the lobby.
The design of the steel framework was governed by the desire to find the most economical solution of preventing damage caused by seismic forces. The external members are placed 18" outside the curtain wall facade.
The only members rising directly from the ground are the main columns which are spaced at 50' while the intermediate columns and the diagonal bracing end above the entrance floor. As the concept did not fit into any of the categories listed in the Building Code, a computer analysis was carried out which disclosed a much greater strength than that postulated in the regulations although steel consumption was no higher than with a conventional structure.
The cladding of the external members of the structure and the framing of the curtain wall are of bronze anodized aluminum, the spandrels and glazing of similarly colored or tinted glass.

Alcoa Building, San Francisco, California

Das Gebäude steht auf einer dreigeschossigen öffentlichen Garage – entworfen von Wurster, Bernardi and Emmons und DeMars and Reay – am Südende des Golden Gate Center, einem neu entwickelten Wohn- und Geschäftsviertel in der Nähe des Hafens. Es bietet in 24 Normalgeschossen eine Bürofläche von insgesamt 37200 qm.
Das Garagendach mit der Eingangshalle liegt zwei Stockwerke über dem Straßenniveau. Der Freiraum ist zu einer reizvoll gestalteten Plaza mit einem großen Brunnen und vier Sitzgruben ausgebaut. Die Verbindung zum Straßenniveau stellen vier Freitreppen und eine geschützt neben der zurückgesetzten Halle liegende Rolltreppenanlage her.
Das Stahlskelett verdankt seine Form dem Wunsch nach einer möglichst wirtschaftlichen Lösung des Problems, Bauschäden durch seismische Erschütterungen zu verhindern. Die äußeren Tragglieder liegen etwa 46 cm vor der raumabschließenden Vorhangfassade. Nur die im Abstand von etwa 15,20 m stehenden Hauptstützen laufen bis zum Boden durch, die aussteifenden Diagonalen und die senkrechten Zwischenglieder enden über dem Eingangsgeschoß. Da das Tragwerkkonzept in keine der bestehenden Bauvorschriften paßte, wurde eine Computeranalyse durchgeführt; sie ergab, daß die Festigkeit wesentlich größer ist, als es die Vorschriften verlangen. Der Stahlverbrauch war dabei nicht höher als bei einer konventionellen Konstruktion.
Die Verkleidung der äußeren Tragglieder und die Profile der Vorhangwand bestehen aus bronzefarben anodisiertem Aluminium, die Brüstungsplatten und Fensterscheiben aus in gleichem Ton eingefärbten, beziehungsweise getönten Glas.

1, 2. The building, constructed as an extremely stiff cage because of the risk of seismic forces, is set astride a public garage. The open space above the garage roof has been converted into an attractive plaza.

1, 2. Das wegen der Gefahr seismischer Erschütterungen als extrem steifer Käfig konstruierte Gebäude erhebt sich über einer öffentlichen Garage. Der Freiraum auf dem Garagendach wurde zu einer reizvollen Plaza ausgebaut.

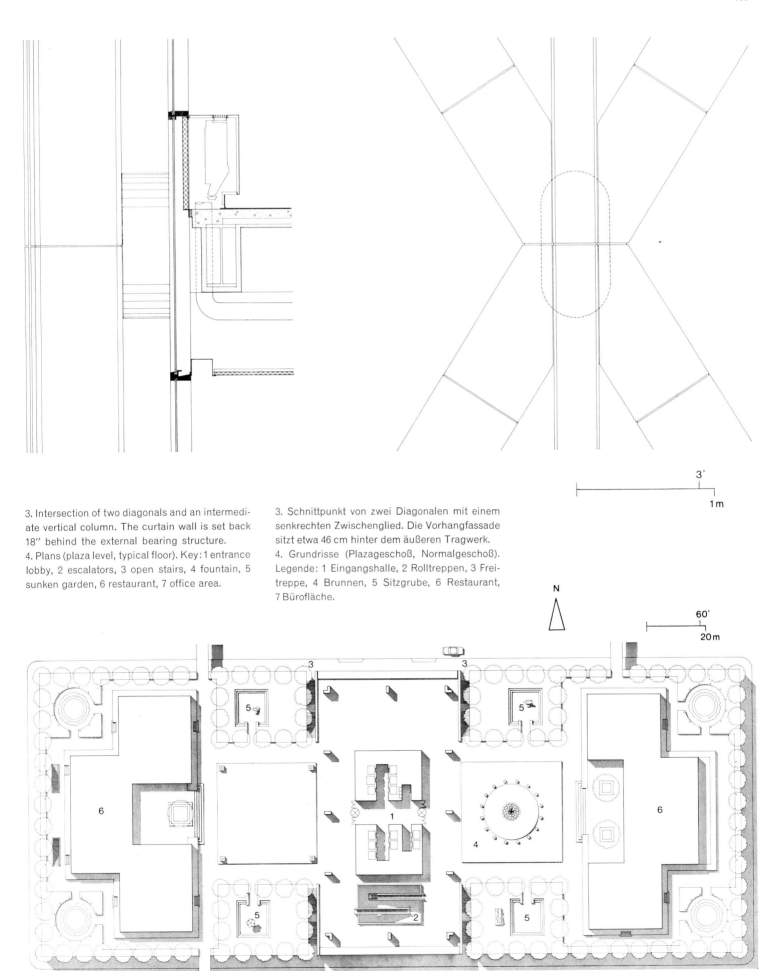

3'

1 m

3. Intersection of two diagonals and an intermediate vertical column. The curtain wall is set back 18″ behind the external bearing structure.
4. Plans (plaza level, typical floor). Key: 1 entrance lobby, 2 escalators, 3 open stairs, 4 fountain, 5 sunken garden, 6 restaurant, 7 office area.

3. Schnittpunkt von zwei Diagonalen mit einem senkrechten Zwischenglied. Die Vorhangfassade sitzt etwa 46 cm hinter dem äußeren Tragwerk.
4. Grundrisse (Plazageschoß, Normalgeschoß). Legende: 1 Eingangshalle, 2 Rolltreppen, 3 Freitreppe, 4 Brunnen, 5 Sitzgrube, 6 Restaurant, 7 Bürofläche.

N

60'

20 m

5. Corner office. In the background, right, is Telegraph Hill.
6. A view of the building from across the fountain. The claddings of the external bearing structure consist of bronze anodized aluminum; spandrels and glazing are of similarly colored or tinted glass.

5. Eckbüro. Rechts im Hintergrund der Telegraph Hill.
6. Blick über den Brunnen auf das Gebäude. Die Verkleidungen des äußeren Tragwerkes bestehen aus bronzefarben anodisiertem Aluminium, die Brüstungsplatten und Fensterscheiben aus in gleichem Ton eingefärbten, beziehungsweise getönten Glas.

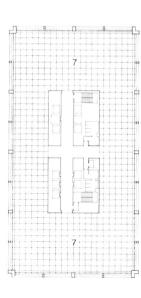

John Hancock Center, Chicago, Illinois

The John Hancock Center – known as "Big John" to the local population – is situated on North Michigan Avenue in a prestigious district with expensive apartments, shops, professional offices, hotels, restaurants, clubs and art galleries. The wish to continue this mixture – a pure office building initially contemplated was found to be unsuited if only because of the long distance from the nearest urban railways – gave rise, in the first planning phase, to the idea of using the site for a 70-story apartment tower and a 45-story, though equally high office tower. But the two towers would have occupied most of the site and would have impaired each other's privacy and daylight conditions. Moreover, the apartments on the lower floors would have suffered from the noise nuisance of the street. It was therefore decided to construct a single tower where the offices would be on the lower floors and the apartments on the higher floors.

The tapered shape of the tower was chosen in order to match the different floor space requirements which decrease from bottom to top – from the entrance and commercial zones at the base and the parking floors above them to the clusters of small apartments at medium height and finally to the large apartments on top where relatively less space is needed for ancillary rooms with artificial lighting.

Structurally, the exterior members of the steel frame represent a tube where the necessary stiffness is provided by diagonal members and by those structural floors which coincide with the intersections of the diagonals and the corner columns. In keeping with the functional organization, this tubular body has its largest cross-section where the stresses caused by wind forces are greatest. Steel consumption, amounting to about 30 lbs per sq ft of floor space, was no greater than for a 45- to 50-story tower of conventional type.

John Hancock Center, Chicago, Illinois

Das John Hancock Center – von den Chicagoern »Big John« genannt – liegt an der North Michigan Avenue, inmitten eines vornehmen Viertels mit teuren Apartments, Luxusläden, Kleinbüros, Hotels, Restaurants, Klubs und Kunstgalerien. Aus der Aufgabenstellung heraus, diese Funktionsmischung fortzuführen – ein reiner Bürobau, wie zu Beginn in Erwägung gezogen, erwies sich schon wegen der großen Entfernung zu Untergrundbahnlinien als ungünstig –, entstand in der ersten Planungsphase die Idee, das Grundstück mit einem 70geschossigen Apartmentblock und einem gleich hohen 45geschossigen Bürogebäude zu bebauen. Die beiden Türme hätten jedoch einen Großteil des zur Verfügung stehenden Geländes in Anspruch genommen, auch hätten sie sich gegenseitig Einsichtsmöglichkeiten geboten und beschattet. Außerdem wäre für die Apartments in den unteren Geschossen die Geräuschbelästigung von der Straße nachteilig gewesen. Man entschloß sich daher zu einem einzigen Gebäude und zur Anordnung der Apartments über den Büros.

Die Verjüngung nach oben ergab sich daraus, daß die Ansprüche der verschiedenen, in ihrer Abfolge von Nutzungszwängen bestimmten Einrichtungen an die Raumtiefe von unten nach oben abnimmt: Die durch eine Außenrampe erschlossenen Garagen über der Eingangs- und Geschäftszone benötigen mehr Tiefe als die darüberliegenden Büros, diese wiederum mehr als die folgenden Kleinapartments, und eine noch geringere Tiefe beanspruchen schließlich die großen Wohnungen im oberen Teil des Turms mit ihrem gegenüber den Kleinapartments geringeren relativen Flächenanteil an künstlich belichtbaren Nebenräumen.

Vom Tragverhalten her stellen die äußeren Glieder des Stahlskeletts ein Rohr dar, wobei die Diagonalen und die Decken in Höhe der Schnittpunkte dieser Diagonalen mit den Eckstützen für die notwendige Steifigkeit sorgen. In Übereinstimmung mit der funktionalen Organisation hat dieses Rohr dort den größten Querschnitt, wo auch die statische Beanspruchung durch Windkräfte am größten ist. Der Stahlverbrauch lag mit etwa 145 kg/qm nicht höher als bei einem 45- bis 50geschossigen Hochhaus konventioneller Bauart.

1. Site plan. Key: 1 court, 2 mechanical installations, 3 car ramp to garages, 4 service ramp, 5 club.
2. The tower is tapered from bottom to top in keeping with the functional requirements. Structurally, the exterior members of the steel frame represent a stiffened tube.

1. Lageplan. Legende: 1 Hof, 2 technische Räume, 3 Rampe zu den Garagen, 4 Anlieferung, 5 Klub.
2. Entsprechend den funktionellen Erfordernissen verjüngt sich der Turm von unten nach oben. Vom Tragverhalten her stellen die äußeren Glieder des Stahlskeletts ein steifes Rohr dar.

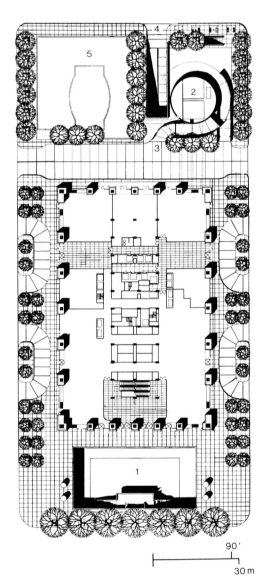

90'
30 m

Pages 164–165:
3. Rising to a height of about 1,100' (excluding the two television aerials), the tower occupies a dominant position on Chicago's skyline.

Seiten 164–165:
3. Mit einer Höhe von etwa 340 m (ohne die beiden Fernsehantennen) nimmt der Bau innerhalb der Skyline Chicagos eine beherrschende Stellung ein.

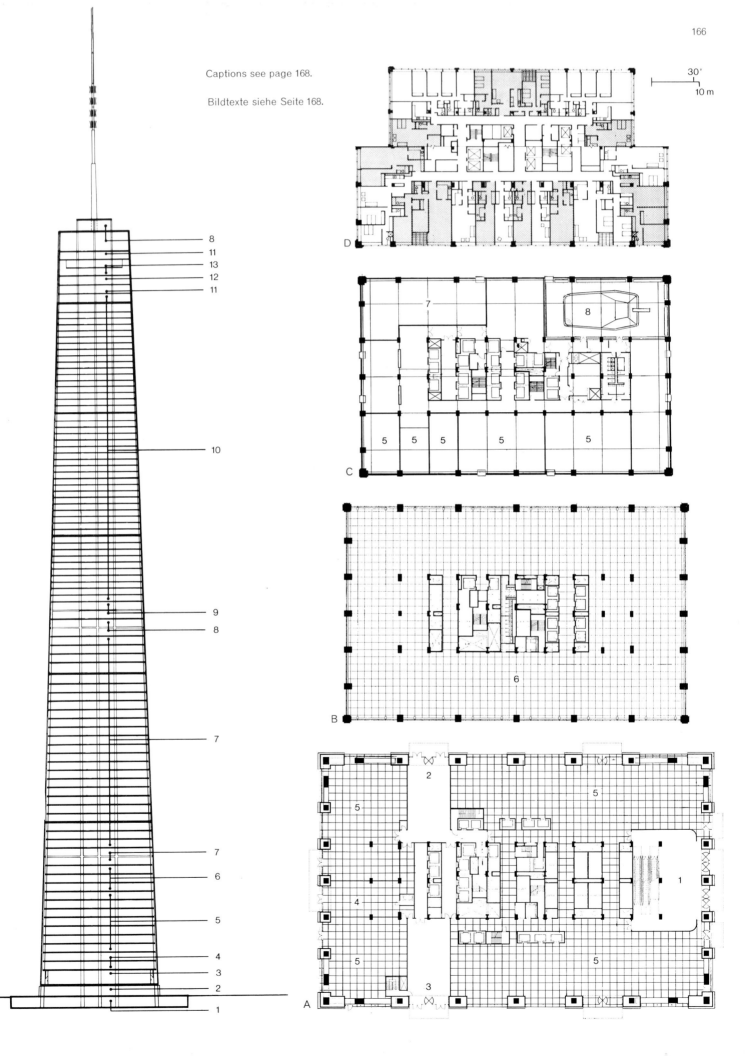

Captions see page 168.

Bildtexte siehe Seite 168.

30'
10 m

Pages 166–167:

4. Section. Key: 1 commercial and service spaces, 2 main lobbies and commercial spaces, 3 office lobby and commercial spaces, 4 commercial spaces, 5 parking, 6 offices, 7 mechanical equipment and offices, 8 mechanical equipment, 9 "sky" lobby, swimming pool, restaurant and shops, 10 apartments, 11 television rooms, 12 observatory, 13 restaurant.

5. Plans (A street level, B typical office floor, C transit floor, D apartment floors). Key: 1 office lobby, 2 restaurant lobby, 3 apartment lobby, 4 car lobby, 5 shops, 6 office area, 7 restaurant, 8 swimming pool.

6. The entrance floor is clad with travertine.

Seiten 166–167:

4. Schnitt. Legende: 1 Geschäfts- und Nebenräume, 2 Hauptzugänge und Geschäftsräume, 3 Büro-Lobby und Geschäftsräume, 4 Geschäftsräume, 5 Parkplätze, 6 Büros, 7 technische Räume und Büros, 8 technische Räume, 9 »Sky«-Lobby, Schwimmbad, Restaurant und Läden, 10 Apartments, 11 Räume für das Fernsehen, 12 Observatorium, 13 Restaurant.

5. Grundrisse (A Straßengeschoß, B typisches Bürogeschoß, C Transitgeschoß, D Apartmentgeschosse). Legende: 1 Eingang zu den Büros, 2 Eingang zu den Restaurants, 3 Eingang zu den Apartments, 4 Eingang für Autofahrer, 5 Läden, 6 Bürofläche, 7 Restaurant, 8 Schwimmbad.

6. Das Straßengeschoß des Gebäudes ist mit Travertin verkleidet.

7. Living room in one of the apartments. In designing the layout of the apartments, a point was made not to place small rooms near the diagonals.
8. Office lobby on the 2nd floor.
9. "Sky" lobby on the transit floor between offices and apartments.

7. Blick in den Wohnraum eines Apartments. Bei der Festlegung der Wohnungs-Grundrisse wurde darauf geachtet, daß im Bereich der Diagonalen keine kleinen Räume liegen.
8. Büro-Lobby im 1. Obergeschoß.
9. »Sky«-Lobby im Transitgeschoß zwischen den Büros und Apartments.

Sears Tower, Chicago, Illinois. Under construction

The site on which the Sears Tower is being erected covers an area of about 129,000 sq ft in a rapidly developing business district at the western edge of the Loop. The gross floor area of the nearly 1,470' high tower – about 4,400,000 sq ft spread over four sub-surface levels and 109 stories – is the largest in any single building in the world, with the exception of the Pentagon. The owner is Sears, Roebuck and Co., the department stores combine whose offices are at present still spread over the entire Chicago area. Initially the owner will only use about 7,000 out of the 16,500 workplaces in the tower for their own requirements.

The space below plaza level will contain commercial areas, a cafeteria with 1200 seats, service areas and – with direct access from the lower level of Wacker Drive on the west side of the block – a loading dock capable of handling 17 trucks at one time.

The tower is composed, in plan, of column-free squares of 75' side length. The first 49 floors which contain the owner's offices, requiring large floor areas, form a solid block of nine squares. Higher up, the tower is "stepped back" with two of the corner squares omitted from the 50th to the 66th floor, the two other corner squares from the 67th to the 90th floor, and a further three squares – leaving no more than two residual squares – from the 91st to the 109th floor. This design was primarily adopted because of the difficulty of renting floor areas of the great depth required by the owners themselves.

The squares are surrounded on all sides by columns spaced at 15' which take part in a cellular-tube frame. As it was not permissible to block the passages between the different units, it was decided not to stabilize them against horizontal forces by means of diagonal members as was done, for instance, in the case of the John Hancock Center. It was therefore necessary to use the more expensive method of rigid joints between columns and floor beams. The steel framework, preassembled in sections extending over several floors, has a cladding of black anodized aluminum and bronze tinted glass.

Sears Tower, Chicago, Illinois. Im Bau

Das Grundstück, auf dem der Komplex im Augenblick errichtet wird, hat eine Größe von etwa 12000 qm. Es liegt am westlichen Rande der Loop in einem sich schnell entwickelnden Geschäftsgebiet. Mit einer Gesamtfläche von etwa 410000 qm in vier Sockelgeschossen und einem 109geschossigen, knapp 450 m hohen Turm wird dieses Bürogebäude in seiner Größe nur vom Pentagon, dem amerikanischen Verteidigungsministerium, übertroffen. Bauherr ist der Warenhauskonzern Sears, Roebuck and Co., dessen Büros im Augenblick noch über das ganze Stadtgebiet verteilt sind. Vorerst werden von den 16500 Arbeitsplätzen nur etwa 7000 vom Bauherrn beansprucht.

In den Sockelgeschossen befinden sich Läden, eine Cafeteria mit 1200 Plätzen, Nebenräume und – mit direkter Zufahrt von der unteren Ebene des im Westen vorbeiführenden zweigeschossigen Wacker Drive – ein Ladedock, an dem gleichzeitig 17 Lastwagen abgefertigt werden können.

Der nach oben zurückgestufte Turm ist im Grundriß aus stützenfreien Quadratfeldern mit einer Seitenlänge von etwa 22,80 m zusammengesetzt. Die ersten 49 Geschosse bilden einen homogenen Block aus neun Quadraten. Hier befinden sich die Büros des Bauherrn, für die große zusammenhängende Flächen gefordert waren. Vom 50. bis zum 66. Geschoß fallen zwei, vom 67. bis zum 90. die restlichen zwei Eckquadrate weg, und vom 91. bis zum 109. Geschoß bleiben schließlich noch zwei Quadrate übrig. Man entschloß sich zu der Rückstufung der oberen Geschosse vor allem deswegen, weil sich sehr tiefe Büroräume, wie sie der Bauherr für sich selbst gefordert hatte, nur schwer vermieten lassen.

Die Grundrißeinheiten werden allseitig von Stützen mit Achsabständen von etwa 4,57 m, die Teil eines zellularen Rohrtragwerks sind, umschlossen. Da die Durchgänge zwischen den einzelnen Einheiten nicht verbaut werden durften, war es nicht möglich, die Rohrwände – wie beim John Hancock Center – durch Diagonalen gegen Horizontalkräfte zu stabilisieren; man mußte vielmehr zu der konstruktiv aufwendigeren Methode greifen, die Knotenpunkte zwischen Stützen und Deckenträgern biegesteif auszubilden. Die äußere Verkleidung des in mehrgeschossigen Einheiten vorgefertigten Stahltragwerks besteht aus schwarz anodisiertem Aluminium und bronzefarben getöntem Glas.

1. View from southeast of the "stepped-back" tower (model). The plan is composed of column-free squares of 75' side length. The first 49 stories form a solid block of nine squares; two corner squares are omitted from the 50th to the 66th floor, two further corner squares from the 67th to the 90th floor, and three more squares – leaving only two residual squares – from the 91st to the 109th floor.

1. Blick von Südosten auf den nach oben zurückgestuften Turm (Modell). Der Grundriß baut sich auf stützenfreien Quadratfeldern mit einer Seitenlänge von etwa 22,80 m auf. Die ersten 49 Geschosse bilden einen homogenen Block aus neun Quadraten, vom 50. bis zum 66. Geschoß fallen zwei, vom 67. bis zum 90. die restlichen zwei Eckquadrate weg, und vom 91. bis zum 109. Geschoß bleiben schließlich noch zwei Quadrate übrig.

173

2–5. Views of the tower from different directions
(model).
6. Plans (A entrance level, B mezzanine level,
C 50th floor, D 67th floor, E 91st to 101st floor).

2–5. Ansichten des Turms aus verschiedenen
Richtungen (Modell).
6. Grundrisse (A Eingangsgeschoß, B Mezzaningeschoß, C 50. Geschoß, D 67. Geschoß, E 91.
bis 101. Geschoß).

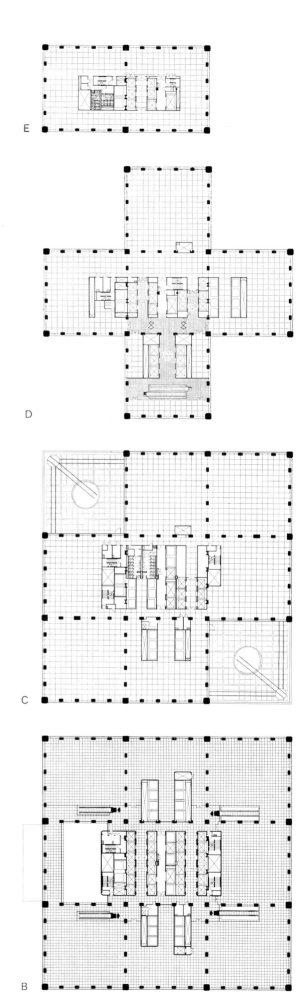

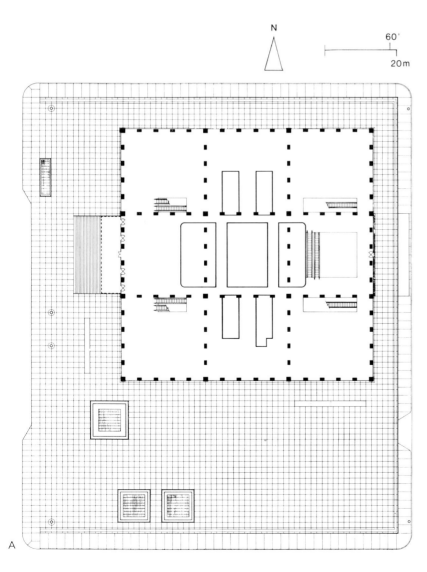

One Shell Plaza, Houston, Texas

With its fifty stories, this office tower is the tallest reinforced concrete building in the world. It is situated on a podium raised by 4' above the ground on a site facing the City Hall Park. The Shell Oil Company is the principal tenant.

On the three lowest levels are storage areas and parking facilities for 365 cars. The "Mall" level immediately below the podium contains shops, cafeteria, loading bays and a post office, and is connected by a tunnel to the existing network of downtown sub-surface shopping arcades. At podium level are the entrance lobbies on the long sides and exhibition areas on the short sides of the tower. The mezzanine level directly above the podium is taken up by banking facilities. On the following 42 floors are freely divisible office areas, averaging 20,000 sq ft each. On the three top floors are a club, a restaurant and an observation gallery.

The structural design of the tower is based on a "tube within a tube" concept. The outer tube is composed of a series of closely-spaced columns and high spandrel beams. The increased depth of columns at eight points around the building provides supplementary wind stiffening while conveying the impression of undulated walls and giving indication of the unconventional system of statics. The inner tube is formed by the core shear walls enclosing building services and elevator shafts. With a maximum deflection from the vertical of 1/1,300th of its height, the tower has an extremely high stability. Even so, it was possible to construct it at the unit price of a conventional 35-story structure. The weight of the tower is spread by means of an about 8' thick, "floating" concrete pad. The need for expensive waterproofing was eliminated by the installation of a special draining system which keeps the water table permanently below the critical level.

The exterior of the building is sheathed in Italian travertine; the windows are glazed with bronze tinted glass; internal partitions are of gypsum.

One Shell Plaza, Houston, Texas

Mit 50 Geschossen ist dieser Büroturm das höchste Stahlleichtbetongebäude der Welt. Er liegt gegenüber dem Stadtpark auf einem um etwa 1,20 m angehobenen Podium. Hauptmieter ist die Shell Oil Company.

In den unteren drei Untergeschossen befinden sich Lagerräume und Parkplätze für 365 Autos, während auf der »Mall«-Ebene, dem Geschoß unmittelbar unter dem Podium, Läden, eine Cafeteria, Laderampen und ein Postamt untergebracht sind. Die Mall ist durch einen Tunnel an das unterirdische Netz innerstädtischer Ladenpassagen angeschlossen. Das Eingangsgeschoß auf dem Podium enthält Lobbies an den Längs- und Ausstellungsflächen an den Querseiten; im darüberliegenden Mezzaningeschoß hat sich eine Bank eingerichtet. Die folgenden 42 Geschosse bieten frei unterteilbare Büroflächen mit einer Größe von jeweils etwa 1850 qm. In den oberen drei Geschossen befinden sich ein Klub, ein Restaurant und eine Aussichtsplattform.

Für das Tragwerk des Gebäudes wurde eine »Rohr-in-Rohr«-Konstruktion gewählt. Das äußere Rohr ist in eng gestellte Stützen und hohe Deckenrandbalken aufgelöst; Verstärkungen, die die Standfestigkeit der Struktur gegenüber Windbelastung erhöhen, verleihen ihm einen leicht schwingenden Umriß und bringen zugleich zum Ausdruck, daß hier andere als die vertrauten statischen Verhältnisse vorliegen. Das innere Rohr wird von den Wänden gebildet, die den Versorgungs- und Aufzugskern umgeben. Mit einer maximalen Ablenkung der Gebäudespitze aus der Vertikalen von 1/1300 der Gebäudehöhe besitzt das Tragwerk eine extrem große Steifigkeit. Trotzdem waren seine Baukosten, bezogen auf die gleiche Einheit, nicht höher als bei einem 35geschossigen Gebäude konventioneller Bauart. Zur Verteilung der Lasten des Turmes auf den Untergrund dient eine »schwimmende« Betonplatte mit einer Dicke von etwa 2,50 m. Aufwendige Grundwasserabdichtungen umging man durch die Installation eines besonderen Entwässerungssystems, das den Wasserstand ständig unter der für das Gebäude kritischen Höhe hält.

Die Außenflächen des Gebäudes bestehen aus italienischem Travertin und bronzefarben getöntem Glas, die inneren Trennwände aus Gips.

1. The tower, seen from the City Hall Park. The structure is a "tube within a tube", with the outer tube composed of closely-spaced columns and high spandrel beams. Deeper columns at eight points provide additional wind bracing for enhanced stability while conveying the impression of an undulating wall.

1. Blick vom Stadtpark auf das Gebäude. Das Tragwerk ist eine »Rohr-in-Rohr«-Konstruktion. Das äußere Rohr ist in eng gestellte Stützen und hohe Deckenrandbalken aufgelöst; Verstärkungen zur Erhöhung der Standfestigkeit der Struktur gegenüber Windbelastung verleihen ihm einen leicht schwingenden Umriß.

2. Banking facilities on mezzanine level.
3. Plans (podium level; typical floor). Key: 1 lobby,
2 exhibition area, 3 core, 4 office area.
4. View, across the City Hall Park, of the northwest side of the building.

2. Bankhalle im Mezzaningeschoß.
3. Grundrisse (Podiumsgeschoß, Normalgeschoß).
Legende: 1 Lobby, 2 Ausstellungsfläche, 3 Kern,
4 Bürofläche.
4. Blick über den Stadtpark hinweg auf die Nordwestseite des Gebäudes.

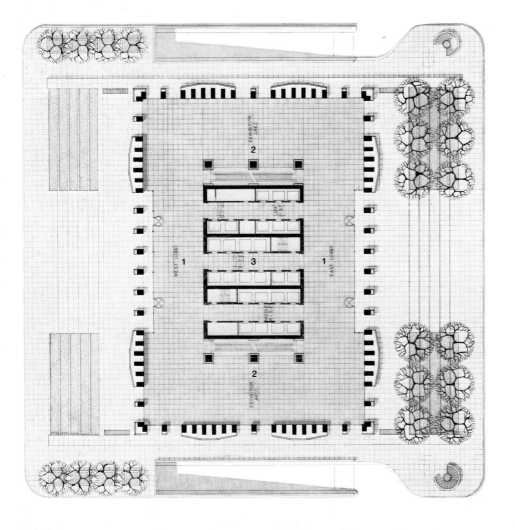

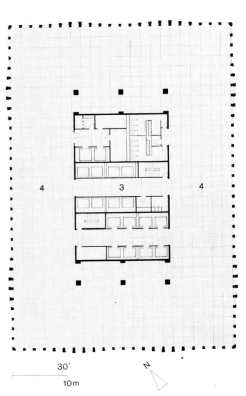

30'
10m

Albright Knox Art Gallery, Buffalo, New York

It was the intention in designing the new wing to enhance and preserve the appearance of the earlier neoclassic marble building designed by Edward B. Green in 1905. This has been achieved by containing all the new spaces – except the transparent glass cubes of auditorium and vestibule – within marble walls which extend from the base of the original building.

The center of the new wing is a large outdoor sculpture courtyard which is on axis with the entrance and enclosed by two exhibition galleries, an office wing and a cafeteria. On its south side, placed several steps lower than the courtyard, is a large exhibition gallery which can be partitioned at will by movable screens. Above the gallery is the auditorium which has a seating capacity of 350 people. The glass walls of the auditorium are of dark grey glass permitting the use of the projector even in daytime without having to draw the curtains.

The entrance to the museum was moved to the new wing so that it could be at ground level. The existing building and the new wing were connected where they overlapped by a large stairway ascending in a two-story well.

Albright Knox Art Gallery, Buffalo, New York

Beherrschend beim Entwurf des Neubaus war der Wunsch, die Wirkung des im Jahr 1905 von Edward B. Green entworfenen Nachbargebäudes nicht anzutasten. Man erreichte dies, indem man alle Räume bis auf die entmaterialisierten Glaskuben des Auditoriums und des Windfangs hinter geschlossenen, am Sockel des Altbaus anschließenden Marmorwänden verbarg.

Mittelpunkt des Neubaus ist ein großer Skulpturenhof. Er liegt axial vor dem Eingang und wird von zwei Ausstellungsgalerien, einem Bürotrakt und einer Cafeteria umgeben. Im Süden schließt sich ein großer, um mehrere Stufen abgesenkter Ausstellungssaal an, der durch bewegliche Stellwände beliebig unterteilt werden kann. Über dem Ausstellungssaal thront das 350 Plätze fassende, in seiner Grundfläche fast genau dem Hof entsprechende Auditorium, im rückwärtigen Teil von zwei kräftigen Kreuzstützen aus Stahl, im vorderen Teil von einem in den Ausstellungs- und Bühnennebenräumen verborgenen Rahmenwerk gehalten. Die Glaswände des Auditoriums sind so dunkel getönt, daß man die Projektionsanlage auch am Tage benutzen kann, ohne die Vorhänge zuziehen zu müssen.

Gemeinsamer Besucherzugang zu beiden Bauteilen ist heute der ebenerdig zu betretende Haupteingang des Neubaus; der Altbau wird von diesem aus über eine in seiner Südwestecke angelegten Treppe erschlossen.

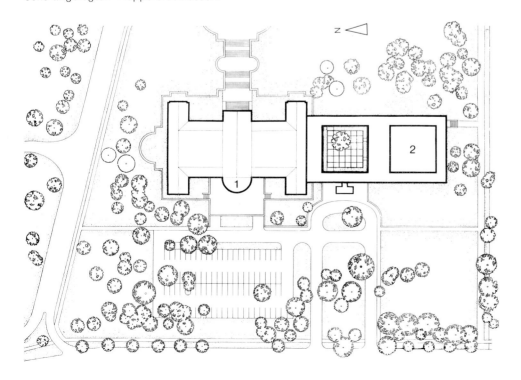

1. Site plan. Key: 1 original building, 2 new wing.
2. View of the museum at night, seen from northwest. The glass-encased auditorium and the new vestibule are the only parts to protrude beyond the marble walls of the new wing which extend the base of the original building.
3. Plans of new wing (ground floor, upper floor). Key: 1 vestibule, 2 gallery, 3 stairs to galleries in original building, 4 cloakroom, 5 offices, 6 sculpture courtyard, 7 dining room, 8 kitchen, 9 stairs to auditorium, 10 exhibition gallery, 11 auditorium.

1. Lageplan. Legende: 1 altes Gebäude, 2 Anbau.
2. Nachtansicht von Nordwesten. Nur das rundum verglaste Auditorium und der neue Eingang heben sich von den geschlossenen, marmorverkleideten Wänden des Flachbaus ab, die den Sockel der alten Architektur fortsetzen.
3. Grundrisse des Anbaus (Erdgeschoß, Obergeschoß). Legende: 1 Windfang, 2 Galerie, 3 Treppe zu den Ausstellungsräumen im alten Gebäude, 4 Garderobe, 5 Büros, 6 Skulpturenhof, 7 Speiseraum, 8 Küche, 9 Treppen zum Auditorium, 10 Ausstellungssaal, 11 Auditorium.

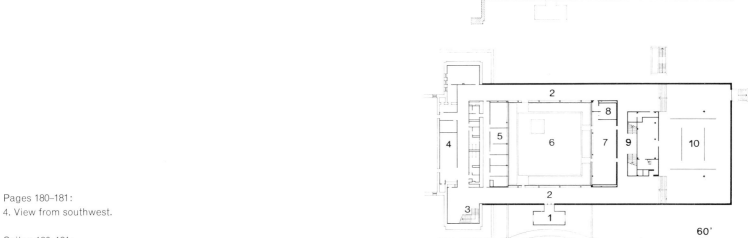

Pages 180–181:
4. View from southwest.

Seiten 180–181:
4. Ansicht von Südwesten.

60'

20 m

5. Exhibition gallery on the entrance side, with the sculpture courtyard on the left.
6. The exhibition gallery below the auditorium is placed several steps below the level of the courtyard and can be partitioned at will. The grid pattern of the ceiling supplies air and electricity.

5. Die auf der Eingangsseite liegende Ausstellungsgalerie. Links der Skulpturenhof.
6. Der Saal unterhalb des Auditoriums ist um mehrere Stufen abgesenkt. Die festen Außenwände werden von runden, in der Decke eingelassenen Leuchten, die beweglichen Trennwände von Leuchten, die an Lichtschienen hängen, erhellt.

7. The auditorium has a capacity of 350 people. The dark grey glass walls permit the use of the projector even in daytime without the necessity of drawing the curtains.
8. The sculpture courtyard is flanked on one side by the auditorium and on the other side by the imposing columned facade of the older building so that an interesting contrast is created.

7. Das Auditorium faßt 350 Personen. Dunkelgrau getöntes Sonnenschutzglas erlaubt den Betrieb der Projektionsanlage auch bei Tage, ohne daß die Vorhänge zugezogen werden müssen.
8. Der Skulpturenhof wird auf der einen Seite vom Auditorium, auf der anderen Seite von einer imposanten Säulenfront des Altbaus gefaßt. Hierdurch entsteht ein spannungsreicher Kontrast.

Joseph H. Hirshhorn Museum and Sculpture Garden, Washington, D. C.
Under construction

The building is to be a public museum under the administration of the Smithsonian Institution, serving as a permanent home for the collection of contemporary art assembled by
Joseph H. Hirshhorn and presented to the American people.

The site made available by Congress crosses the Mall, the great linear park through central
Washington terminated in the east by the Capitol and the west by the Lincoln Memorial to
form a cross axis at the point where the mall widens with the National Archives. One important object of the architects was to avoid any interruption of the visual continuity of the
central lawn of the Mall. Their solution was to place the massive cylinder with the enclosed
exhibition galleries in a position behind the building line of the south side of the Mall with
a sunken sculpture garden penetrating the tree border of the Mall and continuing the line
of the cross axis.

The cylinder, covered in granite aggregate precast concrete and surrounded by a walled
courtyard measuring 360′ × 330′, rests on four monumental supports which with their deep-
cut sculptured ribs merge in a continuous flow with the exposed ceiling structure below
the second floor. Apart from a balcony at third floor level which provides a view on to the
sculpture garden and Mall, the upper floors are without fenestration on the outside. Colon-
naded glass walls open to an eccentrically placed circular inner court.

The visitor enters the museum through the glass-enclosed lobby. From this lobby, escalators
descend to the lower floor which contains gallery space for changing exhibits, an auditorium
seating 280 people, as well as service rooms. Other escalators ascend to the galleries on the
second and third floors. Access to the offices and research areas on the fourth floor is by
elevator connecting also to the lower level service areas. Elevators and emergency stairs
are within the four massive supports.

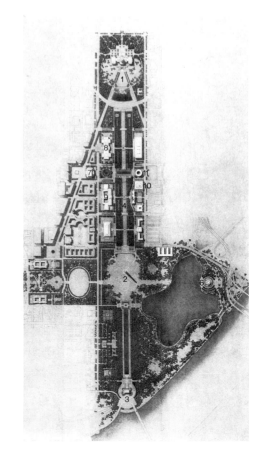

1. Plan of the Washington Mall. Key: 1 Capitol
2 Washington Monument, 3 Lincoln Memorial,
4 Mall, 5 White House, 6 Jefferson Memorial, 7
National Archives, 8 National Gallery of Art, 9
Museum of Natural History, 10 Smithsonian Institution, 11 Joseph H. Hirshhorn Museum.
2. Cross-section of the museum. In the center
Jefferson Drive, on the left the sunken sculpture
garden in the tree border of the Mall.

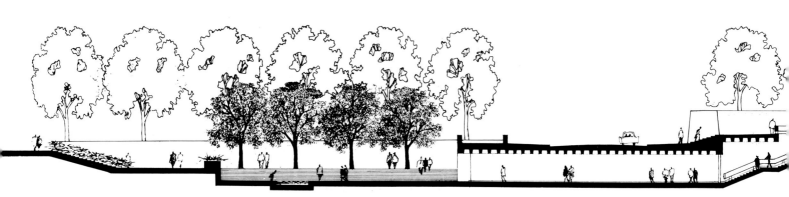

Joseph H. Hirshhorn Museum and Sculpture Garden, Washington, D.C. Im Bau

Der Bau ist dazu bestimmt, als öffentliches Museum unter der Obhut der Smithsonian Institution die von Joseph H. Hirshhorn zusammengetragene und dem amerikanischen Volk gestiftete Sammlung zeitgenössischer Kunst aufzunehmen.

Das vom Kongreß zur Verfügung gestellte Grundstück kreuzt das östliche Stück der Mall, der vom Capitol über das Washington Monument bis zum Lincoln Memorial reichenden Ost-West-Achse des Regierungs- und Museumsviertels, auf der Höhe der etwas zurückgesetzten National Archives. Eine wichtige Aufgabe bestand für die Architekten darin, die Mall in ihrer visuellen Kontinuität nicht zu unterbrechen. Sie ließen daher den gedrungenen Betonzylinder mit den geschlossenen Ausstellungsflächen in der Flucht der die Mall im Süden begrenzenden Gebäudekette und stießen nur mit dem abgesenkten Skulpturengarten in den Freiraum vor.

Der von einer etwa 110 × 100 m großen Plattform umgebene Zylinder ruht auf vier monumentalen Pfeilern, die mit den tiefen, plastisch durchgebildeten Rippen der Decke unter dem 1. Obergeschoß eine formale Einheit bilden. Nach außen sind die oberen Geschosse bis auf einen Aussichtsbalkon im 2. Obergeschoß, von dem man auf den Skulpturengarten und die Mall hinabblicken kann, völlig geschlossen; alle Räume öffnen sich auf einen exzentrisch plazierten runden Innenhof.

Als Besucher betritt man das Museum durch eine verglaste Eingangshalle im Erdgeschoß. Von hier führen Rolltreppen hinab in das Untergeschoß, das Räume für Wechselausstellungen, ein Auditorium mit 280 Plätzen und Serviceeinrichtungen enthält, sowie hinauf in die umlaufenden Galerien des 1. und 2. Obergeschosses. Die Verwaltungs- und Forschungsräume im 3. Obergeschoß erreicht man über Aufzugs- und Treppenkerne, die im Erdgeschoß in die vier Pfeiler hineinmodelliert sind.

1. Ausschnitt aus dem Regierungs- und Museumsviertel von Washington. Legende: 1 Capitol, 2 Washington Monument, 3 Lincoln Memorial, 4 Mall, 5 White House, 6 Jefferson Memorial, 7 National Archives, 8 National Gallery of Art, 9 Museum of Natural History, 10 Smithsonian Institution, 11 Joseph H. Hirshhorn Museum.
2. Schnitt durch das Museum. In der Mitte der Jefferson Drive, links der abgesenkte, in die Mall vorstoßende Skulpturengarten.

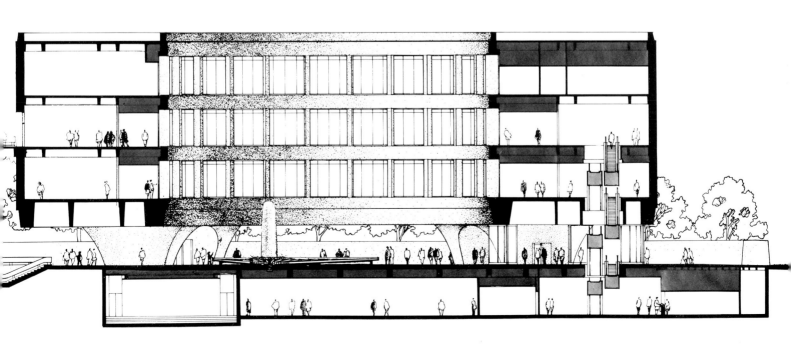

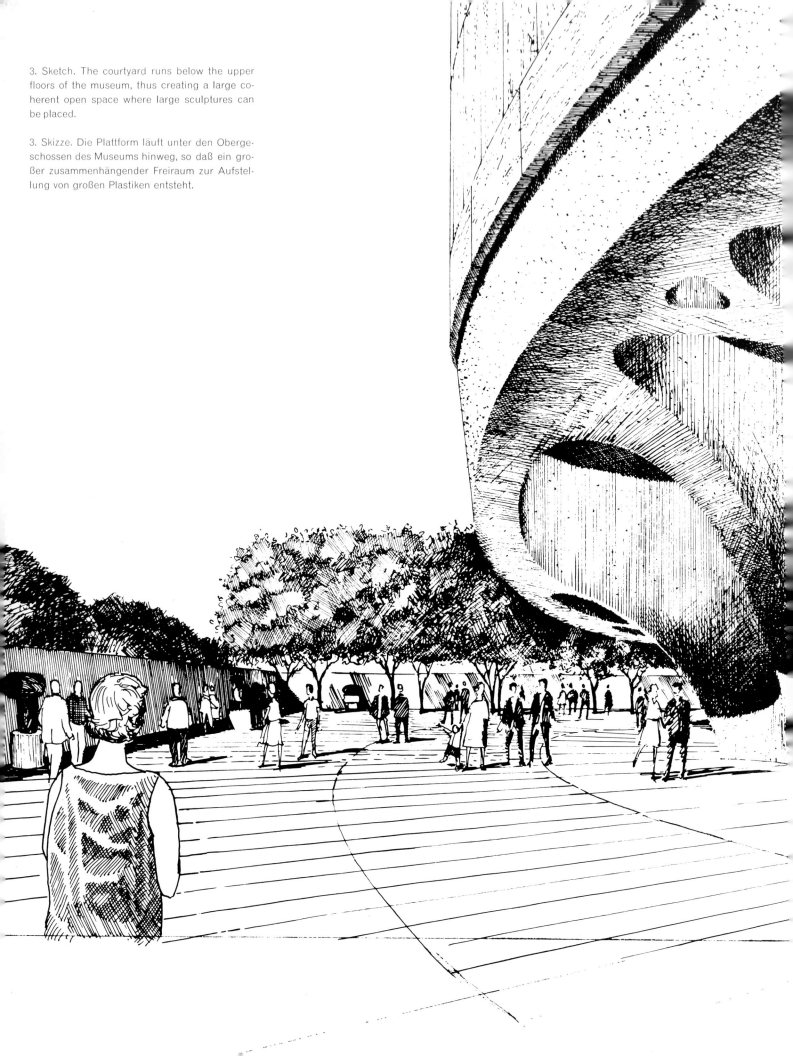

3. Sketch. The courtyard runs below the upper floors of the museum, thus creating a large coherent open space where large sculptures can be placed.

3. Skizze. Die Plattform läuft unter den Obergeschossen des Museums hinweg, so daß ein großer zusammenhängender Freiraum zur Aufstellung von großen Plastiken entsteht.

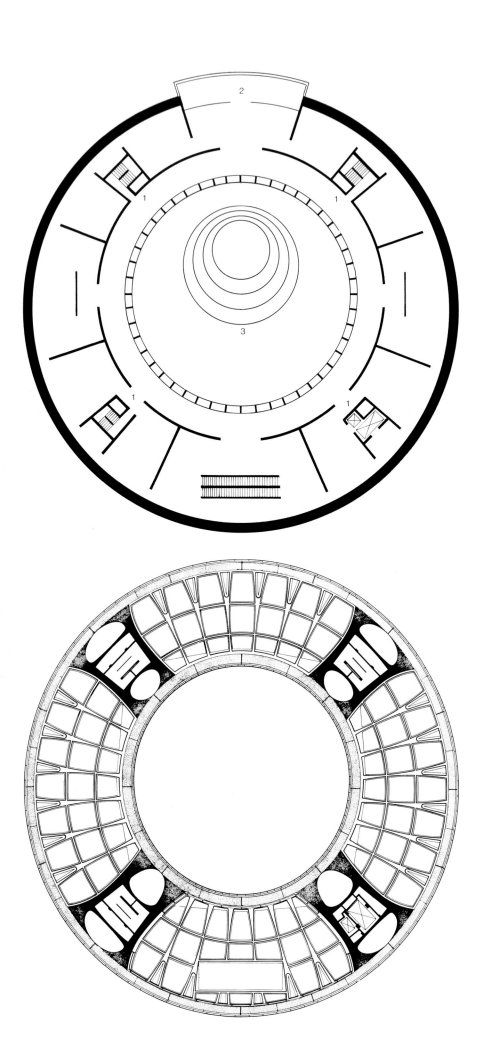

4. Plan (3rd floor). Key: 1 core with elevator and stairs, 2 viewing balcony, 3 central court.
5. Underside of the exposed ceiling below the 2nd floor. The four monumental supports of the building merge in continuous flow with the deep-cut ribs of the ceiling.
6. Site plan. Key: 1 Jefferson Drive, 2 sculpture garden, 3 museum, 4 central court.

4. Grundriß (2. Obergeschoß). Legende: 1 Erschließungskern, 2 Aussichtsbalkon, 3 Innenhof.
5. Spiegel der Decke unter dem 1. Obergeschoß. Die vier monumentalen Pfeiler, auf denen der Bau ruht, bilden mit den tiefen Deckenrippen eine formale Einheit.
6. Lageplan. Legende: 1 Jefferson Drive, 2 Skulpturengarten, 3 Museum, 4 Innenhof.

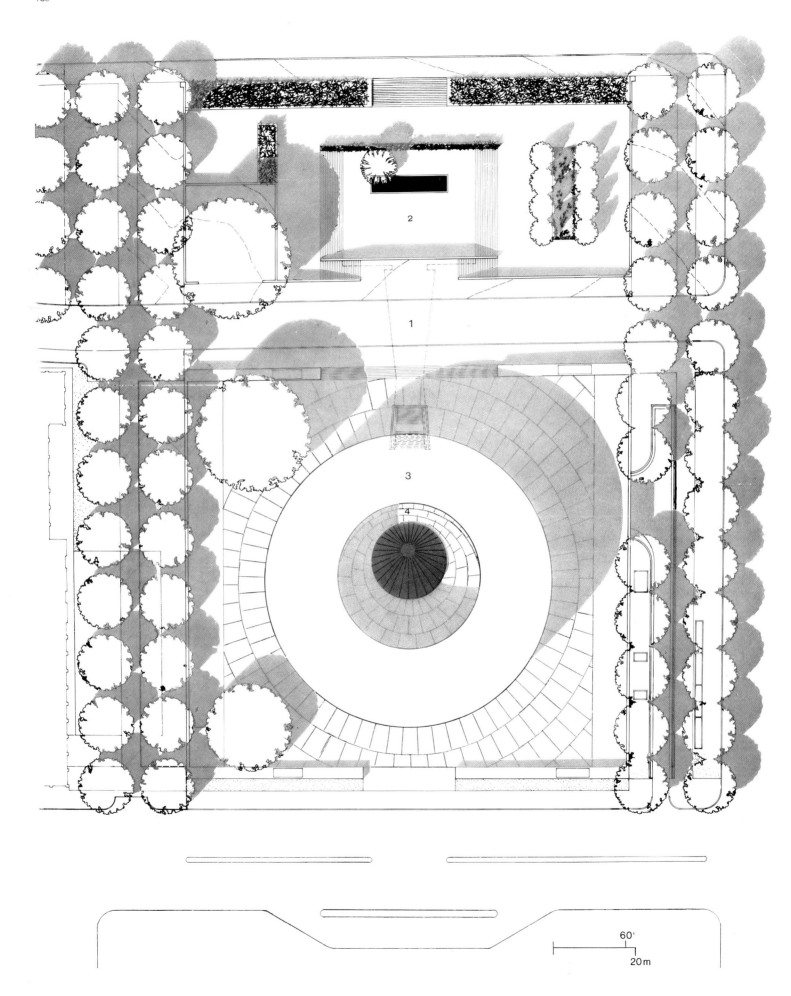

60'

20m

Beinecke Rare Book and Manuscript Library, Yale University, New Haven, Connecticut

All that can be seen of this library, which houses one of the most famous American collections of rare books and manuscripts from the outside is a plaza and a large exhibition hall above an entrance lobby. All other spaces are placed below the plaza, light and too dry an atmosphere being deleterious to the preservation of books and manuscripts.
Below the plaza are two stories. The lower one contains mechanical equipment and a large book stack space, the upper one, an additional smaller stack space, catalog and reference room as well as a reading room and staff offices, around a sunken court designed by Isamu Noguchi. The entrance lobby at plaza level is glass-enclosed and upon entering reveals the vast exhibition hall. Wide twin flights of stairs connect both the floor below and the exhibition balcony above. In the center of the space of the exhibition hall are six stories of illuminated book stacks storing 180,000 volumes out of the total of 820,000 volumes and separated from the hall by glass walls.
The structural facade of the exhibition hall consists of Vierendeel trusses which transfer their loads to four massive corner columns. The trusses are 50' high, and respectively, 88' and 131' long and are composed of prefabricated, tapered steel crosses which are covered with grey granite on the outside and with precast granite aggregate concrete on the inside. Fitted into the bays between these crosses are $1\frac{1}{4}''$ thick panels of white, translucent marble which filter the light and protect the precious books against the sun.
The building is equipped with two independent air-conditioning systems, one for the book stacks and one for all the other rooms.

Beinecke Rare Book and Manuscript Library, Yale University, New Haven, Connecticut

Von der eine der berühmtesten amerikanischen Sammlungen seltener Bücher und Manuskripte beherbergenden Bibliothek tritt nach außen nur eine Plattform sowie die große Ausstellungshalle mit dem daruntergesetzten Eingangsfoyer in Erscheinung; alle übrigen Einrichtungen wurden, um die dem Auge sich darbietende Baumasse möglichst klein zu halten, unter die Plattform verbannt.
Der von der Plattform abgedeckte Bereich umfaßt zwei Stockwerke; im unteren liegen technische Anlagen und ein großes Büchermagazin, im oberen neben einem weiteren, kleineren Magazin zwei Räume mit Katalogen und Bibliographien sowie, um den von Isamu Noguchi gestalteten Hof herum, der Lesesaal und die Verwaltungsräume. Die auf der Plattformebene angeordnete Eingangshalle ist nach außen voll verglast und sowohl mit dem 1. Untergeschoß als auch mit der Empore, über der sich die Ausstellungshalle erhebt, durch eine großzügige Doppeltreppenanlage optisch eng verbunden. Die Ausstellungshalle gliedert sich in einen freien Außenraum und einen mit Glaswänden von diesem getrennten sechsgeschossigen Kern, der etwa 180000 der insgesamt etwa 820000 Bände aufnimmt.
Die seitliche Begrenzung der Ausstellungshalle besteht aus Pfostenfachwerkträgern, die ihre Lasten über die Empore auf vier mächtige Eckpfeiler abgeben. Die Träger sind etwa 15 m hoch und etwa 27 m, beziehungsweise etwa 40 m lang. Die vorgefertigten, sich zu den Spitzen hin verjüngenden Stahlkreuze, aus denen sie sich zusammensetzen, wurden außen mit grauem Granit und innen mit vorgefertigten Betonelementen verkleidet. In den Zwischenfeldern sitzen etwa 3 cm dicke Tafeln aus weißem, durchscheinendem Marmor, die das Licht filtern und die kostbaren Bücher vor direkter Sonneneinstrahlung schützen.
Das Gebäude besitzt zwei voneinander unabhängige Klimaanlagen: eine für die Büchermagazine und eine für die übrigen Räume.

1. A view of the exhibition hall with the glass-encased, separately air-conditioned book stack. Illumination has been kept low to give full effect to the warm tones of the daylight filtering through the marble panels.

1. Blick in die Ausstellungshalle mit dem verglasten, gesondert klimatisierten Bücherturm. Die Ausleuchtung ist sehr zurückhaltend, um das durch die Marmorplatten gefilterte Tageslicht in seinen warmen Tönen voll zur Wirkung kommen zu lassen.

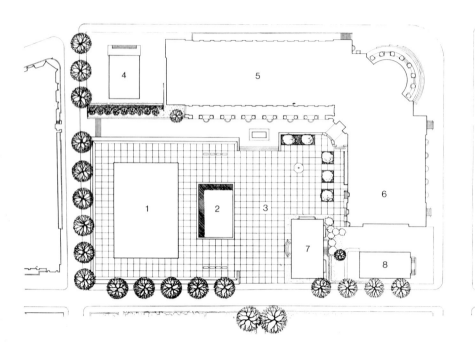

2. Site plan. Key: 1 exhibition hall of the library, 2 sunken court, 3 plaza, 4 Book & Snake Society, 5 University Dining Hall, 6 Woolsey Hall, 7 Woodbridge Hall, 8 Scroll & Key Society.
3. Plans (A court level, B plaza level, C exhibition balcony) and section. Key: 1 sunken court, 2 curators' offices, 3 reading room, 4 cataloging room, 5 catalog and reference books, 6 book stacks, 7 entrance lobby, 8 book stack, 9 exhibition balcony, 10 mechanical equipment.

2. Lageplan. Legende: 1 Ausstellungshalle der Bibliothek, 2 abgesenkter Hof, 3 Plattform, 4 Book & Snake Society, 5 University Dining Hall, 6 Woolsey Hall, 7 Woodbridge Hall, 8 Scroll & Key Society.
3. Grundrisse (A Hofebene, B Plattformebene, C Emporenebene) und Schnitt. Legende: 1 abgesenkter Hof, 2 Kuratorenbüros, 3 Lesesaal, 4 allgemeiner Katalog, 5 Manuskriptkatalog und Bibliographien, 6 Magazin, 7 Eingangsfoyer, 8 Bücherturm, 9 Empore, 10 technische Anlagen.

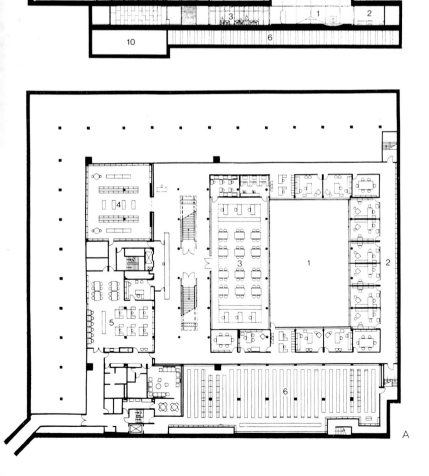

A

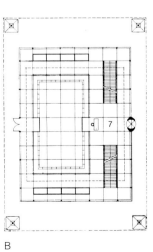

B

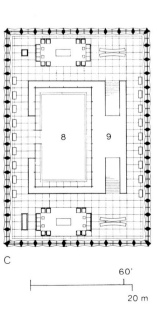

C

60'

20 m

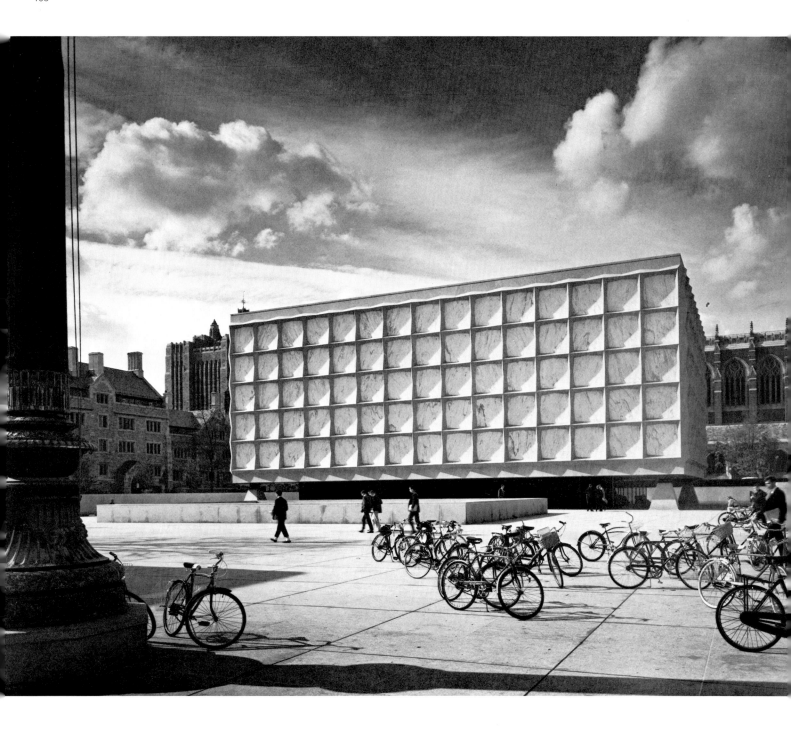

4. View of the entrance from Woolsey Hall. The low wall in the center surrounds the sunken court designed by Isamu Noguchi.

Pages 194–195:
5, 6. Close-ups of the Vierendeel trusses. The steel crosses forming the external load-bearing structure are covered with grey granite on the outside. The panels consist of white, translucent marble.

4. Blick von der Woolsey Hall auf die Eingangsseite der Ausstellungshalle. Die niedrige Brüstungsmauer in Platzmitte umgibt den von Isamu Noguchi gestalteten Lichthof.

Seiten 194–195:
5, 6. Detailansichten der Ausstellungshalle. Die Kreuzelemente, aus denen sich das Tragwerk der Außenwände zusammensetzt, sind außen mit grauem Granit verkleidet. In den Zwischenfeldern sitzen Tafeln aus weißem, durchscheinendem Marmor.

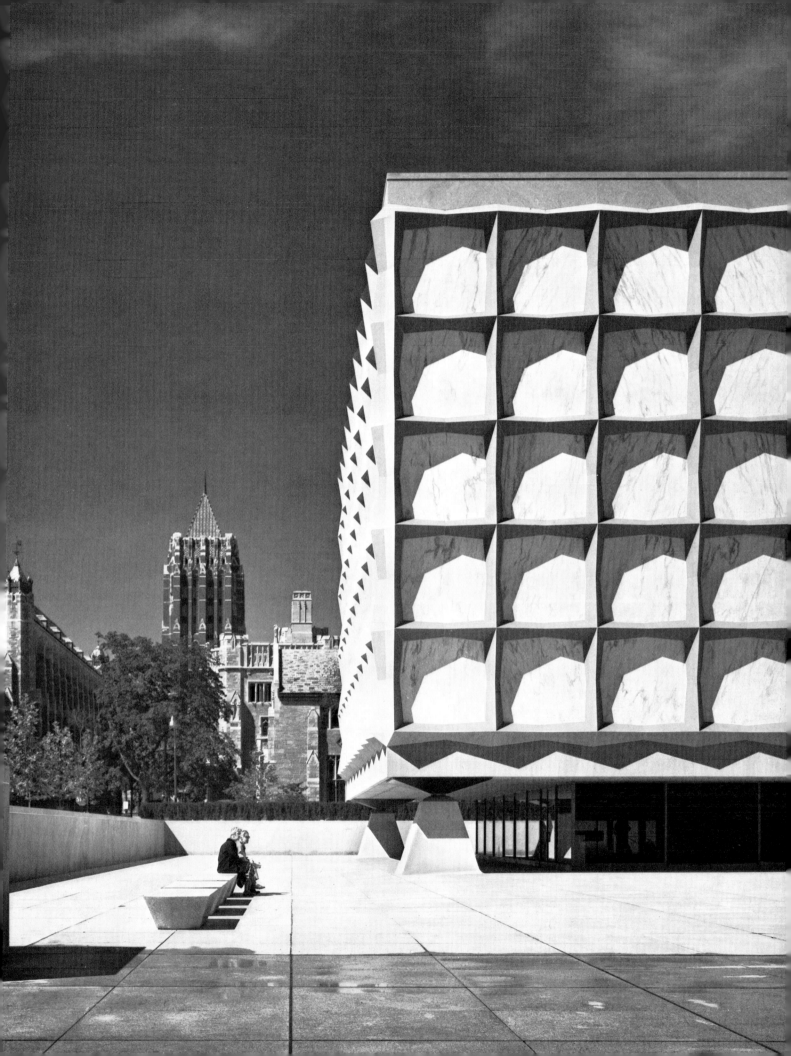

Lyndon Baines Johnson Library, University of Texas, Austin, Texas

The library contains documents and other material from President Johnson's entire political career as well as his term of office as President. Like the Sid W. Richardson Hall to the east of it (which houses the Latin American Colletion Library, the Institute of Latin American Studies, the Eugene C. Barker Texas History Center Library, the Texas State Historical Society as well as the Lyndon Baines Johnson School of Public Affairs), the library has been designed by Skidmore, Owings & Merrill in joint association with Brooks, Barr, Graeber & White. The library is situated in the eastern part of the University of Texas campus which is separated from the central part by the small tree-studded valley of a river.
Two great parallel walls, some 200' long, 65' high and 90' apart, define the main mass of the library. These walls, the end walls, the cantilevered top story, and the podium serving as the base of the building are faced in travertine. The tapering shape of the long walls delineates the shape of the columns which they conceal and which support the load of the top story. The ceiling box girders, together with thin connecting stiffeners, form a strong pattern visible from below and are supported by 3' high steel pins separating the ceiling structure from the wall beneath. The space between girders and walls is of glass so as to provide a visual separation.
The main entrance to the library is at podium level. On this level is an exhibit area with displays relating to the official life of the President. From here, a monumental stairway ascends to the main exhibit hall extending through the whole length and width of the building with audio-visual displays and a small auditorium. The space between this floor and the ceiling girders is left completely free on the north side while the south side contains five floors filled with archives visible through glass walls. In the top story are study rooms, curators' offices, a small research room, reference library, and a suite occupied by the President in his retirement.

Lyndon Baines Johnson Library, University of Texas, Austin, Texas

Die Bibliothek beherbergt Dokumente und anderes Material aus der Zeit der politischen Tätigkeit Präsident Johnsons. Sie ist wie die östlich angrenzende Sid W. Richardson Hall, in der die Latin American Collection Library, das Institute of Latin American Studies, die Eugene C. Barker Texas History Center Library, die Texas State Historical Society sowie die Lyndon Baines Johnson School of Public Affairs untergebracht wurden, ein Gemeinschaftswerk von Skidmore, Owings & Merrill und Brooks, Barr, Graeber & White. Der Komplex liegt im östlichen Teil des Geländes der University of Texas, auf dem sogenannten East Campus, der vom Zentralbereich durch ein kleines baumbestandenes Flußtal getrennt ist.
Zwei große parallele Wände, etwa 61 m lang, 19,80 m hoch und 27,50 m weit voneinander entfernt, definieren den Hauptbaukörper der Bibliothek. Sie sind, genauso wie das ihnen als Basis dienende Podium, die Querabschlüsse und die Längswände des Dachgeschosses, mit römischem Travertin verkleidet. Der wechselnde Querschnitt zeichnet die Form der im Innern verborgenen Stützen nach, welche die Lasten des auskragenden Dachgeschosses aufnehmen. Als Auflager der Dachgeschoßträger, die zusammen mit dünneren Aussteifungen einen tiefen, sichtbar gelassenen Rost bilden, dienen etwa 91 cm hohe Stahlgelenke. Der Auflagerbereich ist verglast, um die beiden Bauteile klar voneinander abzusetzen.
Der Hauptzugang der Bibliothek befindet sich auf der Podiumsebene. Die Raumfolge beginnt mit einer niedrig gehaltenen Halle, in der in ausstellungsartiger Form über die Amtszeit von Präsident Johnson berichtet wird. Von hier führt eine monumentale Treppenanlage auf eine den gesamten Baukörper einnehmende Zwischendecke mit weiteren Ausstellungsvitrinen und einem kleinen Auditorium. Der Raum zwischen dieser Decke und den Trägern des Dachgeschosses blieb auf der Nordhälfte völlig frei, während über der Südhälfte in fünf Geschossen das Archiv untergebracht ist. Im Dachgeschoß liegen Kuratorenbüros, eine Handbibliothek, ein Studienraum sowie eine von Präsident Johnson nach seiner Amtszeit benutzte Suite.

1. Site plan. Key: 1 Lyndon Baines Library, 2 Sid W. Richardson Hall.
2. Plan (A plaza level, B main exhibit floor, C top floor) and section. Key: 1 podium, 2 entrance lobby, 3 exhibit area, 4 main exhibit hall, 5 auditorium, 6 research room, 7 interior court, 8 reference library, 9 curators' offices, 10 President's suite.

1. Lageplan. Legende: 1 Lyndon Baines Johnson Library, 2 Sid W. Richardson Hall.
2. Grundrisse (A Podiumsgeschoß, B Zwischengeschoß, C Dachgeschoß) und Schnitt. Legende: 1 Podium, 2 Eingangshalle, 3 Ausstellungsbereich, 4 große Ausstellungshalle, 5 Auditorium, 6 Studienraum, 7 Innenhof, 8 Handbibliothek, 9 Kuratorenbüros, 10 Präsidentensuite.

Pages 198–199:
3. General view of the library from the south. On the right, the Sid W. Richardson Hall.

Seiten 198–199:
3. Gesamtansicht der Bibliothek von Süden. Rechts die Sid W. Richardson Hall.

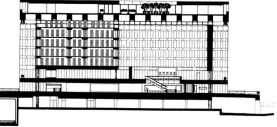

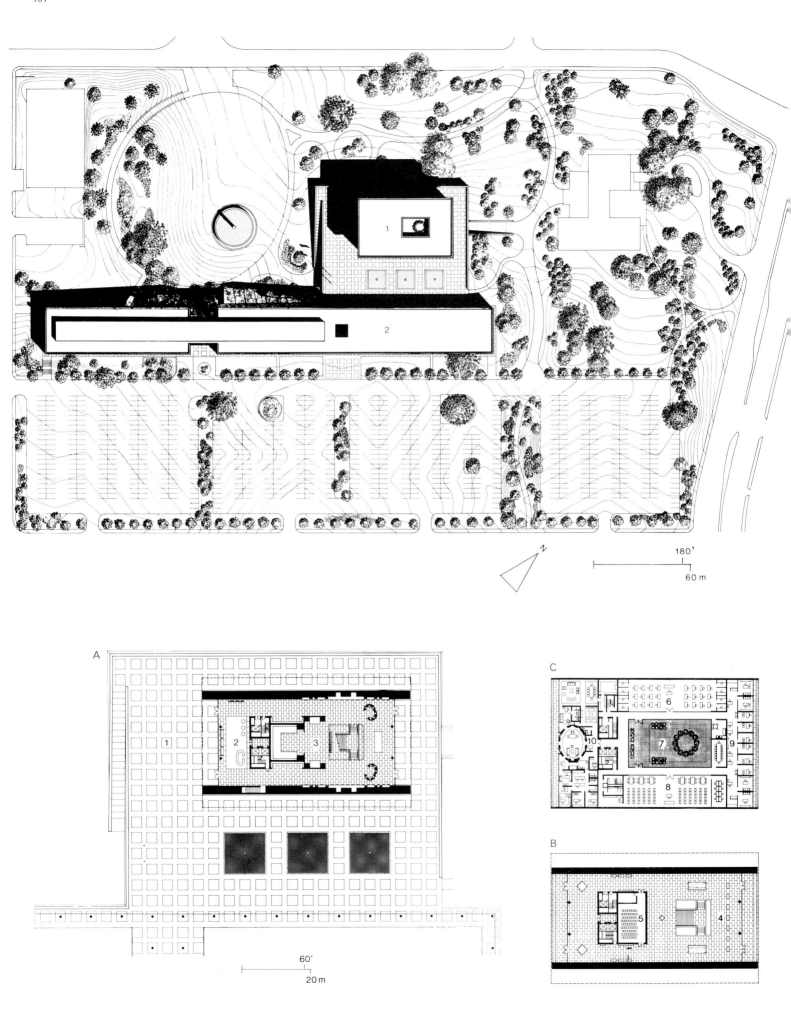

180'
60 m

A

1   2   3

60'
20 m

C

6
10   7   9
8

B

5   4

4. The tapering thickness of the two long walls delineates the shape of the columns within.

5. Because of their long span, the concrete girders carrying the top story were post-tensioned. The tensioning devices are of polished stainless steel.

6. The archives, seen from plaza level exhibit area. The documents are kept in red bound boxes placed like books on shelves.

4. Der wechselnde Querschnitt der beiden Längswände zeichnet die Form der im Innern verborgenen Stützen nach.

5. Die Betonträger, auf denen das Dachgeschoß ruht, wurden wegen der großen Spannweite vorgespannt. Die Spannköpfe bestehen aus poliertem Edelstahl.

6. Blick von der Podiumsebene auf das Archiv. Die Dokumente werden in roten Kästen aufbewahrt, die wie Bücher in Regalen stehen.

Joseph Regenstein Library, University of Chicago, Chicago, Illinois

The library responds to the research requirements of the Social Science and Humanities Division, Business School, Graduate Library School, School of Education, Far Eastern and Asian Studies and the Department of Biology.

The program required that the book collection, readers, faculty studies and library staff related to each discipline should always be located on the same floor. This requirement called for the provision of seven floors, including two below ground, varying in size from 75,000 to 87,000 sq ft – a floor area about ten times as large as the average floor area of the other campus buildings. The resulting scale problem has, however, been overcome by an apparent reduction of the volume through judicious spacings and setbacks. Three primary constituent parts of the building are recognizable: a west wing with the book stacks, a central part with the reading rooms, and an east wing with the faculty studies. There are, however, no strict boundaries between these zones, as the central reading room zones are, where necessary, extended either westwards or eastwards. Moreover, the west and east wings are divided into separate units, with horizontal variation in the west wing and with horizontal as well as vertical variation in the east wing. The facade structures, too, are differentiated, with projecting and recessed parts forming strong contrasts in the vertical direction, the projecting parts being window-less in the wings and glazed in the central parts. The smaller window-less bays are taken up by carrels, locker rooms and service shafts, the larger ones by study rooms and staircases. Finally, a secondary differentiation is provided by story-to-story changes of a few inches in the depth of the projections. As the limestone panels of the exterior walls are in front of the floor slabs, the facades show a clear vertical emphasis which is further accentuated by vertical grooves cut into the stone panels.

Joseph Regenstein Library, University of Chicago, Chicago, Illinois

Die Sammelgebiete der Bibliothek sind Soziologie, Philologie, Volkswirtschaft, Bibliothekswesen, Pädagogik, Fernost- und Asienkunde sowie Biologie.

Im Programm war vorgeschrieben, Buchbestand, Lese-, Studien- und Verwaltungsräume für jedes Gebiet jeweils auf einem Stockwerk unterzubringen. Durch diese Forderung ergaben sich sieben Geschosse, von denen zwei unterhalb der Erdoberfläche und fünf darüber liegen. Die Geschoßgrößen variieren von 7000 bis 8100 qm. Sie übersteigen die der übrigen Bauten des Campus um etwa das Zehnfache. Trotzdem kommt es nicht zu einer Sprengung der bisherigen Dimensionen, da die Baumasse stark gegliedert ist. Zunächst zeichnen sich drei Primärbauteile ab, ein westlicher Magazin-, ein mittlerer Lesesaal- und ein östlicher Verwaltungsteil. Funktional sind diese Bereiche jedoch nicht scharf voneinander geschieden, vielmehr schwingt die zentrale Leseraumzone je nach Bedarf sowohl in den einen, als auch in den anderen Nachbarbereich hinüber. Magazin- und Verwaltungsteil zerfallen weiterhin in einzelne Riegel, die beim Magazinteil nur im Grundriß, beim Verwaltungsteil darüber hinaus auch im Aufriß gegeneinander verschoben sind. Auch die Fassaden zeigen eine aufgelockerte Struktur. Sie gliedern sich einmal in kräftig gegeneinander abgesetzte, senkrecht gereihte Positiv- und Negativformen, wobei in den Gebäudeflanken die geschlossenen und im Mittelteil die verglasten Felder die Rolle der Positivform innehaben. Die kleineren der geschlossenen Felder dienen als Studienkojen, Schrankräume und Installationsschächte, die größeren als Arbeitszimmer und Treppenhäuser. In einer zweiten Gliederungsstufe springen die Fassaden schließlich geschoßweise um einige Zentimeter vor und zurück. Da die aus Kalkstein bestehenden Fassadenplatten vor den Decken vorbeilaufen, ergibt sich in den Außenwänden eine eindeutige Vertikaltendenz; verstärkt wird diese noch durch die in das Gestein eingefrästen senkrechten Riefen.

1. Corner of the building. The window-less parts of the facades consist of grooved limestone panels.
2. South side of the central part of the building with the main entrances.

1. Gebäudeecke. Die geschlossenen Außenwände bestehen aus gerieften Kalksteinplatten.
2. Blick auf die Südseite des Gebäudemittelteils mit den Hauptzugängen.

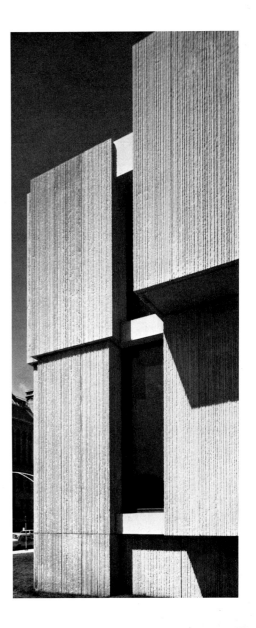

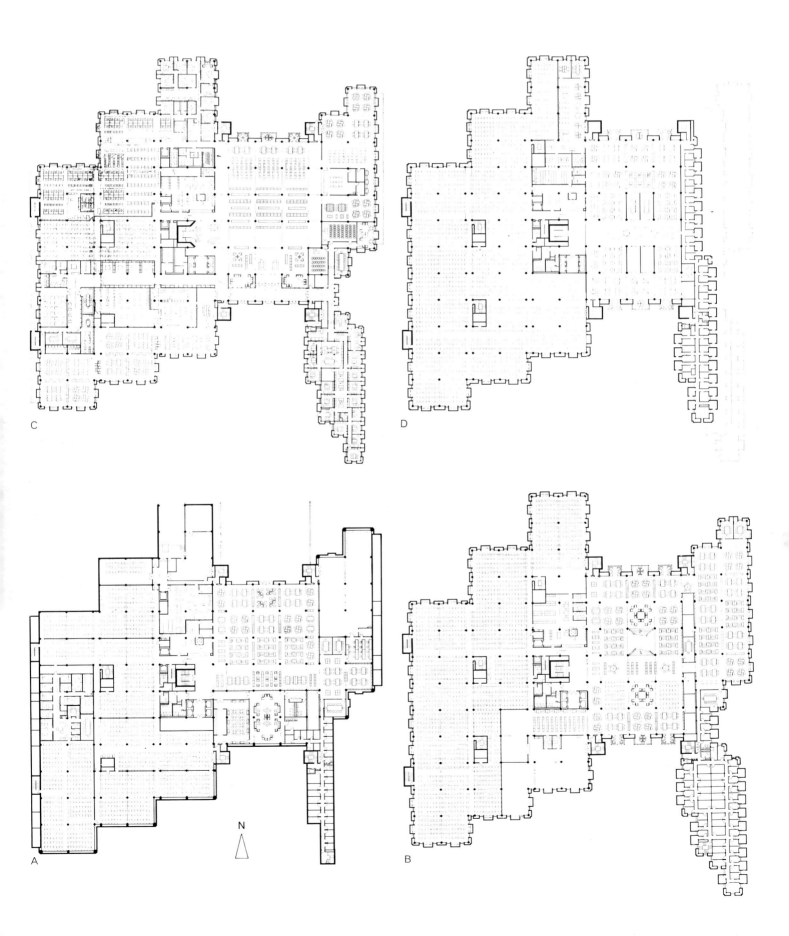

C

D

A

N

B

3. Plans (A 1st basement. B ground floor, C 2nd floor, D 4th floor). The highly differentiated building volume appears to consist of three parts, a west wing with the book stacks, a central part with the reading rooms, and an east wing with faculty studies; depending on requirements, the reading zone may be extended either westwards or eastwards.

4. The library seen from southeast, with the faculty studies in the foreground, right.

3. Grundrisse (A 1. Untergeschoß, B Erdgeschoß, C 1. Obergeschoß, D 3. Obergeschoß). Im Rahmen einer starken Gliederung der verhältnismäßig großen Baumasse zeichnen sich zunächst drei Primärbauteile ab, ein westlicher Magazin-, ein mittlerer Lesesaal- und ein östlicher Verwaltungsteil, wobei die Leseraumzone je nach Bedarf sowohl in den einen, als auch in den anderen Nachbarbereich hinüberschwingt.

4. Blick von Südosten auf die Bibliothek. Vorn rechts der Verwaltungsflügel.

5. Lounge at a bay window of the central part of the building.
6. Reading and rest area in the center of the central part of the building.

5. Ruheplatz in einem Fenstererker des Gebäudemittelteils.
6. Lese- und Ruheplätze im Zentrum des Gebäudemittelteils.

7. The 2nd and 3rd floor of the central part of the building are directly connected by a flight of stairs.

7. Das 1. und das 2. Obergeschoß des Gebäudemittelteils sind durch eine zentrale Treppe direkt miteinander verbunden.

Louis Jefferson Long Library, Wells College, Aurora, New York

The library, covering an area of 55,000 sq ft, has stacking space for about 250,000 volumes, seating accommodation for nearly 350 readers, and a wide variety of group and seminar rooms. Standing on a slope, the building is planned on three levels, with one public entrance at ground level and another one at top level. These entrances are connected by a pedestrian street which runs right across the building and also serves as an exhibition space. To facilitate orientation, the layout of the shelves is different on each floor, following a radial pattern (except for a minor area in the north wing) at ground level and a grid pattern on the intermediate level, while the top level has a composite plan with a radial pattern at the ends and a grid pattern in the middle.

The layout pattern of the building is wholly, and the elevation partly, governed by the "field theory". The module is a square with a side length of 42'. Four of these squares, in staggered arrangement, form the core area, three separate squares each form one small wing, and two squares together one larger wing. The most dramatic architectural feature is no doubt the cedar wood roof which, with its multifaceted planes, matches the complicated layout pattern of the building. It is supported partly by isolated columns and partly by clusters of eight columns. These clusters, which also serve as wind bracing, stand above the centers of the nine basic squares and rest on strong masonry piers which are also used as air distribution ducts.

Consistent with the principle of the "field theory", some of the non-bearing plasterboard walls continue the slope of the faceted roof edges. They are painted either white – like the ceilings – or red or purple so that they form a meaningful contrast to the primary wood or brick materials and to the furnishings attuned to these structural materials.

Louis Jefferson Long Library, Wells College, Aurora, New York

Die Bibliothek bietet bei einer Gesamtfläche von 5100 qm Regalraum für etwa 250000 Bände, Sitzplätze für knapp 350 Leser sowie eine Vielzahl von Gruppen- und Seminarräumen. Das Gebäude ist dreigeschossig in den Hang gesetzt, mit einem unteren Publikumszugang im Erdgeschoß und einem oberen im zweiten Obergeschoß. Die Zugänge stehen durch eine quer durch das Gebäude laufende Fußgängerstraße, die auch als Kunstgalerie dient, miteinander in Verbindung. Zur besseren Orientierung sind die Regale in jedem Geschoß anders ausgerichtet: im Erdgeschoß radial (mit Ausnahme der kleineren Anlage im nördlichen Flügel), im ersten Obergeschoß orthogonal und im zweiten Obergeschoß radial an den Enden sowie orthogonal in der Zwischenzone.

Der Bau folgt in seiner Grundrißstruktur vollständig und im Aufriß teilweise den Prinzipien der »Feldtheorie«. Grundeinheit ist ein Quadrat mit einer Seitenlänge von etwa 12,80 m. Vier Quadrate bilden, gegeneinander verschoben, den Kernbereich, drei Quadrate jeweils einen kleineren und zwei Quadrate zusammen einen größeren Flügel. Das architektonisch dramatischste Element ist zweifellos das Zedernholzdach, das mit seiner vielfach facettierten Oberfläche auf die komplizierte Grundrißstruktur des Gebäudes antwortet. Getragen wird es einerseits von einzeln stehenden, andererseits von zu Achtergruppen zusammengebündelten Pfosten. Die Achtergruppen, die auch die Windkräfte übernehmen, befinden sich über den Zentren der neun Basisquadrate. Sie ruhen auf kräftigen, zugleich als Luftverteiler ausgebildeten Mauerwerkspfeilern.

Die nichttragenden, verputzten Trennwände schließen in Konsequenz des »feldtheoretischen« Prinzips teilweise schräg an die Facettenränder des Daches an. Sie sind entweder weiß – wie die Deckenunterseiten –, rot oder purpur gestrichen und kontrastieren dadurch bewußt zu den Primärelementen aus Holz oder Ziegelstein und der farblich auf diese abgestimmten Einrichtung.

1. Basic layout. Four basic squares form the core area, another five the four wings.
2. Seats and tables on the top floor, providing a lounge between the four central squares.

1. Grundrißschema. Vier Grundeinheiten bilden den Kernbereich, weitere fünf die vier Flügel.
2. Sitzgruppe im zweiten Obergeschoß. Die Gruppe markiert die Restfläche zwischen den vier Kernquadraten.

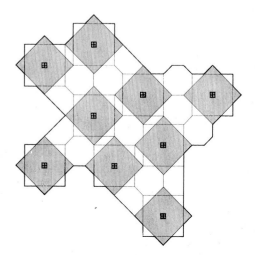

3. Library, seen from the northwest, with the lower public entrance in the center.
4. Site plan. Key: 1 lower public entrance, 2 upper public entrance, 3 staff entrance.
5. Library, seen from northeast.

3. Ansicht der Bibliothek von Nordwesten. In der Mitte der untere Publikumszugang.
4. Lageplan. Legende: 1 unterer Publikumszugang, 2 oberer Publikumszugang, 3 Personalzugang.
5. Ansicht der Bibliothek von Nordosten.

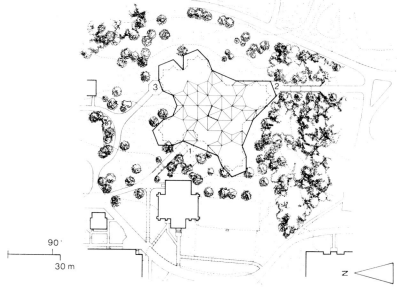

90'
30 m

Z

6. Southwest side of the building, seen from the upper public entrance.
7. Plans (ground floor, 2nd floor, 3rd floor). Key: 1 lower public entrance, 2 group study, 3 seminar room, 4 lounge, 5 newspapers, 6 lending counter, 7 catalog, 8 reference library, 9 administration, 10 staff entrance, 11 periodicals, 12 smoking and study room, 13 central lounge, 14 rare book room, 15 upper entrance.
8. Lower public entrance.

6. Blick vom oberen Publikumszugang entlang der Südwestseite des Gebäudes.
7. Grundrisse (Erdgeschoß, 1. Obergeschoß, 2. Obergeschoß). Legende: 1 unterer Publikumszugang, 2 Gruppenraum, 3 Seminarraum, 4 Lounge, 5 Zeitungen, 6 Ausleihe, 7 Katalog, 8 Handbibliothek, 9 Verwaltung, 10 Personalzugang, 11 Zeitschriften, 12 Rauch- und Studierraum, 13 zentraler Sitzbereich, 14 Rara, 15 oberer Zugang.
8. Unterer Publikumszugang.

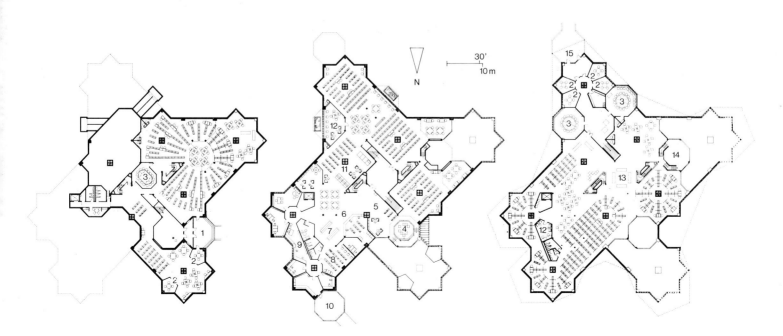

9. Radially orientated shelves on the ground floor.
10. Upper reading room. The wedge conceals the stairs leading from the upper public entrance to the lower floors. In the foreground, right, the easternmost of the internal stairs.
11. Lounge on the first floor.

9. Der radial ausgerichtete Regalbereich im Erdgeschoß.
10. Oberer Leseraum. Der Keil verbirgt die Treppe vom oberen Publikumszugang in die unteren Geschosse. Vorn rechts die östliche der internen Treppen.
11. Die Lounge im ersten Obergeschoß.

Social Sciences Building, Cornell University, Ithaca, New York

The Social Sciences Building at Cornell University provides space not only for social sciences studies and related research facilities, but also for psychology, sociology, economics and international studies departments. Faculty offices, student lounges and an auditorium for 400 people are included as well as the usual supporting secretarial and clerical service areas. The research facilities for the social sciences department are equipped with especially designed acoustical and environmental temperature control provisions.

Large, uninterrupted spaces free from structural supports have been provided to meet the program requirements. This resulted in the development of a steel structural frame which, as the design progressed, materialized in the choice of an exposed Vierendeel truss of weathering steel. A bronze heat-reducing glass and Border Pink granite aggregate in the precast concrete as well as a duranodic bronze finish on the aluminum window enframement were chosen as compatible materials with the weathering steel trusses. The structural steel framing for this building also serves as the curtain wall for the three stories from the second floor to the roof. Each facade of trusses rests on two supports 90' apart and cantilevering 30' beyond to the corners. Glass and window mullions frame into the flanges of the members of the truss to complete the curtain wall. The truss members are rectilinear and all members have an H-shaped cross-section.

The HVAC system is based on an all air reheat system. Outer wall and window heat losses are offset by hot water radiation.

The large, windowless podium on which the entire building rests is naturally used for the laboratories and auditorium, and the absence of windows aids the strict environmental controls required in these areas. Offices and other spaces for instruction are located on the upper floors utilizing the large glass areas.

A large plaza surrounds the ground floor of the building and provides an inviting space for students as well as faculty.

Social Sciences Building, Cornell University, Ithaca, New York

In dem Gebäude, das den Abteilungen Sozialwissenschaften, Psychologie, Wirtschaftswissenschaften und internationale Studien dient, waren neben normalen, von der Benutzung und der Größe her büroartigen Räumen auch ein Auditorium mit 400 Plätzen und besonders abgeschirmte Forschungsräume unterzubringen. Man entschloß sich deshalb für eine Zweiteilung in einen halb versenkten, fensterlosen Sockel mit zwei Geschossen für das Auditorium und die Forschungsräume sowie einen verglasten Oberbau mit vier Geschossen für die übrigen Räume.

Der Oberbau hat eine tragende Pfostenfachwerkfassade mit H-förmig ausgebildeten Profilen aus wetterfestem Stahl. Der Pfostenabstand beträgt etwa 3,05 m. Die Fassade wird auf jeder Seite von zwei Pylonen aus Beton getragen; neun Felder liegen zwischen den Pylonen, drei Felder kragen auf jeder Seite aus. Die inneren Stützen des Gebäudes nehmen im Interesse einer möglichst großen Flexibilität nur jeden dritten Fassadenpfosten auf. In Abstimmung auf das Material des sichtbar gelassenen Außentragwerks bestehen die Fenster aus bronzefarben getöntem Glas und die Rahmen aus in gleichem Ton anodisierten Aluminium; als Zuschlagstoff für die vorgefertigten Betonelemente, mit denen der Sockel verkleidet wurde, wählte man rosafarbenen Granit.

Die Klimaregelung des Gebäudes erfolgt über ein Umlaufsystem. Der Wärmeverlust an den Fenstern wird durch eine Warmwasserheizung mit Radiatoren kompensiert.

Das Eingangsgeschoß wurde gegenüber den oberen Geschossen um anderthalb Pfostenfelder zurückgesetzt, so daß auf dem Sockel eine umlaufende Plaza eingerichtet werden konnte.

1. North side of the building. The site as well as program requirements dictated the use of a concrete podium supporting a four-story upper structure with a Vierendeel framework facade of weathering steel.

1. Nordseite des Gebäudes. Der Zuschnitt des Grundstücks sowie funktionelle Erfordernisse führten zu einer Zweiteilung in einen zweigeschossigen Sockel aus Beton und einen viergeschossigen Oberbau mit einer tragenden Pfostenfachwerkfassade aus wetterfestem Stahl.

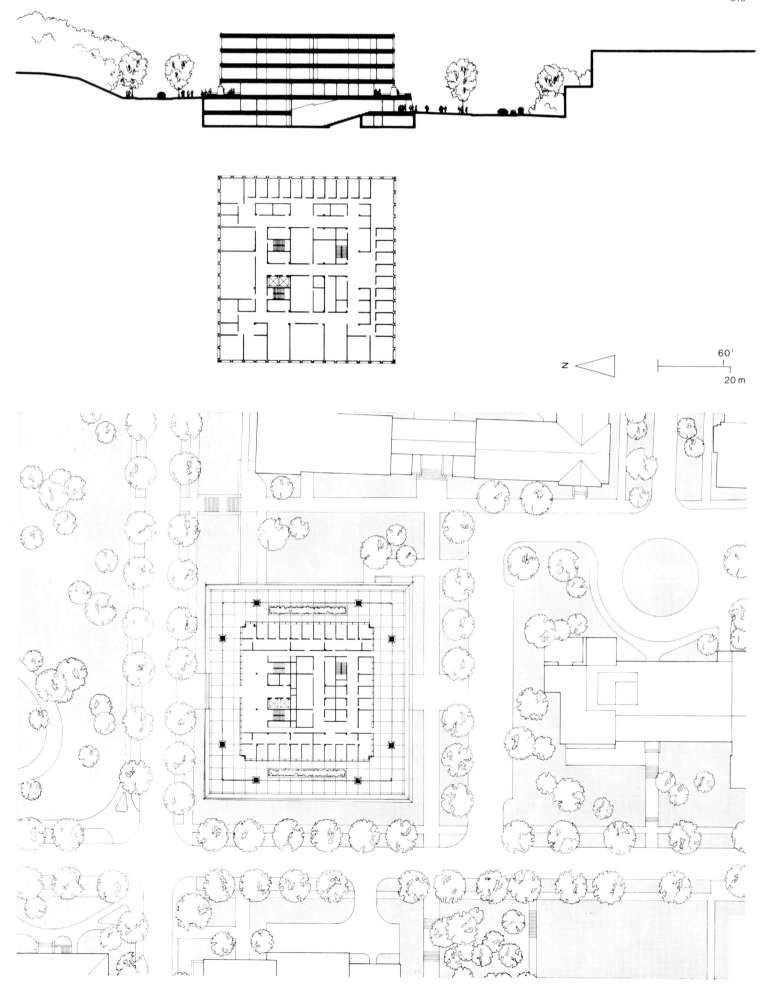

60'

20 m

z

2. Plans (podium floor, typical upper floor) and section. The auditorium on the south side has direct access from the street.
3. North side of the building.
4. The entrance floor above the podium is surrounded by a plaza.

2. Grundrisse (Sockelgeschoß, typisches Obergeschoß) und Schnitt. Das Auditorium auf der Südseite ist direkt von der Straße aus zugänglich.
3. Nordseite des Gebäudes.
4. Das Sockelgeschoß ist als umlaufende Plaza ausgebildet.

Annenberg Building, Mount Sinai Medical Center, New York, New York.
Under construction

The 27-story tower is the first stage of a long-range plan for the extension and renewal of the medical center. The total floor area is 1,047,000 sq ft, of which the medical school occupies 60 per cent, and the remainder is occupied by central services for the hospital. There are no hospital beds in this building. The older structures which now contain beds will be replaced by future construction connected to the north side of the Annenberg Building.
In order to provide a site for the new tower, it was necessary to demolish several old buildings in the center of the site bounded by Madison Avenue on the east, Fifth Avenue on the west, 98th Street on the south and 101st Street on the north. The tower is connected at the subsurface levels and by several bridges to the remaining buildings. Eventually, the Guggenheim Pavilion on Fifth Avenue will also be demolished, thus creating a plaza facing Central Park.
Most of the ground floor is allocated to a 600 seat auditorium. To obtain column-free space for it, the structure of the 9th floor (which, like the top floor and the 3rd basement, is reserved for mechanical equipment) contains special trusses from which the floors below, including the roof of the auditorium, are suspended. All areas above the 9th floor are assigned to the medical school while most areas under the 9th floor are related to the hospital.
A 5' square module is the basic planning unit. Most of the vertical piping and ductwork is placed in triangular shafts integrated with the outer columns. The external cladding of shafts, columns and spandrels consists of weathering steel. All exterior glazing is bronze-tinted.
The ground floor is distinguished from the upper floors not only by its greater height but also by its travertine walls and its floors of brown paving brick, identical with the pavement outside. All the interior furnishings throughout the building were designed by Skidmore, Owings & Merrill.

Annenberg Building, Mount Sinai Medical Center, New York, New York. Im Bau

Der 27geschossige Turm stellt den ersten Bauabschnitt einer Erweiterung und baulichen Erneuerung des medizinischen Zentrums dar. Rund 60% der Gesamtfläche von etwa 97000 qm werden der medizinischen Hochschule zur Verfügung stehen, der Rest ist dem Krankenhaus vorbehalten. In dem Gebäude sind keine Krankenbetten vorgesehen.
Zur Gewinnung eines Bauplatzes für den Neubau mußte man mehrere ältere Gebäude im Zentrum des im Osten von der Madison Avenue, im Westen von der Fifth Avenue, im Süden von der 98th Street und im Norden von der 101th Street begrenzten Blockes abreißen. Mit den erhalten gebliebenen Bauten am Blockrand wird das Hochhaus durch ausladende Untergeschosse sowie durch mehrere Brücken verbunden werden. Später wird man auch den an der Fifth Avenue gelegenen Guggenheim Pavilion abreißen und so einen freien Platz gegenüber dem Central Park schaffen.
Den größten Teil des Erdgeschosses nimmt ein Auditorium mit 600 Plätzen ein; um dafür eine stützenfreie Fläche zu erhalten, sind im 9. Geschoß, das wie das oberste Geschoß und das 3. Untergeschoß haustechnische Anlagen enthält, Sonderträger angeordnet und die entsprechenden Bereiche der Decken zwischen diesem und dem Erdgeschoß daran aufgehängt. Oberhalb des 9. Geschosses befinden sich nur Einrichtungen der medizinischen Hochschule, unterhalb desselben fast ausschließlich solche des Krankenhauses.
Das Gebäude ist auf einem Raster von etwa 152 × 152 cm aufgebaut. Ein Großteil der vertikalen Versorgungsleitungen liegt in äußeren, im Grundriß dreieckigen Schächten, die mit den Außenstützen eine Einheit bilden. Die äußere Verkleidung der Schächte, Stützen und Deckenstreifen besteht aus wetterbeständigem Stahl; das Glas der Fenster ist bronzefarben getönt.
Das Erdgeschoß ist gegenüber den anderen Geschossen nicht nur durch eine größere Höhe, sondern darüber hinaus durch Wände aus Travertin und Böden aus braunem Klinker, die sich auch im Außenbereich fortsetzen, hervorgehoben. Die gesamte Inneneinrichtung des Gebäudes wurde von Skidmore, Owings & Merrill entworfen.

1. Section of the building. Key: B3 mechanical equipment, B2 central sterile supply, pharmacy, medical records, B1 outpatients department, emergency ward, radiology, cystoscopy, 1 lobby, auditorium, student lounge, 2 outpatients department, nuclear medicine, cardiopulmonary, 3, 4 outpatients department, 5 administration, faculty dining, public relations, 6 operating rooms, anesthesiology, 7 operating rooms, cardiopulmonary center, anesthesiology, 8 cardiopulmonary center, intensive care, anesthesiology, 9 mechanical equipment, 10, 11 library, 12 multi-discipline teaching laboratories, mail room, 13 multi-discipline teaching laboratories, book store, 14 neurology, pathology, 15 pathology, 16 microbiology, 17 pediatrics, orthopaedics, 18 otolaryngology, anatomy, 19 biochemistry, 20 biochemistry, obstetrics and gynecology, 21 physiology, 22 ophthalmology, medicine, 23 medicine, 24 hematology, medicine, 25 surgery, animal institute, 26 animal institute, 27 mechanical equipment.
2. View from the north.

1. Querschnitt durch das Gebäude. Legende: B3 haustechnische Anlagen, B2 zentrale Sterilisation, Pharmazie, medizinisches Archiv, B1 Ambulanz, Unfallstation, Radiologie, Zystoskopie, 1 Eingangshalle, Hörsaal, Aufenthaltsraum für Studenten, 2 Ambulanz, Strahlenabteilung, Herz-Lungen-Zentrum, 3, 4 Ambulanz, 5 Verwaltung, Mensa, Abteilung für Öffentlichkeitsarbeit, 6 Operationsräume, Anästhesie, 7 Operationsräume, Herz-Lungen-Zentrum, Anästhesie, 8 Herz-Lungen-Zentrum, Intensivstation, Anästhesie, 9 haustechnische Anlagen, 10, 11 Bibliothek, 12 interdisziplinäre Laboratorien, Post, 13 interdisziplinäre Laboratorien, Buchhandlung, 14 Neurologie, Pathologie, 15 Pathologie, 16 Mikrobiologie, 17 Pädiatrie, Orthopädie, 18 Otolaryngologie, Anatomie, 19 Biochemie, 20 Biochemie, Geburtshilfe und Gynäkologie, 21 Physiologie, 22 Ophthalmologie, innere Medizin, 23 innere Medizin, 24 Hämatologie, innere Medizin, 25 Chirurgie, Tierinstitut, 26 Tierinstitut, 27 haustechnische Anlagen.
2. Ansicht von Norden.

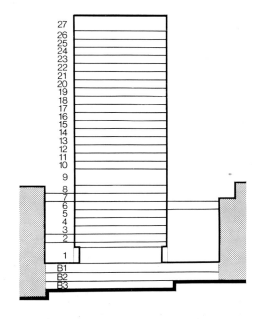

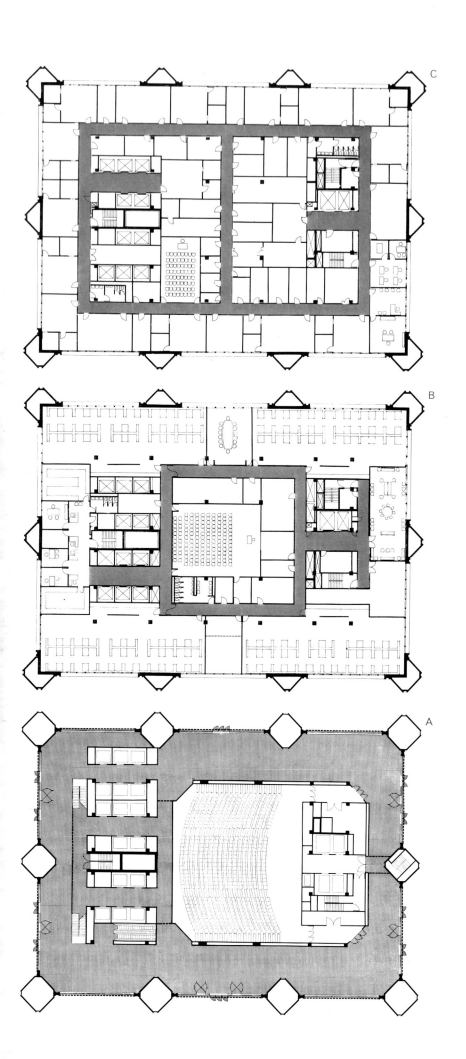

3. Plans (A ground floor, B 13th floor, C 19th floor).
With its large plan area of 140′×200′, the building
permits many variations in the layout.
4. View of the planned plaza (model).

3. Grundrisse (A Eingangsgeschoß, B 13. Geschoß, C 19. Geschoß). Mit einer Grundrißfläche
von etwa 43×61 m erlaubt das Gebäude mannig-
fache Einrichtungsvarianten.
4. Blick auf die geplante Plaza (Modell).

University of Illinois, Chicago Circle Campus, Chicago, Illinois

At the Chicago Circle directly adjacent to the Loop, three of Chicago's expressways converge, providing direct connections between the downtown area, the suburbs and outlying areas. Being located in the immediate vicinity of this important focal point and of a specially constructed rapid transit station, the new campus of the university, previously situated at the shore of Lake Michigan, is one of the most readily accessible sites in the city.

Instruction began in 1965 with 7,000 students; by 1975, this number will have been increased to 25,000. Apart from a very rapid progress of building activities, this enormous expansion rate has been made possible by the high degree of flexibility achieved, during the first phase and most of the second phase, by concentrating on buildings designed to serve specific functions – lectures, laboratory work, etc. – rather than specific disciplines. All the functions with mass movements of students were placed in low-rise buildings, all the others in high-rise buildings.

The first stage of construction comprised the following buildings: the Lecture Center, the first sections of the Central Library and the Science and Engineering Laboratories, the headquarters of the Students Union, the 28-story administration building as well as the central heating and refrigeration plants.

The second phase of construction, designed for an increase in the number of students from 9,000 to 14,000, comprised extensions of the Central Library and the Science and Engineering Laboratories as well as two new buildings, the initial phase of the Architecture and Art Laboratories and the 13-story administration building for the Science and Engineering Offices.

The third phase, just concluded, comprised the construction of the first mixed-use, interdisciplinary buildings – the Science and Engineering South Building, the Behavioral Sciences Building, and the Education and Communications Building. These new buildings are exclusively destined for the more advanced students in their respective fields of study while the undergraduates remain in the central academic area created during the first phase.

University of Illinois, Chicago Circle Campus, Chicago, Illinois

Im unmittelbar vor der Loop liegenden Chicago Circle treffen drei Schnellstraßen, die die Vororte und das Hinterland mit dem Stadtzentrum verbinden, zusammen. Durch seine direkte Nachbarschaft zu diesem wichtigen Verkehrsknoten sowie durch eine eigens eingerichtete Stadtbahnstation ist der neue Campus der zuvor am Lake Michigan gelegenen Universität einer der am besten zugänglichen Plätze der Stadt.

Der Lehrbetrieb begann im Jahr 1965 mit 7000 Studenten, 1975 werden es bereits 25000 sein. Die Voraussetzung für dieses enorme Wachstum der Studentenzahlen ist neben einem äußerst zügigen Baufortschritt dadurch gegeben, daß im Sinne einer maximalen Flexibilität die in der ersten und bis auf wenige Ausnahmen auch in der zweiten Bauphase für die Lehre errichteten Anlagen nicht, wie sonst üblich, auf einzelne Fachdisziplinen, sondern auf einzelne Aktivitäten – Vorlesungen, Laborübungen und so weiter – zugeschnitten sind. Alle Einrichtungen mit sehr starkem Publikumsverkehr wurden in niedrigen Gebäuden, alle Einrichtungen mit weniger starkem Verkehr in Hochhäusern zusammengefaßt.

In der ersten Bauphase wurden folgende Gebäude errichtet: das Lecture Center, die ersten Abschnitte der Central Library und der Science and Engineering Laboratories, das Studentenhaus, die 28geschossige Universitätsverwaltung sowie die Heiz- und Kühlzentrale.

In der zweiten Bauphase, die eine Erhöhung der Studentenzahl von 9000 auf 14000 ermöglichte, kamen Erweiterungen der Central Library und der Science and Engineering Laboratories sowie zwei neue Gebäude, der erste Abschnitt der Architecture and Art Laboratories und das 13geschossige Verwaltungsgebäude der naturwissenschaftlich-technischen Abteilung, hinzu.

In der dritten, gerade abgeschlossenen Bauphase begann man mit der Errichtung der ersten interdisziplinär angelegten Institute, des Science and Engineering South Building, des Behavioral Sciences Building sowie des Education and Communications Building. Diese neuen Institute sind ausschließlich für die älteren Studenten der entsprechenden Abteilungen bestimmt, die jüngeren werden weiterhin im während der ersten Bauphase errichteten Kernbereich unterrichtet.

1. University campus, seen from the north. In the foreground, the 28-story tower of the University Administration, known as University Hall. All the buildings frequented by students are linked by a raised walkway system.

2. Site plan. Key: 1 University Hall, 2 Jefferson Hall, 3 Grant Hall, 4 Douglas Hall, 5 Lincoln Hall, 6 Chicago Circle Center (designed by C. F. Murphy and Associates), 7 Lecture Center, 8 Central Library, 9 Jane Addams' Hull House, 10 Taft Hall, 11 Burnham Hall, 12 Addams Hall, 13 Science and Engineering Laboratories, 14 Utilities Building, 15 Services Building (designed by Epstein and Company), 16 Roosevelt Road Building, 17 Commonwealth Edison Substation, 18 raised walkway, 19 Racine Avenue Building, 20 Science and Engineering Offices, 21 Stevenson Hall, 22 Henry Hall, 23 Plant Research Laboratories, 24 Architecture and Art Laboratories, 25 Behavioral Sciences Building, 26 Science and Engineering South Building, 27 Physical Education Building (designed by Harry M. Weese and Associates), 28 Education and Communications Building (designed by Harry M. Weese and Associates), 29 rapid transit station.

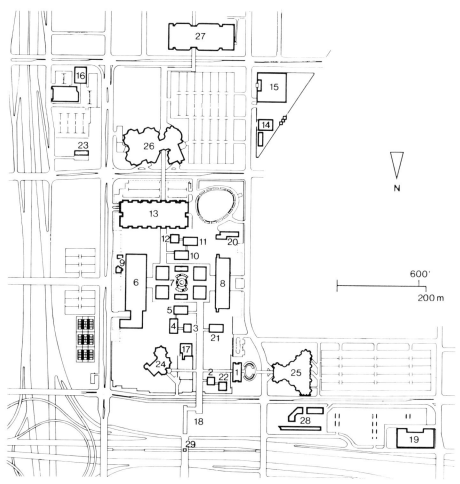

1. Blick vom Norden auf das Universitätsgelände. Im Vordergrund das 28geschossige Hochhaus der Universitätsverwaltung, die University Hall. Alle von den Studenten benutzten Gebäude sind durch ein angehobenes Fußgängerwegesystem miteinander verbunden.

2. Lageplan. Legende: 1 University Hall, 2 Jefferson Hall, 3 Grant Hall, 4 Douglas Hall, 5 Lincoln Hall, 6 Chicago Circle Center (entworfen von C. F. Murphy and Associates), 7 Lecture Center, 8 Central Library, 9 Jane Addams' Hull House, 10 Taft Hall, 11 Burnham Hall, 12 Addams Hall, 13 Science and Engineering Laboratories, 14 Utilities Building, 15 Services Building (entworfen von Epstein and Company), 16 Roosevelt Road Building, 17 Commonwealth Edison Substation, 18 Fußgängerbrücke, 19 Racine Avenue Building, 20 Science and Engineering Offices, 21 Stevenson Hall, 22 Henry Hall, 23 Plant Research Laboratories, 24 Architecture and Arts Laboratories, 25 Behavioral Sciences Building, 26 Science and Engineering South Building, 27 Physical Education Building (entworfen von Harry M. Weese and Associates), 28 Education and Communications Building (entworfen von Harry M. Weese and Associates), 29 Stadtbahnstation.

Architecture and Art Laboratories, University of Illinois,
Chicago Circle Campus, Chicago, Illinois

The Architecture and Art Laboratories are among the first of a series of buildings designed on the basis of the "field theory". The basic unit of the structure is a square of about 80' side length, superimposed at an angle of 45° on a second square of about 85' side length. Each of these units is vertically offset about 3' from the adjoining ones. The units contain studio laboratories, work shops and a library. In the small intermediate spaces are stairs while the expanded octagonal spaces contain rooms for display, teaching, conference and storage purposes.

Initially, no more than three units have been built, providing accommodation for about 680 students. Another five units can be added in a second phase. After completion of the third and last phase, some 1,200 students can be accommodated.

As far as the layout is concerned, the building will not represent a fully functional entity before the second phase is completed. At that time, the unit at present containing the architectural department and the library will become a central core, surrounded by the other units forming a continuous spiral.

The bearing structure consists of reinforced concrete; the outer walls and most of the internal walls are of brick. To let the general design become apparent as clearly as possible, the outer walls are taken up in front of the structural floors (no more than a slight change in the brickwork indicates the floor levels) and contain only a few panoramic windows, shaped to match the geometry of the building.

The furnishings, developed by Dolores Miller & Associates, provide the students with variable workplaces in portable metal components.

Architecture and Art Laboratories, University of Illinois,
Chicago Circle Campus, Chicago, Illinois

Die Architecture and Art Laboratories sind eines der ersten aus einer Serie von Gebäuden, die auf der Basis der »Feldtheorie« entworfen wurden. Die Grundeinheiten des Bauwerkes bestehen aus Quadraten mit einer Seitenlänge von etwa 24,40 m, die in einem Winkel von 45° jeweils von einem zweiten Quadrat mit einer Seitenlänge von etwa 25,90 m überlagert werden. Innerhalb dieser Einheiten, die gegeneinander in der Höhe jeweils um etwa 91,5 cm versetzt sind, befinden sich Studios, Werkstätten und eine Bibliothek; die schmalen Zwischenräume nehmen Treppen, die erweiterten achteckigen Ausstellungs-, Seminar-, Konferenz- und Lagerräume auf.

Vorerst wurden nur drei Einheiten errichtet; etwa 680 Studenten finden darin Platz. In einer zweiten Bauphase sollen weitere fünf Einheiten hinzukommen. Nach Abschluß der dritten und letzten Bauphase soll das Gebäude schließlich 1200 Studenten aufnehmen können.

Ein von der Grundrißorganisation her voll funktionsfähiges Gebilde wird das Gebäude erst nach Abschluß der zweiten Bauphase darstellen. Die jetzt die Architekturabteilung und die Bibliothek aufnehmende Einheit wird dann zum zentralen Kern, um den sich die übrigen Einheiten in einer kontinuierlichen Spirale herumwinden.

Das Tragwerk des Gebäudes besteht aus Stahlbeton; die äußeren sowie die meisten inneren Wände sind aus Ziegelsteinen gemauert. Um die Gesamtform so klar wie möglich hervortreten zu lassen, wurden die äußeren Wände vor den Decken vorbeigeführt (lediglich ein leichter Wechsel im Mauerwerk deutet die Geschosse an) und nur durch wenige, in ihrer Form der Geometrie des Gebäudes folgende Aussichtsfenster unterbrochen.

Das von Dolores Miller & Associates entwickelte Möbelsystem aus beweglichen Metallelementen erlaubt den Studenten, sich ihre Arbeitsplätze nach eigenen Vorstellungen zu bauen.

1. Phase I building, seen from the west. In the foreground, the bridge connecting the Lecture Center with the rapid transit station.

1. Ansicht des ersten Bauabschnittes von Westen. Im Vordergrund die Brücke zwischen dem Lecture Center und der Station der Stadtbahn.

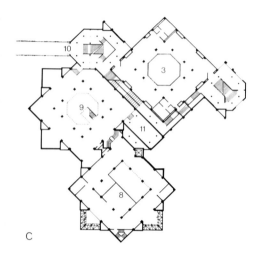

C

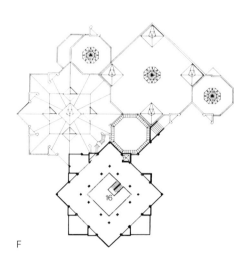

F

2. Plans of phase I building. Key: 1 mechanical equipment, 2 stores, 3 architectural studio, 4 workshop, 5 photographic studio, 6 ground floor entrance, 7 exhibition room, 8 graphics studio, 9 art studio, 10 bridge entrance, 11 conference room, 12 seminar, 13 architecture and art studio, 14 library, 15 graphics studio, 16 plastics and graphics studio.

2. Grundrisse des ersten Bauabschnittes. Legende: 1 technische Anlagen, 2 Lager, 3 Architekturatelier, 4 Werkstatt, 5 Fotoatelier, 6 Erdgeschoßeingang, 7 Ausstellungsraum, 8 Graphikwerkstatt, 9 Kunstatelier, 10 Brückeneingang, 11 Konferenzraum, 12 Seminarraum, 13 Architektur- und Kunstatelier, 14 Bibliothek, 15 Graphikatelier, 16 Plastik- und Graphikstudio.

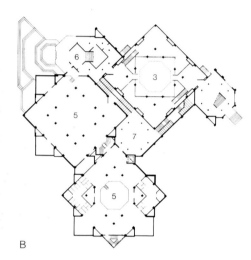

B

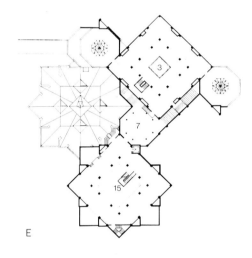

E

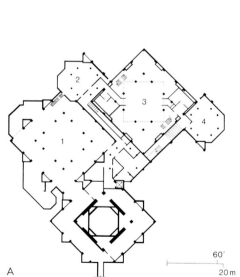

A

60'
20 m

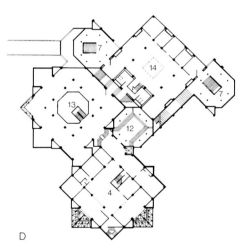

D

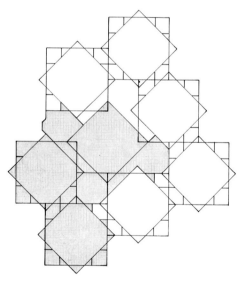

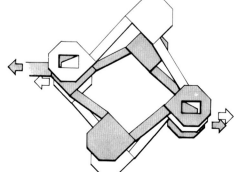

3. Schematic plan of building on completion of phase II.
4. Concourse and display areas after completion of phase II.

3. Grundrißschema der ersten beiden Bauabschnitte.
4. Schema der Verkehrs- und Ausstellungsflächen in den ersten beiden Bauabschnitten.

5. View of phase I building from the south.

5. Ansicht des ersten Bauabschnittes von Süden.

6. Art studio, with the graphics studio in the background.

6. Das Kunstatelier. Im Hintergrund die Graphikwerkstatt.

7. Architecture studio. The furnishing system developed by Dolores Miller & Associates enables the students to design their own workplaces.
8. One of the octagonal spaces outside the basic units is used as a seminar.

7. Das Architekturatelier. Das von Dolores Miller & Associates entwickelte Möbelsystem erlaubt den Studenten, sich ihre Arbeitsplätze selbst zu bauen.
8. Einer der achteckigen Räume außerhalb der Grundeinheiten wurde zu einem Seminarraum ausgebaut.

Behavioral Sciences Building, University of Illinois,
Chicago Circle Campus, Chicago, Illinois

The building contains offices and laboratories for the departments of sociology, psychology, anthropology, geography and urban studies as well as a number of lecture halls and a cafeteria with 700 seats, which are available for general university use.
Main access is via a pedestrian bridge, connected by a "traffic interchange" ramp to the raised walkway system of the central campus.
The zones carrying the heaviest traffic – lecture halls and cafeteria – are located in the eastern half of the building adjacent to the bridge. To distribute the traffic flows, the bridgehead at the level above ground has direct entrances to the floors directly below and above. The internal circulation space in the eastern zone has been designed as a concourse for spontaneous congregations of students. The main stairway connecting the lower floors is flanked by seats, used by students before and after the lectures. The offices and laboratories in the western half of the building are screened from the lecture halls by the elevator landing. Each office sector can be individually controlled and arranged without impairing the general system. The offices are located along the periphery and are clustered in star-shaped patterns around secretarial work areas inside. The laboratories are in the center. They are mechanically serviced from a roof-top penthouse and suspended from twelve triangular shafts which are, at roof level, connected to the penthouse in two separate groups.
Like the other two buildings of the University of Illinois described here, this building, too, has a layout based on the "field theory". The structure is of poured-in-place concrete, most of the walls are of brick.

Behavioral Sciences Building, University of Illinois,
Chicago Circle Campus, Chicago, Illinois

Das Gebäude enthält Büros und Laboratorien der Abteilungen Soziologie, Psychologie, Anthropologie, Geographie und Urbanistik, eine Hörsaalgruppe und eine Cafeteria mit 700 Plätzen. Die Hörsäle und die Cafeteria stehen der gesamten Universität zur Verfügung.
Die Haupterschließung erfolgt über eine Brücke, die mit dem Fußgängersystem der Kernzone durch eine vor der University Hall liegende »Verkehrsaustausch«-Rampe in Verbindung steht.
Die Bereiche mit dem stärksten Studentenverkehr – Hörsäle und Cafeteria – liegen in der östlichen Hälfte des Gebäudes, an die die Brücke anschließt. Zur Entflechtung der Bewegungsströme führen vom Brückenkopf im 1. Obergeschoß direkte Zugänge sowohl zum Erd- als auch zum 2. Obergeschoß. Die inneren Verkehrsflächen des östlichen Bereichs wurden so angelegt, daß hier Studenten in spontaner Weise zusammentreffen können. Die zentrale Treppe etwa, die die beiden unteren Geschosse miteinander verbindet, begleiten Sitztribünen, die zum Verweilen vor und nach den Vorlesungen einladen. Die Büros und Laboratorien in der westlichen Gebäudehälfte sind durch eine Aufzugshalle gegen die Hörsäle abgeschirmt. Jeder Sektor dieses Teils kann individuell organisiert und verändert werden, ohne das übergeordnete System zu beeinträchtigen. Die Büros liegen an den Außenwänden und scharen sich sternförmig um interne Sekretariatsbereiche; die Laboratorien nehmen das Gebäudeinnere ein. Die Versorgung erfolgt von einem Dachaufbau aus; die Laboratorien hängen an zwölf dreieckigen Schächten, die auf dem Dach zu zwei Gruppen zusammengefaßt an diesen Dachaufbau anschließen.
Wie die beiden anderen hier vorgestellten Bauten der University of Illinois ist auch dieser in seiner Grundrißstruktur nach der »Feldtheorie« organisiert. Das Tragwerk wurde aus Beton gegossen, die geschlossenen Wände bestehen zum größten Teil aus Ziegelmauerwerk.

1. The building, seen from University Hall. The areas most frequently used by the students are located in the eastern half, adjacent to the bridge connecting with the central campus. To disentangle the traffic flows, direct entrances lead from bridge level both to the cafeteria on the ground floor and to the lecture halls on the floor above bridge level.

1. Blick von der University Hall auf das Gebäude. Die Bereiche mit dem stärksten Studentenverkehr liegen in der östlichen Hälfte, an die die Brücke zur Kernzone der Universität anschließt. Zur Entflechtung der Bewegungsströme führen vom 1. Obergeschoß direkte Zugänge sowohl zur Cafeteria im Erdgeschoß als auch zu den oberen Hörsälen im 2. Obergeschoß.

2. South side of the western part of the building. On the left a stairwell which – unlike most of the outer walls which are of brick – is in concrete.

3. Plans (ground floor, 2nd floor, 3rd floor, 4th floor). The eastern half of the building contains a cafeteria and lecture rooms, the western half offices and laboratories.

4. View of the building across the bridge. In the center the main lecture hall, flanked by terraces leading to the floor above.

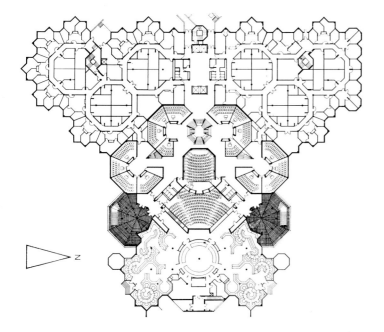

2. Blick auf die Südseite des westlichen Gebäude-teils. Links ein Treppenturm, der nicht wie die meisten Außenwände gemauert, sondern beto-niert wurde.

3. Grundrisse (Erdgeschoß, 1. Obergeschoß, 2. Obergeschoß, 3. Obergeschoß). In der östlichen Gebäudehälfte befinden sich eine Cafeteria und Hörsäle, in der westlichen Gebäudehälfte Büros und Laboratorien.

4. Blick über die Brücke auf das Gebäude. In der Mitte der große Hörsaal, flankiert von Terrassen, die in das 2. Obergeschoß führen.

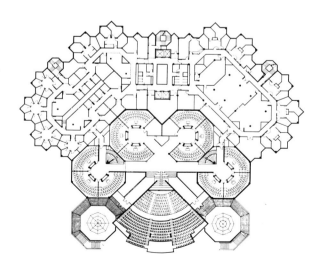
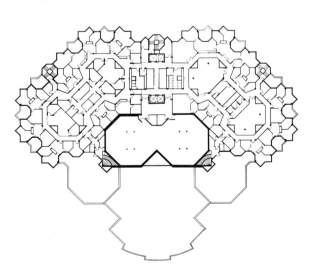

Science and Engineering South Building, University of Illinois, Chicago Circle Campus, Chicago, Illinois

This complex represents the first phase of an extension to the Science and Engineering Laboratories which are part of the original university campus.

The two parts are linked by a bridge which, in the new building, touches down in a passage that widens out to form a kind of forum. To the east of this passage is the laboratory zone, to the west the "public" zone, above it a library.

The five-story laboratory zone contains laboratories, workshops and offices for the chemistry, biology, physics and geology sections. On the typical floors, four principal distribution shafts form the centers of four clusters of laboratories, each consisting of twelve module units; another eight shafts of smaller cross-section serve the offices and ancillary laboratories along the outer walls. The four central clusters of laboratories can be divided by removable partitions into rooms of different sizes. The partitions are fitted with horizontal piping for hot, cold and chilled water, ordinary air, compressed air, vacuum, nitrogen, natural gas and steam. Not only in the partitioning of the rooms but also in the selection of fixtures, much emphasis has been laid on maximum flexibility. The laboratory furniture, for instance, can be readily re-arranged at short notice, if desired.

In the public zone, one-half of the area is assigned to lecture rooms of different sizes, the other to a cafeteria and book store.

The structural frame of the building – which is laid out in accordance with the "field theory" – is of reinforced concrete, the non-bearing outer walls are of brick.

Science and Engineering South Building, University of Illinois, Chicago Circle Campus, Chicago, Illinois

Der Komplex ist der erste Bauabschnitt einer Erweiterung der noch in der Anfangsphase der Universität errichteten Science and Engineering Laboratories.

Die Verbindung zwischen den beiden Bauten stellt eine Brücke her. Sie endet beim Neubau in einer Passage, die sich im Zentrum zu einem forumartigen Platz erweitert. Östlich schließt an diese Passage der Laborbereich, westlich der »öffentliche« Bereich an. Über der Passage liegt eine Bibliothek.

Der fünfgeschossige Laborbereich enthält Laboratorien, Werkstätten und Büros für die Abteilungen Chemie, Biologie, Physik und Geologie. Vier Hauptinstallationsschächte bilden in den Normalgeschossen die Zentren von vier Laborgruppen aus jeweils zwölf Moduleinheiten, weitere acht Schächte mit kleinerem Querschnitt bedienen die an den Außenwänden liegenden Büros und die Nebenlaboratorien. Die vier zentralen Laborgruppen lassen sich durch demontierbare Trennwände in verschieden große Räume unterteilen. Die Trennwände sind mit horizontal geführten Leitungen für heißes, kaltes sowie gekühltes Wasser, Normalluft, Druckluft, Vakuum, Stickstoff, Naturgas und Dampf ausgestattet. Nicht nur bei der Raumgliederung, sondern auch bei der Wahl der Einrichtungsgegenstände wurde auf größtmögliche Flexibilität geachtet. So können die Labormöbel bei Bedarf in kürzester Zeit umarrangiert werden.

Der öffentliche Bereich enthält in der einen Hälfte verschieden große Hörsäle, in der anderen Hälfte eine Cafeteria und einen Buchladen.

Das Tragwerk des in seiner Grundrißstruktur nach der »Feldtheorie« organisierten Gebäudes besteht aus Stahlbeton, die nichttragenden geschlossenen Außenwände wurden aus Ziegelsteinen gemauert.

1. General view of the building from northwest.
2. Plans (ground floor, 2nd floor, 3rd floor). Key: 1 passage, 2 bridge, 3 cafeteria, 4 lecture rooms, 5 book store, 6 library, 7 workshops, 8 laboratories and offices.

1. Gesamtansicht des Gebäudes von Nordwesten.
2. Grundrisse (Erdgeschoß, 1. Obergeschoß, 2. Obergeschoß). Legende: 1 Passage, 2 Brücke, 3 Cafeteria, 4 Hörsäle, 5 Buchladen, 6 Bibliothek, 7 Werkstätten, 8 Laboratorien und Büros.

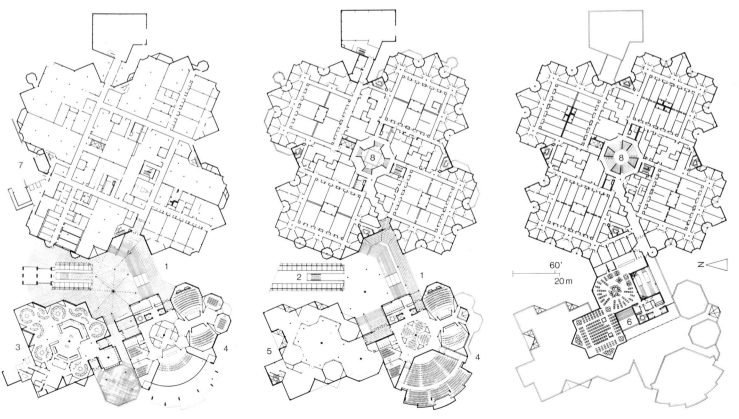

60'
20 m

N

3, 4. Central stairs in the laboratory zone.
5. Large lecture hall.

3, 4. Die zentrale Treppe im Laborbereich.
5. Der große Hörsaal.

Laney College, Oakland, California

Laney College is the largest of several campuses simultaneously built for the six-city Peralta Junior College District. The site is located in a down-town redevelopment area in the immediate vicinity of the new Oakland Museum, designed by Kevin Roche and John Dinkeloo. Covering about 67 acres, the site is bisected by a channel which will be developed into a green-belt connection between Lake Merritt and the Oakland Estuary. The population resident in the surrounding district mainly belongs to the lower-income group which would not normally seek college-level training but may well be prompted by the immediate proximity of the college to make use of its facilities.

The college is designed for a total daytime enrollment of about 7,500 students and provides facilities not only for the usual academic subjects but also for a wide range of vocational subjects with special emphasis on inter-disciplinary contacts.

The building complex forms a compact group on an approximately square site. In the center is an open court, surrounded by library, students center, gymnasium and a base for a future theater. The outer corners of this cross are taken up by an outdoor work area, a combination dance and lecture hall, a physical training center and a nine-story tower for administrative and academic offices. In the outer zone are the teaching premises – with workshops on the ground floor and classrooms surrounding small patios on the upper floor – as well as a science forum and an outdoor swimming pool.

With its untreated concrete and brick facades, the complex has an appearance of strength and warmth.

Laney College, Oakland, California

Das Laney College ist die größte von mehreren Campusanlagen, die gleichzeitig für den sechs Städte umfassenden Peralta Junior College District errichtet wurden. Es liegt in einem innerstädtischen Sanierungsgebiet, in unmittelbarer Nachbarschaft des von Kevin Roche und John Dinkeloo erbauten Oakland Museum. Das etwa 27 ha große Grundstück wird in Querrichtung von einem Kanal durchschnitten, der den Lake Merritt mit der San Francisco Bay verbindet und dessen Uferzone später einen durchgehenden Grüngürtel bilden wird. Die Bewohner der umgebenden Viertel gehören größtenteils einer Bevölkerungsschicht an, in der normalerweise nicht an eine qualifizierte Schulbildung gedacht wird – durch die unmittelbare Konfrontation mit einer entsprechenden Institution hofft man jedoch, sie zu einer solchen anzuregen.

Das College bietet etwa 7500 Studienplätze. Unterrichtet werden sowohl die üblichen akademischen Fächer als auch die unmittelbarer auf eine Berufspraxis bezogenen, wobei besonderer Wert auf interdisziplinäre Begegnungen gelegt wird.

Die sehr kompakt gehaltene Gebäudegruppe ist auf einem annähernd quadratischen Grundriß aufgebaut. Im Zentrum liegt ein offener Hof, umgeben von der Bibliothek, dem Studentenzentrum, einer Sporthalle und der Basis eines noch zu errichtenden Theaters. Die Eckzwickel dieses Kreuzes sind durch einen Arbeitshof, einen kombinierten Vorlesungs- und Tanzbau, einen Sportbau sowie einen neungeschossigen Turm für die Verwaltung gefüllt. In der Außenzone liegen die Unterrichtsgebäude – mit Werkräumen im Erdgeschoß und Klassenräumen, die kleine Höfe umschließen, im Obergeschoß –, ein Forum sowie ein offenes Schwimmbad.

Sichtbeton und unverputztes Ziegelsteinmauerwerk geben dem Komplex ein kräftiges, warmes Gepräge.

1. View of the college from the west (model). In the center are the jointly used facilities, in the outer zone the classrooms and workshops. In the foreground the main entrance with direct access from a station of the new rapid transit railway (BART).
2. View from northwest of the nine-story tower containing the administrative offices.

1. Blick von Westen auf die Anlage (Modell). Im Zentrum befinden sich die allgemeinen Einrichtungen, in der Außenzone die Unterrichtsräume und Werkstätten. Im Vordergrund der Hauptzugang; direkt an diesem Zugang liegt eine Station der neuen regionalen Schnellbahn (BART).
2. Blick von Nordwesten auf den neungeschossigen Turm, in dem die Verwaltung untergebracht ist.

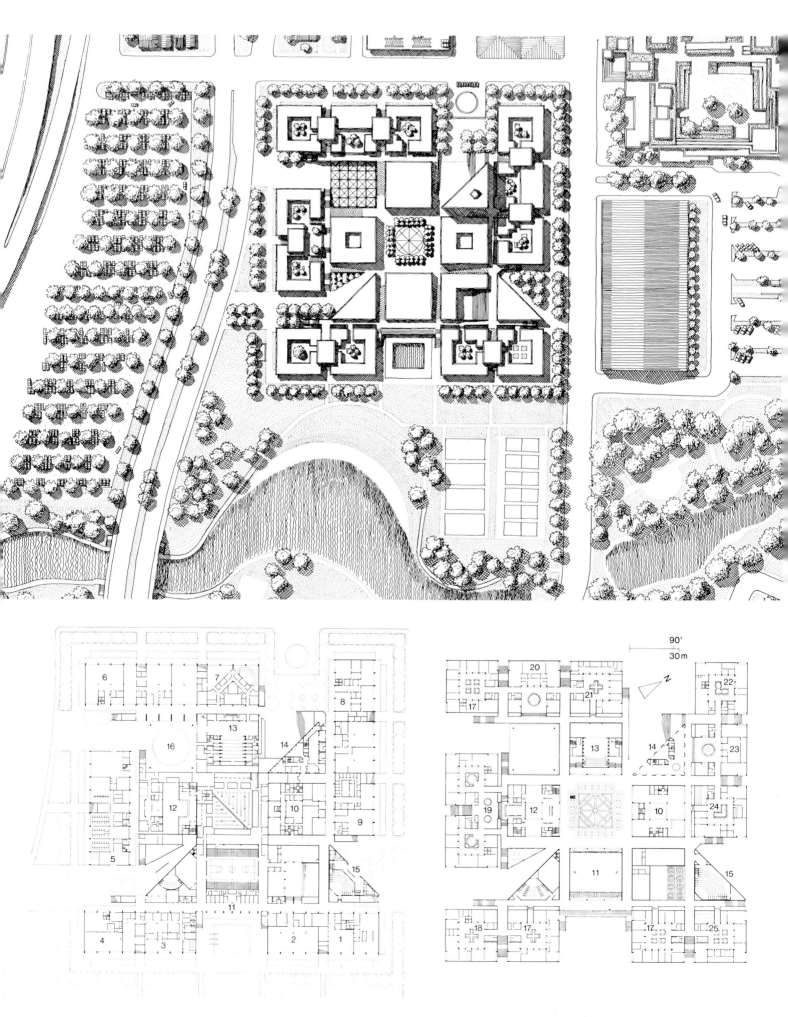

90'
30 m

3. Site plan. At the bottom, the channel bisecting the site.
4. Plans (ground floor, 2nd floor). Key: 1 electrical engineering, 2 air-conditioning technology, 3 cooking, 4 mechanical center, 5 metal work, 6 workshops, 7 music, 8 electronics, 9 graphic arts, 10 library, 11 sports center, 12 student center, 13 theater, 14 administration, 15 forum, 16 open work area, 17 classrooms, 18 nursing, 19 commercial subjects, 20 drawing, 21 metallurgy, 22 arts, 23 chemistry, 24 physics, 25 biology.
5. View of the library across the central court.
6. Theater under construction.

3. Lageplan. Unten der Kanal, der das Collegegelände in Querrichtung durchschneidet.
4. Grundrisse (Erdgeschoß, 1. Obergeschoß). Legende: 1 Elektrotechnik, 2 Klimatechnik, 3 Kochen, 4 Betriebszentrale, 5 Metallbearbeitung, 6 Werkstätten, 7 Musik, 8 Elektronik, 9 Graphik, 10 Bibliothek, 11 Sport, 12 Studentenzentrum, 13 Theater, 14 Verwaltung, 15 Forum, 16 Arbeitshof, 17 Klassenräume, 18 Krankenpflege, 19 Handelslehre, 20 Zeichnen, 21 Metallurgie, 22 Kunst, 23 Chemie, 24 Physik, 25 Biologie.
5. Blick über den zentralen Hof auf die Bibliothek.
6. Das Theater im Bau.

Robert R. McMath Solar Telescope, Kitt Peak National Observatory, Kitt Peak, Arizona

Named after its initiator who died in 1962, the telescope is primarily designed for studying the physical and chemical features of the sun. It is owned by the "Association of Universities for Research in Astronomy".

The heliostat, weighing almost 50 tons, is placed on a concrete tower of about 100' height and circular cross-section. The tube is a shaft of about 500' length, inclined at an angle of 32° with the horizontal, and for the most part buried in the ground where the temperature fluctuates less than in the air. The upper end of the part emerging from the ground is supported by a steel jacket which surrounds the concrete tower but has its own separate foundation so that the heliostat is well protected against wind movements. Unwelcome thermal air flows in the open part of the shaft exposed to solar heat are counteracted by a cooling system mounted below the outer cladding. This system works with a liquid which will not freeze up even at extremely low winter temperatures. The jackets of the upper part of the shaft and of the concrete tower have square cross-sections, and their center lines are set at an angle of 45° to minimize the surface exposed to the wind.

Robert R. McMath Solar Telescope, Kitt Peak National Observatory, Kitt Peak, Arizona

Das nach seinem 1962 verstorbenen Initiator benannte Teleskop dient in erster Linie der Erforschung der physikalischen und chemischen Eigenschaften der Sonne. Eigentümer ist die Association of Universities for Research in Astronomy.

Der knapp 50 t wiegende Heliostat sitzt auf einem etwa 30 m hohen Rundturm aus Beton. Als Tubus dient ein etwa 152 m langer, um 32° gegen die Waagrechte geneigter Schacht, der zum größeren Teil unter die Erde gelegt wurde, weil hier die Temperatur konstanter ist als an der Luft; der aus der Erde herausragende Teil lagert mit seinem oberen Ende auf einer den Betonturm umgebenden Stahlhülle, die unabhängig gegründet wurde und dadurch den Heliostaten weitestgehend vor Windbewegungen schützt. Unerwünschten thermischen Aufwinden im freien, der Sonneneinstrahlung ausgesetzten Teil des Schachtes begegnete man mit einem unter der äußeren Verkleidung installierten Kühlsystem. Es arbeitet mit einer Flüssigkeit, die auch bei extrem niedrigen Wintertemperaturen nicht einfriert. Die im Querschnitt quadratischen Umhüllungen des oberen Schachtabschnittes und des Betonturmes wurden in ihren Längsachsen um 45° verkantet, um dem Wind eine möglichst kleine Angriffsfläche zu bieten.

1. Section of telescope. Key: 1 heliostat support tower, 2 heliostat, 3 optical tunnel, 4 mirror, 5 observation room, 6 spectrograph, 7 aluminisation room for the mirror.
2. Close-up view. The square jackets of the upper part of the shaft and of the concrete tower are set at an angle of 45° to minimize the surface exposed to the wind.

1. Schnitt durch das Teleskop. Legende: 1 Unterbau des Heliostaten, 2 Heliostat, 3 Tubus, 4 Spiegel, 5 Beobachtungsraum, 6 Spektrograph, 7 Aluminisierraum für die Spiegel.
2. Detailansicht. Die im Querschnitt quadratischen Umhüllungen des oberen Schachtabschnittes und des Betonturmes wurden in ihren Längsachsen um 45° verkantet, um dem Wind eine möglichst kleine Angriffsfläche zu bieten.

Pages 246–247:
3. General view. From the distance, the telescope seems like a gigantic sculpture.

Seiten 246–247:
3. Gesamtansicht. Das Teleskop erscheint aus größerer Entfernung wie eine gigantische Skulptur.

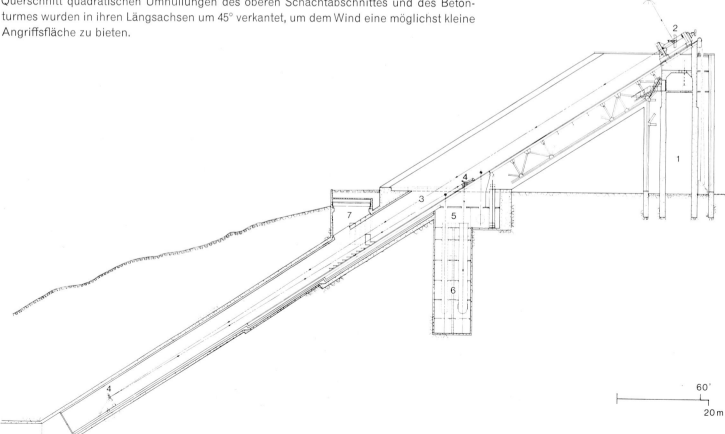

60'

20 m

Lindheimer Astronomical Research Center, Northwestern University, Evanston, Illinois

The building, erected on a tongue of filled land projecting into Lake Michigan, houses two reflector telescopes – one large instrument with a diameter of 40″ for research purposes, and a smaller one of 16″ diameter for teaching purposes.

One prime requirement was to protect the telescopes as effectively as possible against temperature changes, vibrations and wind movements. The designers solved this problem by completely separating the telescopes and their concrete piers from the enclosure.

The larger telescope is carried on a hollow pier of circular cross-section, the smaller instrument on one of square cross-section which also provides the access facilities – a small lift and a spiral flight of stairs cantilevered from the outer walls.

The steel pipe framework supporting the enclosure stands on its four bases with such a wide stance that it cannot be deformed even by very strong wind forces. The pipes are weld-assembled by means of circular steel discs or segments. The vertical parts of the enclosure consist of corrugated steel panels. The size of the units and position and size of the windows are adapted to a module of the corrugations – a detail which contributes greatly to the impression of machine-like perfection.

The lower floor, surrounding a small court, is partly below ground level so that it has the appearance of a base rather than a story. It contains workshops and service rooms. To reveal the structural independence of the enclosure, the lower end of the latter is placed so high above the top of the lower floor that it can be recognized even from a long distance.

Lindheimer Astronomical Research Center, Northwestern University, Evanston, Illinois

Das Gebäude steht auf einer künstlich geschaffenen Landzunge im Lake Michigan. Es beherbergt zwei Spiegelteleskope, ein größeres mit einem Durchmesser von etwa 102 cm für Forschungszwecke und ein kleineres mit einem Durchmesser von knapp 41 cm für die Lehre.

Eine wichtige Forderung war, die Teleskope so gut wie möglich gegen Temperaturschwankungen, Vibrationen und Windbewegungen zu schützen. Die Architekten lösten diese Aufgabe, indem sie die Teleskope und die sie tragenden Betonschäfte vollständig von der Hüllkonstruktion trennten.

Der Schaft unter dem größeren Teleskop ist eine runde, der unter dem kleineren Teleskop eine quadratische Hohlsäule. Die quadratische Säule dient zugleich der Erschließung: Im Innern befindet sich ein kleiner Aufzug, und von den Außenwänden kragt eine umlaufende Treppe aus.

Das die Hülle tragende Raumfachwerk aus Stahlrohren steht so breitbeinig auf seinen vier Fundamenten, daß es auch von sehr starken Windkräften nicht verformt werden kann. Die Rohre sind über runde Stahlscheiben, beziehungsweise entsprechende Scheibenabschnitte miteinander verschweißt. Für die senkrechten Teile der Hülle verwendete man Paneele aus gewelltem Stahlblech. Die Elementgrößen sowie die Lage und die Abmessung der Fenster sind genau auf das Wellenmaß abgestimmt – ein Detail, das wesentlich zu dem Eindruck apparatehafter Perfektion, den das Gebäude vermittelt, beiträgt.

Das einen kleinen Hof umschließende Basisgeschoß ist halb in den Erdboden versenkt; dadurch wirkt es nicht wie ein eigenes Geschoß, sondern wie ein Sockel. Es enthält Werkstätten und Maschinenräume. Um die konstruktive Unabhängigkeit der Hülle ganz deutlich werden zu lassen, wurde ihr unterer Abschluß so weit über die Oberkante des Basisgeschosses gelegt, daß man ihn auch aus größerer Entfernung noch erkennen kann.

1. The building, seen from across the lake. It contains two reflector telescopes – a larger one for research purposes, and a smaller one for teaching purposes.
2. Section. The two telescopes are supported on concrete piers. As a protection against temperature changes, vibrations and wind movements, the surrounding enclosure is a completely separate structure.

1. Blick über den See auf das Gebäude. Es enthält zwei Spiegelteleskope, ein größeres für Forschung und ein kleineres für die Lehre.
2. Schnitt. Die beiden Teleskope ruhen auf Betonschäften. Um sie gegen Temperaturschwankungen, Vibrationen und Windbewegungen zu schützen, ist die sie umgebende Hülle vollständig von ihnen gelöst.

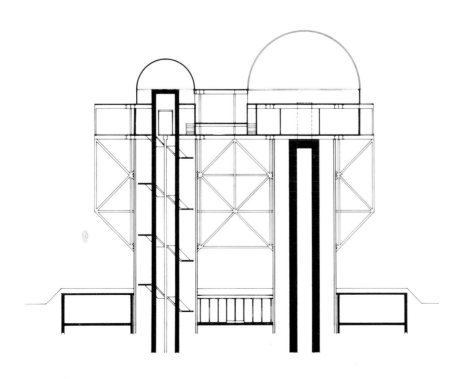

3. The framework supporting the enclosure stands on its four bases with such a wide stance that it cannot be deformed even by strong wind forces.
4. The two telescope rooms, seen from below. The pipes of the steel framework are welded together with circular steel discs or segments.

3. Das die Hülle tragende Raumfachwerk steht so breitbeinig auf seinen vier Fundamenten, daß es auch von starken Windkräften nicht verformt werden kann.
4. Blick von unten auf die beiden Teleskopräume. Die Rohre des Stahlfachwerkes sind über runde Stahlscheiben, beziehungsweise entsprechende Scheibenabschnitte miteinander verschweißt.

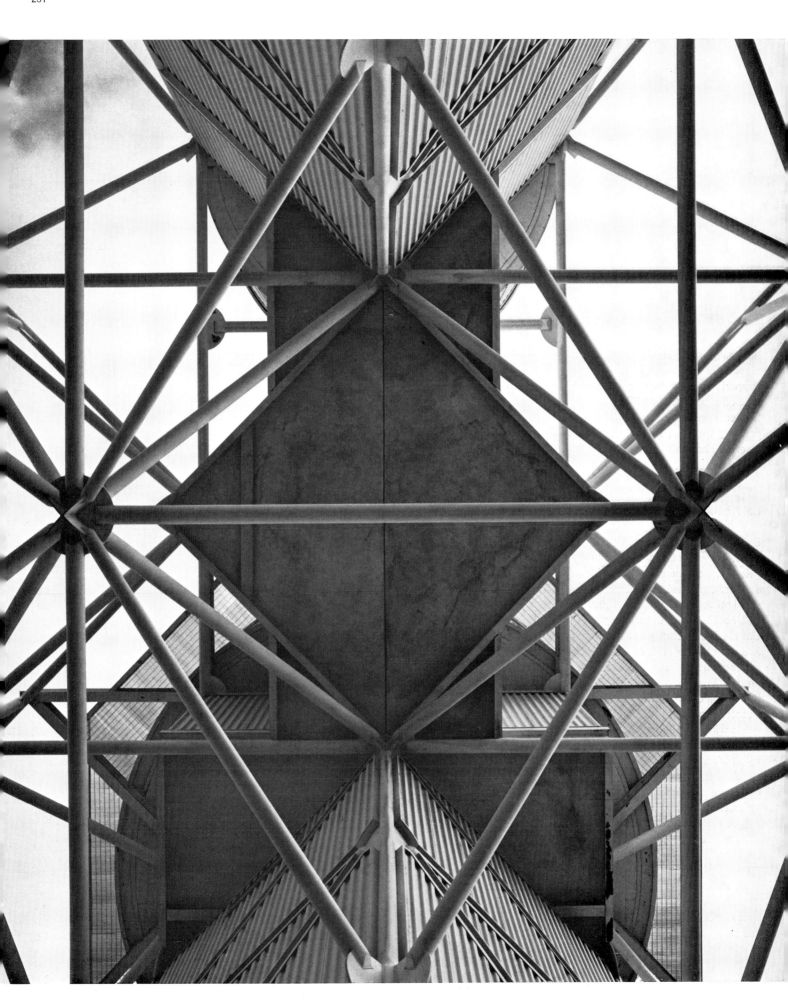

Oakland-Alameda County Coliseum, Oakland, California

Favorably situated alongside a major inter-city freeway near the population center of the Bay Region, this complex – designed for a whole range of sports and recreation facilities – consists of a stadium, an enclosed multi-purpose arena and an intermediate exhibition hall, flanked by two outdoor exhibition areas.

The circular stadium, with a maximum seating capacity for 53,000 spectators and an outside diameter of 770', is primarily designed for baseball, football and soccer. To facilitate access to the seats, the playing field was lowered 29' below ground level. The lower rows of the grandstands make use of the slopes of the excavated bowl, forming a ring around the entire playing field, while the upper rows are supported by a reinforced concrete structure extending around two-thirds of the playing field. Access to the upper grandstand is from the roof of the exhibition hall and a ring-shaped earth berm connecting with it. For football and soccer matches, a removable grandstand of tubular steel is erected in the eastern part of the playing field, and the pitch runs from north to south while baseball is played from east to west.

The exhibition hall has a floor space of 50,000 sq ft. By combining it with the immediately adjacent multi-purpose arena, a contiguous indoor exhibition area of about 110,000 sq ft can be obtained.

Like the stadium, the multi-purpose arena is circular in plan. It has an outer diameter of 420' and seating accommodation for up to 15,000 spectators. Of particular interest is the design of the roof which spans the entire space without intermediate columns. A ring of diagonally intersecting columns of reinforced concrete, which also take up lateral forces, supports an external ring of compression members, likewise consisting of reinforced concrete. Suspended from this compression ring are 96 galvanized steel cables, linked to a steel tension ring in the center. These cables support a system of slender precast concrete ribs carrying the roof, as well as a steel-framed penthouse 260' in diameter. Because of the inverted shape of the roof, the rain water is collected at the outer wall of the penthouse from which it is pumped up to the gutters along the compression ring.

Oakland-Alameda County Coliseum, Oakland, California

Der für vielerlei Arten von Sport- und anderen Freizeitbetätigungen ausgelegte Komplex, günstig an einer Schnellstraße in der Nähe des Bevölkerungsschwerpunktes der Bay-Region gelegen, besteht aus einem Stadion, einer Mehrzweckhalle und einem dazwischengeschobenen Ausstellungsbau mit zwei flankierenden Ausstellungsflächen im Freien.

Das kreisförmige, maximal 53000 Zuschauerplätze bietende Stadion, das primär für Baseball, Football und Fußball ausgelegt wurde, hat einen äußeren Durchmesser von etwa 235 m. Um die Erschließung der Zuschauerplätze möglichst einfach zu halten, wurde das Spielfeld um etwa 9 m in den Boden abgesenkt. Der untere, direkt von der Parkplatzebene aus zugängliche Teil der Tribünenanlage liegt an der Schräge des Erdaushubs und umgibt ringförmig das gesamte Spielfeld, während der obere, als Stahlbetonkonstruktion ausgeführte Teil einen Drittelkreis offen läßt. Erschlossen wird der obere Teil über das Dach des Ausstellungsbaus und einen daran anschließenden Erdwallring. Für Football- und Fußballspiele wird im östlichen Bereich des Spielfeldes eine Stahlrohrtribüne aufgestellt. Die Spielachse verläuft dann in Nord-Süd-Richtung, während Baseball von Osten nach Westen gespielt wird.

Der Ausstellungsbau bietet eine Fläche von rund 4650 qm. Durch Hinzunahme der unmittelbar angrenzenden Arena der Mehrzweckhalle läßt sich die überdachte Ausstellungsfläche auf etwa 10200 qm erweitern.

Wie das Stadion hat auch die Mehrzweckhalle einen kreisförmigen Grundriß. Bei einem äußeren Durchmesser von etwa 128 m bietet sie maximal 15000 Zuschauerplätze. Eine besondere Beachtung verdient die Konstruktion des den gesamten Raum frei überspannenden Daches: Ein auch gegen Seitenkräfte stabiler Kranz aus X-förmig sich kreuzenden Stahlbetonstützen trägt einen ebenfalls aus Stahlbeton bestehenden äußeren Kompressionsring. Zwischen diesem und einem inneren Zugring aus Stahl sind 96 verzinkte Stahlkabel gespannt, auf denen ein schlankes Stahlbetonrippenwerk ruht. Die Stahlkabel tragen nicht nur das Dach, sondern auch einen stählernen Dachaufbau mit einem Durchmesser von etwa 79 m. Da das Dach nach innen geneigt ist, muß das Regenwasser, das sich am Rande des Dachaufbaus sammelt, mit Pumpen zu den Abläufen am Kompressionsring gehoben werden.

1. Aerial photograph of the Coliseum complex, with the stadium in the foreground, the exhibition hall in the center, and the multi-purpose arena in the background. For football and soccer matches, a grandstand of tubular steel is erected in the eastern part of the playing field.

1. Luftaufnahme des Komplexes. Im Vordergrund das Stadion, in der Mitte der Ausstellungsbereich, im Hintergrund die Mehrzweckhalle. Für Football- und Fußballspiele wird im östlichen Teil des Stadions eine Stahlrohr-Tribüne aufgestellt.

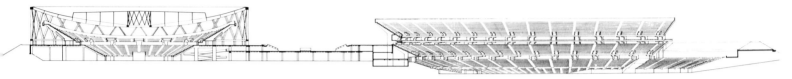

2. Section of stadium, exhibition hall and multi-purpose arena.
3. Details of the arena roof. Top: system plan. Bottom: plan of two bays, and sections of the outer compression ring (A), two longitudinal ribs with steel cable insertions (B), and the inner tension ring (C).
4. Site plan of the complex, with the stadium arranged for baseball.

2. Schnitt durch Stadion, Ausstellungsbau und Mehrzweckhalle.
3. Details des Daches der Mehrzweckhalle. Oben Übersichtsplan, unten Grundriß von zwei Feldern und Schnitte durch den äußeren Kompressionsring (A), zwei Längsrippen mit eingelegten Stahlkabeln (B) und den inneren Zugring (C).
4. Lageplan des Komplexes. Das Stadion ist hier für Baseball eingerichtet.

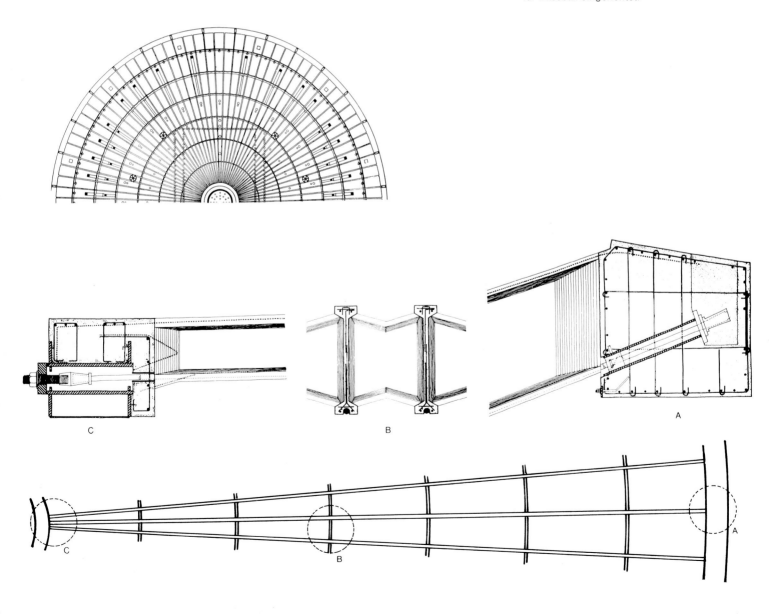

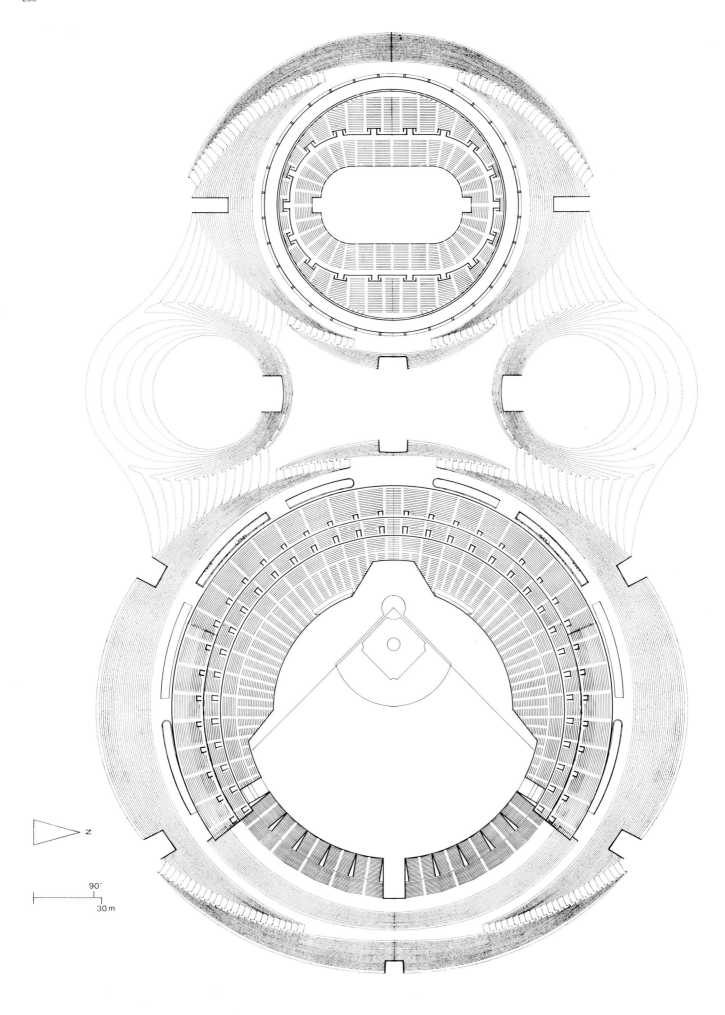

90'
30 m

5. View of the complex from the north.
6. Nighttime view of the multi-purpose arena.

5. Ansicht des Komplexes von Norden.
6. Die Mehrzweckhalle am Abend.

7. Outer concourse of the arena. The upper glass
wall is braced by trusses.
8. Interior of the multi-purpose arena.
9. Ramps for the grandstands of the stadium.

7. Blick in den äußeren Umgang der Mehrzweckhalle. Die obere Glaswand wird durch Fachwerk-
träger ausgesteift.
8. Blick auf die Arena der Mehrzweckhalle.
9. Rampen im Tribünenbereich des Stadions.

Housing Units at the Winnebago Children's Home, Neillsville, Wisconsin

The home, designed for emotionally disturbed children from seven to eighteen years of age, stands in particularly attractive grounds which cover an area of 180 acres on the bank of the Black River. The four new houses have been built to replace obsolete dormitory facilities. In addition, there are a large administration and dormitory building, a school, and two older housing units.

Within the grounds, the children have complete freedom. Their daily routine is much the same as in a normal family. They go to school in the morning – either to public school in Neillsville if possible, or to the special school on the grounds; they come home for lunch and return to school in the afternoon. The therapy mainly takes the form of informal, spontaneous communication.

In keeping with this pedagogical and therapeutic principle, the four new houses, each of them accommodating ten children and their house parents, are organized like large family houses. The individual rooms – four double rooms and two single rooms – are placed in ascending helical configuration around a continually rising common space where the children, supervised by the house parents, can follow their daytime routine – reading and study, hobbies and crafts. The exterior covered areas beneath the higher rooms along the periphery are used as terraces for outdoor meals and play and for the storage of bicycles, toboggans and other outdoor accessories.

Despite their emotionally stimulating spatial complexity, the houses are composed of individually simple elements. Each of the rooms on the periphery is a square box with a diagonally oriented gable roof. The common room in the middle is covered by four roof elements which are supported by three circular columns in the center and by the inner walls of the peripheral rooms. Bearing structure and cladding of the houses are of wood.

Wohneinheiten im Winnebago Children's Home, Neillsville, Wisconsin

Das Heim, das geistig behinderte Kinder im Alter von 7 bis 18 Jahren aufnimmt, liegt auf einem außergewöhnlich schönen, etwa 73 ha großen Gelände am Ufer des Black River. Die vier Neubauten wurden anstelle überalterter Wohneinheiten errichtet. Neben diesen umfaßt die Anlage ein großes Verwaltungs- und Wohnheimgebäude, eine Schule sowie zwei ältere Wohneinheiten.

Auf dem Gelände haben die Kinder völlige Freiheit; den älteren wird teilweise sogar individueller Ausgang gewährt. Das tägliche Leben verläuft fast genauso wie in einer normalen Familie: Morgens gehen die Kinder zur Schule – wenn möglich in die öffentliche Schule von Neillsville oder aber in die Spezialschule des Heimes –, mittags kommen sie zum Essen nach Hause, um dann am Nachmittag wieder zum Unterricht zu gehen. Die Behandlung erfolgt primär über spontane, informelle Kontakte.

Entsprechend diesem pädagogischen und therapeutischen Prinzip sind die vier Neubauten, die jeweils zehn Kinder und ihre Hauseltern beherbergen, wie große Einfamilienhäuser organisiert. Die privaten Räume – vier Doppel- und zwei Einzelzimmer – umschließen in wendeltreppenartiger Form einen gleichlaufend ansteigenden Gemeinschaftsraum, in dem die Kinder unter Aufsicht der Hauseltern ihrer Tagesbeschäftigung – Lesen, Lernen, Basteln und so weiter – nachgehen können. Die Freiflächen unter den höhergelegenen Außenräumen werden als Spiel- und Speiseterrassen sowie zum Abstellen von Fahrrädern, Schlitten und anderen größeren Geräten benutzt.

Die Häuser haben trotz ihrer emotional stimulierenden räumlichen Komplexität einen sehr einfachen Aufbau. Die Außenräume sind gleichgroße quadratische Boxen mit einem diagonal aufgesetzten Giebeldach. Der zentrale Gemeinschaftsraum wird von vier Dachelementen, die in der Mitte auf drei Rundstützen und am Rand auf den Innenwänden der Außenräume aufliegen, überdacht. Das Tragwerk der Häuser besteht wie ihre Verkleidung aus Holz.

1. Perspective plan of a house. In the middle the common room, on the outside the bedrooms.

1. Perspektivischer Grundriß einer Wohneinheit. Im Zentrum der Gemeinschaftsraum, außen die Schlafräume.

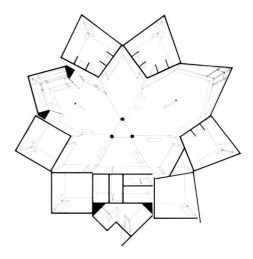

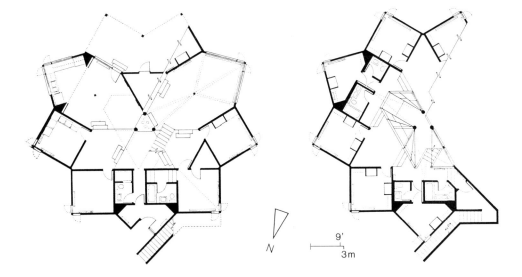

2. Entrance sides of two of the houses. On the right of each house, the outdoor stairs leading to the upper end of the common room.
3. Plans (lower level, upper level).

2. Blick auf die Eingangsseiten von zwei Häusern. Rechts jeweils die Außentreppe zum oberen Ende des Gemeinschaftsraumes.
3. Grundrisse (untere Ebene, obere Ebene).

N

9'
3m

4. The common room ascends helically in keeping with the bedrooms on the outside.
5. Stairs leading to the upper end of the common room.
6. Common room. In the background, left, the circular columns in the center of the house.

4. Der Gemeinschaftsraum steigt gleichlaufend mit den außenliegenden Schlafräumen wendeltreppenförmig an.
5. Treppe zum oberen Ende des Gemeinschaftsraumes.
6. Der Gemeinschaftsraum. Links im Hintergrund die zentralen Rundstützen.

7. Two houses, seen from across the river.

7. Blick über den Fluß auf zwei Häuser.

Carmel Valley Manor, Carmel Valley, California

This village for the elderly is situated 7 miles outside Carmel, a small coastal town south-west of Monterey, which has given its name to the isolated, very attractive valley in the Santa Lucia Range. Covering 26 acres, the site begins on the south side with a low meadow along the valley road and rises fairly rapidly towards the center before swinging gently towards the foothills on the right-hand side of the valley.

The general facilities for the village are located in the center of the site. The cruciform main building contains the administrative offices, a lounge, a dining room, an infirmary as well as craft rooms. In the two ancillary buildings are smaller lounges, reading rooms and laundry facilities. The chapel is designed so that it can also be used for other social activities.

Among the 170 residential units are 48 units for single persons without cooking facilities (but with sink and refrigerator), 72 two-room units with kitchenette, 32 three-room units with separate kitchen and 18 three-room units with separate kitchen and additional bathroom. The single-room units are located in three two-story buildings, connected to the main building by covered walks, the two-room units in nine single-story buildings, the smaller three-room units in eight single-story buildings with open courts, and the larger three-room units in nine pairs of cottages separated by carports.

Except for the chapel which has a wooden roof supported by steel trusses, and the two-story townhouses where regulations called for steel frames, all buildings have timber frames. The walls have a cladding of gypsumboard on the inside and white stucco coating on the outside. The roofing consists of redwood shingles.

The architectural design was clearly influenced by traditional Californian styles and their Mediterranean, especially Spanish, forerunners. One of the reasons for this choice was the original requirement to integrate with the new complex a colonial-style house dating back to the 1920s which was, however, destroyed by fire during the planning stage.

Carmel Valley Manor, Carmel Valley, California

Das Altenzentrum liegt ungefähr 11 km außerhalb von Carmel, der kleinen Küstenstadt südwestlich von Monterey, die dem abgeschiedenen, landschaftlich sehr reizvollen Tal innerhalb der Santa Lucia Range den Namen gab. Das etwa 10,5 ha große Grundstück beginnt im Süden an der schmalen Durchgangsstraße mit einer flachen Wiese, steigt dann zur Mitte verhältnismäßig rasch an, um dann nach Norden langsam gegen den rechten Rand der Talsohle auszuschwingen.

Im Zentrum des Geländes befinden sich die allgemeinen Einrichtungen des Heimes. Das kreuzförmige Hauptgebäude enthält die Verwaltung, einen Aufenthaltsraum, einen Speisesaal, eine Krankenstation sowie Handwerksräume; in den beiden Nebengebäuden sind kleinere Aufenthaltsräume, Lesezimmer und Räume zum Wäschewaschen untergebracht. Die Kapelle gestattet in ihrer räumlichen Organisation neben Gottesdiensten auch andere gemeinschaftliche Aktivitäten.

Die 170 Wohneinheiten gliedern sich in 48 Einzimmerwohnungen ohne Kochgelegenheit (aber mit Ausguß und Kühlschrank), 72 Zweizimmerwohnungen mit Kochnische, 32 Dreizimmerwohnungen mit separater Küche sowie 18 Dreizimmerwohnungen mit separater Küche und einem zusätzlichen Bad. Die Einzimmerwohnungen liegen in drei zweigeschossigen, mit dem Hauptgebäude durch überdachte Gänge verbundenen Häusern, die Zweizimmerwohnungen in neun eingeschossigen Häusern, die kleineren Dreizimmerwohnungen in acht eingeschossigen Häusern mit zentralem Innenhof und die größeren Dreizimmerwohnungen in neun eingeschossigen Doppelhäusern mit zwischengeschalteten Autounterständen.

Bis auf die Kapelle, deren Holzdach auf Stahlträgern ruht, und die zweigeschossigen Häuser, die entsprechend den Bauvorschriften Stahltragwerke erhalten mußten, werden alle Bauten von reinen Holzskeletten getragen. Die Wände sind innen mit Gipsplatten verkleidet und außen weiß verputzt, als Dachdeckungsmaterial wählte man Schindeln aus Redwood.

In ihrem formalen Vokabular bezogen sich die Architekten auf traditionelle kalifornische Bauformen und deren Vorläufer im Mittelmeerraum, besonders in Spanien. Motiv hierfür war nicht zuletzt die ursprünglich gestellte Aufgabe, ein um 1920 im Kolonialstil errichtetes Haus, das jedoch während der Planungsarbeiten durch Feuer vernichtet wurde, in die Anlage zu integrieren.

1. General view of the retirement village from the north.
2. Site plan. Key: 1 main road, 2 main building, 3 ancillary buildings, 4 chapel, 5 two-story house with 16 single-room units, 6 single-story house with eight two-room units, 7 single-story house with four smaller three-room units, 8 single-story house with two larger three-room units separated by carports, 9 carports, 10 swimming pool.

1. Gesamtansicht des Altenzentrums von Norden.
2. Lageplan. Legende: 1 Durchgangsstraße, 2 Hauptgebäude, 3 Nebengebäude, 4 Kapelle, 5 zweigeschossiges Haus mit 16 Einzimmerwohnungen, 6 eingeschossiges Haus mit acht Zweizimmerwohnungen, 7 eingeschossiges Haus mit vier kleineren Dreizimmerwohnungen, 8 eingeschossiges Haus mit zwei größeren Dreizimmerwohnungen und zwischengeschalteten Autounterständen, 9 Autounterstände, 10 Schwimmbad.

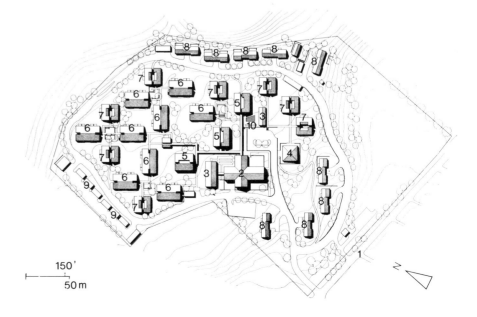

150'
50 m

3. One of the single-story houses with two-room units.
4. Court of one of the single-story houses with smaller three-room units.
5. Plans of the different types of residential units (A single-room unit, B two-room unit, C three-room unit with one bathroom, D three-room unit with two bathrooms and carport).

3. Blick auf eines der eingeschossigen Häuser mit Zweizimmerwohnungen.
4. Blick in den Hof eines der eingeschossigen Häuser mit kleineren Dreizimmerwohnungen.
5. Grundrisse der verschiedenen Wohnungstypen (A Einzimmerwohnung, B Zweizimmerwohnung, C Dreizimmerwohnung mit einem Bad, D Dreizimmerwohnung mit zwei Bädern und Autounterstand).

6. Main building, seen across the swimming pool from northeast.
7. Chapel.

6. Blick von Nordosten über das Schwimmbad auf das Hauptgebäude.
7. Die Kapelle.

A

B

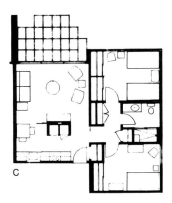

C

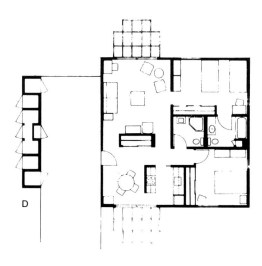

D

Portland Center, Portland, Oregon

The Portland Center rises as a combined residential and commercial district on a site of nearly 83 acres at the fringe of the central business district. It is regarded as one of the most outstanding urban renewal projects in the United States and has already received several awards.

Now occupied are three high-rise apartment blocks, 24 low-rise town houses, a parking garage with a restaurant and a stockbroker's office on the top floor, a shopping center, and three office complexes.

Each of the three apartment blocks stands on a podium which is used as a garage. Their plan is nearly square, with elevators, stairs and refuse shafts placed in the center, surrounded by corridors. Two of the towers have 25 stories, the third has 22. A typical floor contains eight apartments with two to three-and-a-half rooms; on each of the upper floors are four apartments with four to five rooms.

Because the balconies do not extend into continuous galleries, they provide a strong feature of the facades. To ensure privacy and to prevent air draughts, the balconies are flanked to their full depth by the projecting wall panels of the bearing structure.

The low-rise town houses form two clusters of twelve around the two 25-story towers. They are located along the edges of the garage podiums whose landscaped roofs provide access to high-rise and low-rise houses alike. Bedrooms and bathrooms are half-a-story below the entrance while sitting rooms and kitchens are half-a-story above it.

Of the office complexes erected so far, one belongs to the Boise Cascade Corporation and another to the Blue Cross of Oregon. The seven-story main building of the latter is connected by a bridge with a free-standing parking garage where further stories are planned to be added for additional office space.

Outdoor facilities were designed by Lawrence Halprin & Associates, with Charles Moore and William Turnbull as architectural consultants for one of the two parks. In the center is a terrace with two pools of water on different levels, connected by a sprouting cascade.

Portland Center, Portland, Oregon

Das Portland Center entsteht als kombiniertes Wohn- und Büroviertel auf einem fast 34 ha großen Gelände am Rande des Hauptgeschäftsgebietes der Stadt. Es gilt als eines der hervorragendsten Beispiele der Vereinigten Staaten für großflächige innerstädtische Sanierungen und wurde bereits mehrfach ausgezeichnet.

Bis heute sind drei Wohnhochhäuser, 24 Reihenhäuser, ein Parkhaus mit Restaurant und Börsenmaklerbüro im Obergeschoß, ein Einkaufszentrum und drei Bürokomplexe bezogen.

Die auf ausgedehnten Garagensockeln ruhenden drei Wohnhochhäuser sind im Grundriß annähernd quadratisch, wobei Aufzüge, Treppen und Müllschlucker jeweils einen zentralen Kernbereich mit umlaufenden Korridoren bilden. Zwei der Häuser sind 25geschossig, das dritte hat drei Geschosse weniger. Die Normalgeschosse enthalten acht Wohnungen mit zwei bis dreieinhalb Zimmern, die oberen Geschosse vier Wohnungen mit vier und fünf Zimmern.

Die Balkone geben den Fassaden, da sie nicht als umlaufende Galerien ausgebildet sind, eine kräftige Gliederung; zum Schutz gegen Einblick und Zugerscheinungen werden sie seitlich in voller Breite von den entsprechend weit vorgezogenen tragenden Wandscheiben gefaßt.

Die 24 Reihenhäuser sind je zur Hälfte den beiden 25geschossigen Wohnhochhäusern zugeordnet. Sie sitzen auf den Rändern der Garagensockel, deren gärtnerisch gestaltete Dächer sowohl ihnen als auch den Hochhäusern als Zugangsebene dienen. Die Schlafräume und Bäder liegen ein halbes Geschoß unter dem Zugang, die Wohnräume und Küchen ein halbes Geschoß darüber.

Von den bisher errichteten Bürokomplexen gehört einer der Boise Cascade Corporation und ein anderer dem Blue Cross of Oregon. Der Komplex des Blue Cross besitzt ein frei stehendes, mit dem siebengeschossigen Hauptgebäude über eine Brücke verbundenes Parkhaus; dieses soll später aufgestockt werden, um Platz für weitere Büros zu schaffen.

Die Außenanlagen wurden von Lawrence Halprin & Associates entworfen. Ihr Zentrum bildet eine unter Mitwirkung der Architekten Charles Moore und William Turnbull entstandene Terrassenanlage mit zwei auf verschiedenen Höhen liegenden und durch eine rauschende Kaskade verbundenen Wasserbecken.

1. The apartment blocks, seen from the south. In the foreground, the lower part of the terrace with the cascade.

1. Blick von Süden auf die Wohnhäuser. Im Vordergrund der untere Bereich der Terrassenanlage mit der Kaskade.

2. Site plan. Key: 1 apartment block, 2 townhouses, 3 terrace with cascade, 4 parking garage,
with restaurant and stockbroker's office on the
top floor, 5 shopping center, 6 general office
building, 7 office block of the Boise Cascade
Corporation, 8 office block and parking garage of
the Blue Cross of Oregon.
3. A view of the cascade, looking north.

2. Lageplan. Legende: 1 Wohnhochhaus, 2 Reihenhäuser, 3 Terrassenanlage mit Kaskade,
4 Parkhaus mit Restaurant und Börsenmaklerbüro im obersten Geschoß, 5 Einkaufszentrum,
6 allgemeines Bürogebäude, 7 Bürogebäude der
Boise Cascade Corporation, 8 Bürogebäude und
Parkhaus des Blue Cross of Oregon.
3. Blick über die Kaskade nach Norden.

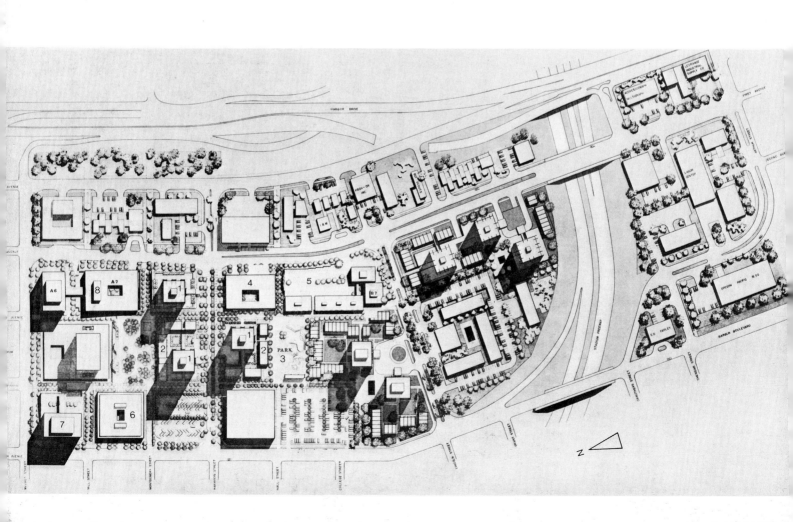

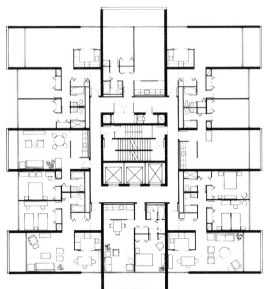

4. Plans of the northernmost of the two 25-story apartment blocks and its associated townhouses (roof level of garage podium with the entrance floor of the tower; lower and upper level of the townhouses; typical floor of the tower).

4. Grundrisse des nördlichen der beiden 25geschossigen Wohnhochhäuser und der diesem zugeordneten Reihenhäuser (Dachebene des Garagensockels mit Eingangsgeschoß des Hochhauses sowie Unter- und Obergeschoß der Reihenhäuser, Normalgeschoß des Hochhauses).

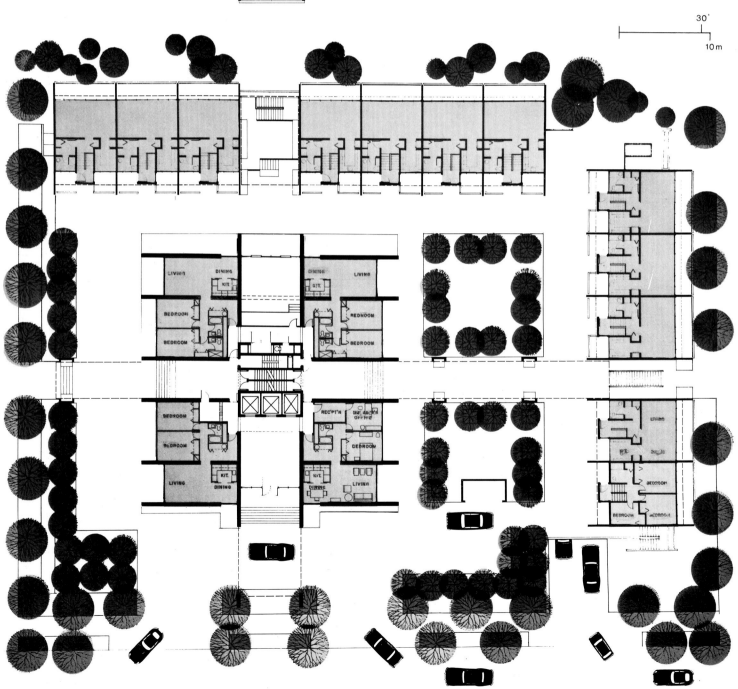

5. As the balconies are not extended into continuous galleries, they provide strong features of the facades.
6. Access to the townhouses is from the landscaped terraces of the garages on which they are erected. Bedrooms and bathrooms are half-a-story below the entrance, sitting room and kitchen half-a-story above it.

5. Die Balkone geben den Fassaden der Wohnhochhäuser, da sie nicht als umlaufende Galerien ausgebildet sind, eine kräftige Gliederung.
6. Die Reihenhäuser werden über die Dachgärten der ihnen als Basis dienenden Garagen erschlossen. Die Schlafräume und Bäder liegen ein halbes Geschoß unter dem Zugang, die Wohnräume und Küchen ein halbes Geschoß darüber.

Mauna Kea Beach Hotel, Kamuela, Hawaii

The hotel is situated at the northwest coast of Hawaii at the foot of Mauna Kea which rises to 13,796' above sea level. It was created through the initiative of Laurance S. Rockefeller, who had been asked to support the local efforts to extend the tourist industry vital to the islands.

The complex consists of three buildings, a building with the public rooms in the lower portion and 154 guest rooms in the upper portion, a free-standing dining pavilion, and a buried service wing.

The long main building, asymmetric in relation to the transverse axis marked by the main entrance, stands on the brow of a hill sloping down to the beach. Good use has been made of the topography by placing the public rooms on different levels, the entrance level containing reception lounge and administrative offices is on top, levels with shops, bar and buffet below. The guest rooms are arranged in three stepped-back tiers affording generous space for terraces which are protected by horizontal wooden trelliswork against the sun and against view from above. On the inside, the guest rooms blend with three open-air galleries filled with luxuriant vegetation. The dominant structural feature of the main building is the white-painted poured-in-place concrete, marked at regular intervals with V-shaped linear beads on the surface. The further range of building materials is restricted: Mexican flagstone, Italian quarry tile, local lava and sand-finish plaster.

Within the dining pavilion, the floor level rises in two tiers towards the interior so that all the guests have an unobstructed view of the sea. The inner zone, sheltered by a dark wooden ceiling, has accommodation for 200 diners; many more can be served on the outside terraces. The service block as well as an auditorium which can also be used as a banqueting hall are built into the slope behind the dining pavilion.

Mauna Kea Beach Hotel, Kamuela, Hawaii

Das Hotel liegt an der Nordwestküste von Hawaii, direkt unter dem 4200 m hohen Mauna Kea. Es entstand auf Initiative von Laurance S. Rockefeller, der gebeten worden war, die örtlichen Bemühungen um eine Ausweitung des für die Inseln lebensnotwendigen Tourismus zu unterstützen.

Der Komplex gliedert sich in drei Teile, den Hauptbau mit den öffentlichen Räumen im unteren und 154 Apartments im oberen Teil, das pavillonartige, abseits stehende Restaurant sowie den in die Erde eingegrabenen Serviceblock.

Der langgestreckte, in seiner vom Haupteingang angedeuteten Querachse leicht versetzte Hauptbau ist auf den Rand einer zum Strand abfallenden Bodenschwelle gesetzt. Der Geländeverlauf wurde dazu ausgenutzt, im öffentlichen Bereich zwei Ebenen zu schaffen, eine obere eingeschossige mit Empfang und Verwaltung sowie eine untere zweigeschossige mit Läden, Bar und Buffet. Die Apartments sind auf beiden Gebäudeseiten nach oben zurückgestaffelt. Auf den Außenseiten geben sie so Raum für terrassenartige Balkone, die durch waagrechte Holzjalousien gegen Sonneneinstrahlung und Einblick von oben geschützt sind. Die Innenseiten bilden eine lebendige Begrenzung der drei reich bepflanzten, gewächshausartigen Gartenhöfe. Beherrschendes Element des Hauptbaus ist in gleichmäßigen Abständen V-förmig reliefierter, weiß gestrichener Ortbeton. Die weitere Materialskala ist knapp: mexikanische Steinfliesen, italienische Keramikplatten, örtliche Lava und Feinputz.

Das Restaurant bietet durch die leichte Staffelung seines Bodens allen Gästen einen ungestörten Ausblick auf das Meer. In dem von einer dunklen Holzdecke geschützten Innenbereich finden 200 Gäste Platz, weit mehr können auf den vorgelagerten Terrassen untergebracht werden.

Der Serviceblock liegt zusammen mit einem Auditorium, das auch als Bankettraum genutzt werden kann, hinter dem Restaurant im Absatz der Bodenschwelle.

1. Main entrance to the hotel, viewed across the central court.

1. Blick über den mittleren Gartenhof auf den Haupteingang des Hotels.

2. Plans (A promenade level, B reception level, C 3rd guest room level). Key: 1 main entrance, 2 reception, 3 administrative offices, 4 garden court, 5 promenade, 6 buffet, 7 bar, 8 restaurant, 9 auditorium, 10 service area, 11 guest rooms.

2. Grundrisse (A Promenadenebene, B Empfangsebene, C 3. Bettengeschoß). Legende: 1 Haupteingang, 2 Empfang, 3 Verwaltung, 4 Gartenhof, 5 Promenade, 6 Buffet, 7 Bar, 8 Restaurant, 9 Auditorium, 10 Servicebereich, 11 Gästezimmer.

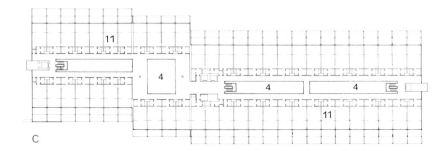

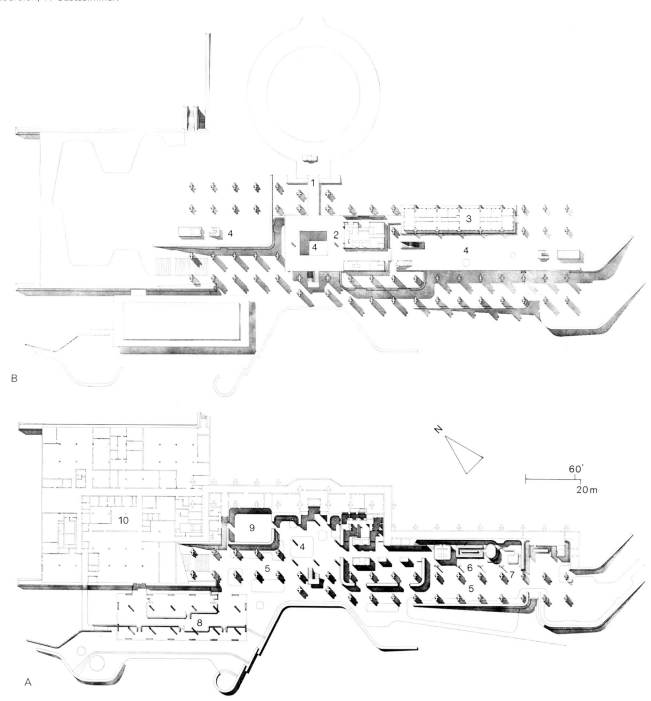

3. Entrance zone. The guest room balconies are protected by horizontally mounted wooden trelliswork against the sun and against view from above.
4. Cross-section.
5. Side view.

3. Blick auf den Eingangsbereich. Die Balkone der Gästeapartments sind durch waagrechte Holzjalousien gegen Einblick und Sonneneinstrahlung geschützt.
4. Schnitt.
5. Seitenansicht.

6. Two-story promenade zone. On the right, on an intermediate level, is the entrance zone.
7. Garden court at the northwestern end.
8. Garden court at the southeastern end, seen from the promenade zone.

6. Die zweigeschossige Promenadenebene. Rechts schließt auf halber Höhe die eingeschossige Empfangsebene an.
7. Der nordwestliche Gartenhof.
8. Blick von der Promenadenebene in den südöstlichen Gartenhof.

Pages 280–281:
9. General view of the hotel, with the dining pavilion on the left.

Seiten 280–181:
9. Gesamtansicht des Hotels. Links das Restaurant.

Photo Credits / Fotonachweis

Morley Baer, Monterey, California   16, 33 (3), 158, 161, 264–266, 267, 269, 273
Jeremiah O. Bragstad, San Francisco, California   71, 73, 138 (8), 139, 141, 143

Orlando R. Cabanban, Chicago, Illinois   30, 225, 227, 229–231, 233–239, 249, 250, 251, 261, 262, 263

Carlton Centre Ltd., Johannesburg, South Africa   32, 129
Louis Checkman, Jersey City, New Jersey   52, 53, 81–83

Diesel Construction, A Division of Carl A. Morse, Inc., Chicago, Illinois   19 (1)

Dwain Faubion, San Francisco, California   240
Yukio Futugawa, Tokyo   116, 117

Hedrich-Blessing, Chicago, Illinois   163, 171, 172

Robert E. Logan, New York, New York   221
Fred Lyon Pictures, Sausalito, California   243 (5)

Walter A. Netsch, Chicago, Illinois   209

Whitson M. Overcash, New York, New York   132

Bo Parker, New York, New York   19 (2), 23, 151, 155, 156
Photo-Art Commercial Studios, Washington, D.C.   271
Lewis M. Pitzely, New York, New York   33 (2)

Louis Reens, New York, New York   31, 209–215
Cervin Robinson, New York, New York   147–149 (8)

J. Walter Severinghaus, New York, New York   280, 281
Ezra Stoller Associates, Inc., Mamaroneck, New York   12, 13 (2), 14, 15, 17, 21, 24, 25, 35–37, 43–45, 47, 48, 49, 61–64, 65, 67, 68, 69, 75–77, 79, 85, 86, 88–93, 96–98, 100–107, 109–111, 113–115, 118, 119, 121, 123–127, 135, 137 (5), 138 (7), 145, 149 (7), 152, 153, 157, 159, 164, 165, 167–169, 175–177, 179–183, 193–195, 198–203, 206, 207, 217, 219, 223, 241, 243 (6), 245–247, 256–259
Roger Sturtevant, Alameda, California   137 (6)
Sunderland Aerial Photographers, Oakland, California   253

Philip Turner, Chicago, Illinois   205

Tanya Vinogradov, London   191

R. Wenkam, Honolulu, Hawaii   34, 275, 277–279
Lawrence S. Williams, Inc., Upper Darby, Pennsylvania   13 (1), 55–59